The Arctic

WORLD BIBLIOGRAPHICAL SERIES

General Editors:
Robert G. Neville (Executive Editor)
John J. Horton   Ian Wallace
Hans H. Wellisch   Ralph Lee Woodward, Jr.

John J. Horton is Deputy Librarian of the University of Bradford and currently Chairman of its Academic Board of Studies in Social Sciences. He has maintained a longstanding interest in the discipline of area studies and its associated bibliographical problems, with special reference to European Studies. In particular he has published in the field of Icelandic and of Yugoslav studies, including the two relevant volumes in the World Bibliographical Series.

Ian Wallace is Professor of Modern Languages at Loughborough University of Technology. A graduate of Oxford in French and German, he also studied in Tübingen, Heidelberg and Lausanne before taking teaching posts at universities in the USA, Scotland and England. He specializes in East German affairs, especially literature and culture, on which he has published numerous articles and books. In 1979 he founded the journal *GDR Monitor*, which he continues to edit.

Hans H. Wellisch is Professor emeritus at the College of Library and Information Services, University of Maryland. He was President of the American Society of Indexers and was a member of the International Federation for Documentation. He is the author of numerous articles and several books on indexing and abstracting, and has published *The Conversion of Scripts* and *Indexing and Abstracting: an International Bibliography*. He also contributes frequently to *Journal of the American Society for Information Science*, *The Indexer* and other professional journals.

Ralph Lee Woodward, Jr. is Chairman of the Department of History at Tulane University, New Orleans, where he has been Professor of History since 1970. He is the author of *Central America, a Nation Divided*, 2nd ed. (1985), as well as several monographs and more than sixty scholarly articles on modern Latin America. He has also compiled volumes in the World Bibliographical Series on *Belize* (1980), *Nicaragua* (1983), and *El Salvador* (1988). Dr. Woodward edited the Central American section of the *Research Guide to Central America and the Caribbean* (1985) and is currently editor of the Central American history section of the *Handbook of Latin American Studies*.

VOLUME 99

The Arctic

H. G. R. King

Compiler

CLIO PRESS
OXFORD, ENGLAND · SANTA BARBARA, CALIFORNIA
DENVER, COLORADO

British Library Cataloguing in Publication Data

King, H.G.R. (Harold Godfrey Rudolf). *1921 –*
Arctic. — (World bibliographical series; 99)
I. Arctic. Bibliographies
I. Title   II. Series
016.998

ISBN 1–85109–072–X

Clio Press Ltd.,
55 St. Thomas' Street,
Oxford OX1 1JG, England.

ABC-Clio Information Services,
Riviera Campus, 2040 Alameda Padre Serra,
Santa Barbara, CA 93103, USA.

Designed by Bernard Crossland.
Typeset by Columns Design and Production Services, Reading, England.
Printed and bound in Great Britain by
Billing and Sons Ltd., Worcester.

THE WORLD BIBLIOGRAPHICAL SERIES

This series, which is principally designed for the English speaker, will eventually cover every country in the world, each in a separate volume comprising annotated entries on works dealing with its history, geography, economy and politics; and with its people, their culture, customs, religion and social organization. Attention will also be paid to current living conditions – housing, education, newspapers, clothing, etc.– that are all too often ignored in standard bibliographies; and to those particular aspects relevant to individual countries. Each volume seeks to achieve, by use of careful selectivity and critical assessment of the literature, an expression of the country and an appreciation of its nature and national aspirations, to guide the reader towards an understanding of its importance. The keynote of the series is to provide, in a uniform format, an interpretation of each country that will express its culture, its place in the world, and the qualities and background that make it unique. The views expressed in individual volumes, however, are not necessarily those of the publisher.

VOLUMES IN THE SERIES

World Bibliographical Series

Contents

Contents

Contents

Contents

Introduction

The Arctic and Subarctic regions (Circumpolar North would be an acceptable alternative name) cover an area of some forty-one million km^2 and constitute about eight per cent of the earth's surface. The lands within the area make up about fifteen per cent of the land area of the world, and the sea about five per cent of the world's ocean. Seven countries claim sovereignty over the region; the USSR, Denmark, the USA, Norway, Sweden, Finland and Iceland (a volume on *Iceland* has already been published in the *World Bibliographical Series*). The human population of the regions is less than nine million.

Rapid economic changes have characterized the Circumpolar North during the past thirty years. World hunger for oil, natural gas, and the scarcer minerals, have made it profitable to apply the most advanced technology to the development of the vast and scarcely-tapped resources of the Arctic Ocean and the adjacent lands. As a hub of communications the Arctic Ocean is a familiar sight to the thousands of air passengers who fly the polar route over Greenland and the North Pole *en route* from Heathrow to Kennedy Airport. The development of high-powered icebreakers enables the Soviet government to maintain an almost year-round navigation of their Northern Sea Route (Northeast Passage) whilst in the west, navigation of the Northwest Passage linking the Atlantic with the Pacific to the north of continental America may soon become a routine.

The opening up of the Arctic for the benefit of western man is an irreversible process, but one must consider the effects of this on the Arctic's original inhabitants, the Eskimos, Aleuts, Indians, Lapps and other northern peoples. In North America, Greenland and Scandinavia there is a great political ferment in process, arising from the aspirations of these peoples to regain something of their autonomy, and to have a greater say in the exploitation of the renewable and non-renewable resources of the lands they claim as their own. Affecting all who live in the Arctic is the ever-present danger of disturbing irreparably nature's balance in this region of snow, ice and permafrost. No major oil spill has yet polluted the Arctic Ocean, but the Chernobyl disaster brought bankruptcy to many Lapp herdsmen whose reindeer were declared unfit for human consumption.

These, and other, issues are discussed in the literature that is included in this volume. Other topics covered include the archaeology, history and current social problems of the native peoples and the narrative accounts of those many intrepid explorers, from the Norsemen onwards, who for reasons of commerce, national prestige or pure adventure have helped to open our eyes to the reality of this unique region.

The Arctic regions can be defined in a number of ways depending on one's particular viewpoint. An obvious boundary might seem to be the Arctic Circle (latitude 66°33′N) above which line the sun does not set at the summer solstice or rise at the winter solstice. A study of the atlas shows that this is not a practical limitation if one wishes to indicate such arctic characteristics as regions of treelessness, typical flora and fauna, presence of permanently frozen ground, or low average temperatures. Accordingly, the Arctic and Subarctic boundaries must be flexible. For the purposes of this bibliography the Arctic and southward-extending Subarctic together include the following land areas: in North America the northern part of the Canadian provinces including Labrador, the Northwest Territories (including the Canadian Arctic islands), and the Yukon Territory; in the USA the State of Alaska; in the USSR, Kamchatka and the region south of the Asiatic coast to roughly 60° latitude and the region south of the European coast to roughly 66° latitude; and in Scandinavia the northern parts of Norway, Sweden and Finland. Also covered are Greenland, Bjørnøya (Bear Island), Svalbard (Spitsbergen) and Jan Mayen. Moreover, the following oceans and seas are included: the Arctic Ocean, part of the North Pacific Ocean, part of the North Atlantic Ocean, the Greenland Sea, the Barents Sea, the White Sea, the Kara Sea, the Laptev Sea, the East Siberian Sea, the Sea of Okhotsk, the Chukchi Sea, the Bering Sea, Aleutian waters, the Gulf of Alaska, the Beaufort Sea, Hudson Bay, Baffin Bay and the Labrador Sea.

The lack of any concise, selective guide to the literature of the Arctic and Subarctic has been made evident from the needs of a postgraduate course in polar studies held for a number of years at the Scott Polar Research Institute, University of Cambridge. The published literature on the Arctic is voluminous. The classified catalogue of the Institute's library lists well over 100,000 items, and the sixteen published volumes of the now defunct *Arctic Bibliography* list over 108,000 items. Currently, computerized bibliographies such as *Recent Polar and Glaciological Literature* (Cambridge) and the Arctic Science and Technology Information Service's *Current Awareness Bulletin* and *Bibliography* (Calgary, Alberta), attempt to control an ever increasing flow of polar publications. Confronted by a proliferation of bibliographies and other listings, often lacking in critical selection, beginners and non-specialists often find themselves lost for a reliable starting point. The object of this addition to the *World Bibliographical Series* is to meet this need by listing and annotating a selection of the relevant literature, culled largely from the resources of the Scott Polar Research Institute, whose library is considered, justly, to be the largest and most comprehensive of its kind in the world. Hopefully, this bibliography will meet the needs not only of university students and researchers, but also those of a far larger general readership which is becoming increasingly aware of the relevance of the polar regions to our understanding of the world.

The difficulties of making a balanced selection of publications in so broad a field as the Arctic cannot be overemphasized; inevitably the final choice of items was mine alone and that choice will, to a certain extent, reflect my interests and areas of special knowledge. In addition, the publishers have set limitations on the number of bibliographic entries to be included in volumes in the *World Bibliographical Series*. The series essentially seeks to meet the needs of the English-language user and to list material available in the larger public or university libraries, thereby excluding the extensive literature of by far the largest national unit within the Arctic, the Soviet Union, which is, in the main, untranslated and often inaccessible to western readers. The same difficulty, though on a smaller scale, applies to Greenland, where publications are largely in Danish, to Svalbard, where they are in Norwegian and to the Scandinavian Lapps, where books can be in Norwegian, Swedish or Finnish. In all these cases, I have sought to include as many worthwhile translations as possible but the necessary omission of much original material has inevitably caused a degree of distortion.

The bulk of the publications selected are books and monographs, together with a number of government publications. New editions and reprints of historical narratives have been included wherever possible. Excluded are newspaper articles and ephemera. Listed under the relevant subject headings will be found the titles of over fifty serial publications all relevant to Arctic studies. The annotations are intended to expand and shed light on the titles rather than to serve as full abstracts.

In general, each section of the bibliography has been arranged alphabetically by author, editor or compiler, or, in their absence, by title. Periodicals are listed alphabetically at the ends of sections following the author sequence. Occasionally, a chronological listing has been considered more useful, as in the voyages and expeditions subsection of the 'History' chapter. Numerous subject bibliographies have been included, which will be found under their topics or regions.

The bibliography is grouped under two main headings: the Arctic region as a whole (entries 1–506) and the Arctic regions considered as political divisions (entries 507–935). Under the first heading the sub-divisions are arranged by topic modelled on the headings customarily used in this series. The regional sub-divisions in the second half are themselves divided by topic, following, where practicable, those headings used in the first half. The two parts are complementary, and much of the material listed under the general section will be relevant to specific regional divisions. Nowhere is this more true than in the historical sections where, inevitably, there is much overlapping. However, rather than group all arctic expedition narratives under one broad heading I have split them up. Thus, those voyages directed towards the North Pole, or with broad objectives, are grouped under 'History' in the general section, whereas those concerned with particular regions will be found at those regions. For example, expeditions to the Northwest Passage will be listed under Canadian Arctic, those to the Northeast Passage under Soviet Arctic. The subject index appended brings together these and other related topics.

Finally users should refer to other related volumes in this series. These are: *Russia/USSR* (vol. 6), *Finland* (vol. 31), *Iceland* (vol. 37), *Atlantic Ocean* (vol. 61), *Norway* (vol. 67), and *Sweden* (vol. 68). Volumes on *Greenland* and *Canada* are in the course of preparation and volumes on *Alaska* and *Siberia* are also planned.

Acknowledgements

I would like to express my thanks to the librarian of the Scott Polar Research Institute for allowing me unfettered access to the collections and to the members of the library staff for their willing cooperation in this enterprise. Once again I am indebted to Dr. Robert Neville, Executive Editor of the *World Bibliographical Series* and to Rachel Houghton, Assistant Editor, for their help, guidance and encouragement at all stages of production. Finally, I would like to record the debt of gratitude I owe to my wife, Barbara, whose customary forebearance and loyal support with proof reading and advice have made my path less stony than it might have been.

H.G.R. King
Cambridge 1989

The Arctic Region in General

1   **The arctic world.**
    Fred Bruemmer, edited by William E. Taylor, Jr.   London: Century
    Publishing, 1985. 256p.
The author, an experienced arctic writer, traveller and photographer, contributed not
only the first part of this book dealing with the history of the Arctic but also many of
the superb photographs which are an important feature of this volume. Part two,
dealing with arctic wildlife, and part three, which reviews arctic archaeology,
exploration and northern peoples in a changing world, are chapters contributed by
experts.

2   **Crown of the world: a review of the inner Arctic.**
    Cora Cheney, Ben Partridge.   New York: Dodd, Mead, 1979. 223p.
    bibliog.
The authors, having attended the Inuit Circumpolar Conference at Barrow, Alaska, in
June 1977, then spent eighteen months travelling in Alaska, Siberia, Lapland,
Spitsbergen, Greenland, Canada and Iceland. This book is a personal view of the
Arctic and serves as a useful introduction to the region at a popular level.

3   **Pôle Nord 1983. North Pole 1983. History of its conquest and
    contemporary problems of maritime and air transportation.**
    Edited by Sylvie Devers.   Paris: Éditions du Centre National de la
    Récherche Scientifique, 1987. 385p. maps. bibliog.
Presents the proceedings (in French and English) of the Tenth International
Conference of the Centre d'Études Arctiques (Centre of Arctic Studies), Paris, with a
preface by the founder of the series, Professor Jean Malaurie. The papers, contributed
by an international body of specialists and covering various aspects of the Arctic, are
grouped under six headings. These are: (1) Geophysics and geography; (2)
Oceanography and climatology; (3) Myths, history, history of circumpolar cartography;
(4) History of exploration 16th-20th centuries; (5) Museums, films and philately
dealing with the North Pole conquest; and (6) Contemporary problems: maritime and
air transportation, economic future and sea law.

The Arctic Region in General

4 **The hot Arctic.**
John Dyson. Boston, Massachusetts: Little, Brown, 1979. 290p.

A personal view of the Arctic by a professional writer, which is based on travel in northern Canada and Greenland. The Arctic is 'hot' for the author because he regards it as causing contention and as being the focus of several kinds of economic spotlight. Essentially, it is a book about the technological changes that affected the Arctic in the 1970s and the effect of these on the native peoples.

5 **Arctic pilot.**
Hydrographer of the Navy, Great Britain. Taunton, England: The Author, 1975-85. 3 vols. maps.

Though primarily intended for navigators, Admiralty Pilots contain a mine of information for the general reader, including, in this case, arctic history, maritime topography, climate and weather conditions, glossaries of foreign terms and much else. These three volumes are available from official agents for charts and cover specific regions of the Arctic. These are: volume one: The coasts of the USSR; volume two: Iceland, Jan Mayen, Bjørnøya (Bear Island) and the east coast of Greenland; and volume three: Davis Strait and Baffin Bay with the west and north-west coasts of Greenland, the north coast of Canada, including Hudson Bay and the Arctic archipelago. All three volumes are continually updated with regular supplements.

6 **Arctic dreams; imagination and desire in a northern landscape.**
Barry Lopez. London: Macmillan, 1986. 464p. bibliog.

This absorbing book contains an extremely perceptive and intelligent account of the author's reactions to the arctic scene. Lopez has travelled extensively, from Bering Strait in the west to Davis Strait in the east. He has lived and hunted with the Eskimos and conversed with the geologists and engineers working on the oil pipeline. He is an acute observer of the natural scene – the animal life, tundra landscape and the weather patterns. He is as conversant with the history of the Arctic as he is prescient in optimistic forecasts for its immediate future. Appendixes include 'Geographic place-names', 'Scientific names for animals and plants' and 'Human culture and civilization'.

7 **Ship in the wilderness.**
J. Snyder, Keith Shackleton. London: Dent, 1986. 208p.

An account of M.S. *Lindblad Explorer's* tourist cruises to such obscure places as the Aleutian Islands, Bering Strait, the Northwest Passage, Iceland, Greenland and Svalbard (Spitsbergen), as well as islands in the Southern Ocean and Antarctica. The book is illustrated with many of Keith Shackleton's evocative paintings.

8 **Microfilm edition of encyclopedia arctica.**
Edited by Vilhjalmur Stefansson. Sponsored by the Office of Naval Research, Department of the Navy. Ann Arbor, Michigan: Xerox University Microfilms in collaboration with Dartmouth College Library, Hanover, New Hampshire, 1974.

This encyclopaedia, compiled by North America's most famous arctic explorer at the end of World War II, was never completed for publication. Eventually the manuscript, held by the Stefansson Collection at Dartmouth College, was prepared for publication in microfilm format, filling twenty-seven reels. There are five main categories into which the work is divided: (1) Biography from earliest times to the 1940s including exploration history; (2) Geography together with the resources and industrial development of the places described, population figures, transportation, and so on; (3) Government departments of all countries dealing with the Arctic; (4) Scientific institutions; (5) Articles on scientific and technological subjects and general history of arctic exploration. Many of the contributions were by the leading experts of their day, with the first section being by far the most valuable. A detailed index is provided at the beginning of reel one.

9   **The northward course of empire.**
    Vilhjalmur Stefansson.   London: Harrap, 1922. 274p. map. bibliog.
A development of the author's theory that man has steadily advanced northwards from his original habitat – the tropics. Stefansson discusses what was then the prevailing view, that the North is inhospitable to life, and demonstrates its potential productivity and habitability, indicating existing established industries. He suggests its future potential, including, for example, trans-polar air routes and domestication of such animals as the musk-ox.

10   **Acta Arctica.**
    Copenhagen: Arktisk Institut, 1943- . irregular.
Features scientific articles, mostly in the English language, ranging over a broad spread of topics relevant to the circumpolar Arctic, in such fields as folklore, natural history and anthropology, among others.

11   **Arctic.**
    Calgary, Alberta: University of Calgary, Arctic Institute of North
    America, 1948- . quarterly.
Includes informed articles on all aspects of arctic interest, including natural history, archaeology, anthropology, history, geography, economic development, native arts and crafts and biographical profiles. Book reviews and obituaries are also featured.

12   **Geographical Journal.**
    London: Royal Geographical Society, 1893- . quarterly.
A scholarly journal which frequently publishes articles relating to aspects of the Arctic and sub-Arctic. Of special value are the regular book reviews and cartographic surveys.

13   **Musk-Ox.**
    Saskatoon, Saskatchewan: University of Saskatchewan, Department of
    Sciences, 1967- . twice-yearly.
A journal covering scientific, cultural, economic and historical aspects of the North. Although the emphasis is on the Canadian North there are also articles dealing with aspects of Alaska, Greenland, the Soviet North and Scandinavia. Also included are other items, such as book reviews, news items and biographies.

14   **Norsk Polarinstitutt Meddelser.**
    Oslo: Norsk Polarinstitutt, 1926- . irregular.
A series of monographs, covering various disciplines dealing with the Arctic, published by the Norwegian Polar Institute in both Norwegian and English.

The Arctic Region in General

15 **Polar Record.**
   Cambridge, England: Scott Polar Research Institute, 1931- . quarterly.

This long-established polar journal publishes articles of a review nature on a wide range of topics ¬ scientific, historical and social. Under the heading 'Notes' briefer contributions cover matters of current interest in Arctic and Antarctic studies. Also included are book reviews and obituaries.

16 **Polar Times.**
   Rego Park, New York: American Polar Society, 1933- . twice-yearly.

Offers extracts from the press relating to the Arctic and Antarctic regions.

17 **Polarforschung.**
   Münster, Federal German Republic: Institut der Geophysik der
   Universität, German Society of Polar Research, 1931- . irregular.

Includes scientific papers in English and German covering a wide variety of subjects dealing with both the Arctic and Antarctic. Book reviews and obituaries are also included.

Geography

General

18 **The circumpolar north; a political and economic geography of the Arctic and sub-Arctic.**
Terence Armstrong, George Rogers, Graham Rowley. London: Methuen, 1978. 303p. maps. bibliog.
A study of the northern regions of our planet, covering geographical, economic, social and political aspects, by acknowledged experts in the field. An introductory chapter covering the general geographical background is followed by regional studies of the northern USSR, Canada, Alaska, Greenland, northern Scandinavia, including Svalbard and Jan Mayen, and the circumpolar oceans. A concluding chapter discusses the North in world affairs. The book was also issued in paperback format.

19 **The polar world.**
Patrick D. Baird. London: Longmans, 1964. 325p. maps. bibliog.
The greater part of this textbook is devoted to a discussion of the physical geography, fauna and flora and peoples of the Arctic.

20 **Symposium: geography of polar countries. Selected papers and summaries.**
Edited by Jerry Brown. Hanover, New Hampshire: US Army, Corps of Engineers, Cold Regions Research and Engineering Laboratory, 1977. 61p. bibliog. (Special Report 77-6).
Offers either the full text, or extended summaries, of a number of United States contributions to a symposium on polar geography held in Leningrad in 1976, together with English and Russian summaries of Soviet contributions. The papers and summaries reflect the participation of members of the joint US–USSR environmental protection agreement project, *Protection of northern ecosystems*. The US papers deal with land-use planning, the impact of resource development on native peoples, fish and

wildlife, and permafrost, and the impact of pipelines and roads on the environment. The Soviet summaries deal with the subjects of properties and changes in the Arctic and Subarctic, flora, treeline, permafrost and methods of predicting changes in the environment.

21 **Polar regions atlas.**
Central Intelligence Agency. Washington, DC: Superintendent of Documents, 1979. 66p. maps.

An invaluable summary of the geography of both polar regions, presented in textual and graphic form. Arctic topics covered include discovery and exploration, climate, physical features, sea ice, climatic change, permafrost, northern development, aboriginal people, fisheries, mining, oil and gas, transportation, environmental protection, science programmes and sovereignty problems. A gazetteer of populated places, administrative divisions, hydrographic features and oil and gas fields is appended.

22 **Problems of physiographic zoning of polar lands.**
Edited by L. S. Govorukha, Yu A. Kruchinin. New Delhi: Amerind Publishing for the Division of Polar Programs and the National Science Foundation, Washington, DC, 1981, 242p. (TT75-52080).

A translation of the Russian original which was published as *Trudy arkticheskogo i antarkticheskogo nauchno-issledovatel'skogo instituta*, Leningrad, 1971, no. 304. The volume consists of a collection of specialist articles devoted to the complex physiographic zoning of the polar regions, both terrestrial and oceanic. Included are papers on the principles of determining the boundaries of the arctic regions themselves, the boundaries of the arctic seas, natural zones in the Arctic on a hydrometeorological basis, climatic zoning of the Arctic and zoogeographical zoning of the Arctic, among others.

23 **Arctic and alpine environments.**
Edited by Jack D. Ives, Roger G. Barry. London: Methuen, 1974. 999p. bibliog.

In this substantial volume, thirty-one specialist authors (mostly North American) cover many aspects of the earth and biological sciences in arctic and alpine regions. Slightly under one half of the book is devoted to reviews of the paleo-environment, covering, for example, climatology, hydrologic régimes and groundwater prediction, and the delimitation and definition of permafrost areas. Nine chapters cover ecological and biological aspects, including the role of climate in the floristic composition and location of northern forest borders, the control of timberlines, plant adaptation and primary productivity in tundra zones. Controversial issues on the origin and evolution of arctic and alpine floras and the evidence for biological refugia during glacial episodes are also discussed. A final section deals with man's adaptation to, and impact on, cold and high latitude environments. Case studies highlight the impact of western technology on northern native peoples and the precarious ecological environment.

24 **The world of ice; the natural history of the frozen regions.**
Brian S. John. London: Orbis, 1979. 120p. maps. bibliog.

A profusely illustrated popular reference book of the polar regions, by an expert on snow and ice, which also covers such factors as climate, geology and animal and plant life.

25 **Polar mirages.**
W. G. Rees. *Polar Record*, vol. 24, no. 149 (July 1988), p. 193-98.
bibliog.
After a brief explanation of how mirages are formed in polar regions, this paper
discusses several kinds of mirages noted in the literature of polar exploration – those
creating illusory land, the 'Novaya Zemlya' effect, long-range and multiple images and
the Fata Morgana.

26 **The arctic basin.**
Edited by John E. Sater. Washington, DC: Arctic Institute of North
America, 1969. 337p. map.
A summary review of arctic geography and technology, derived from research carried
out for the Untied States Army. In addition to the environmental chapters there are
sections dealing with physiology and health, psychological problems, logistics (land,
sea and air) and communications. A detailed folding map accompanies the volume.

27 **Polar deserts and modern man.**
Edited by Terah L. Smiley, James H. Zumberge. Tucson, Arizona:
University of Arizona Press, 1974. 173p. bibliog.
Includes fourteen papers that were presented by experts in various disciplines at the
Polar Deserts Symposium, Philadelphia, Pennsylvania, 1971. These examine polar
deserts with respect to their physical and biological characteristics in relation to
intensified development in polar areas. Analyses are given of the natural setting and
dynamic processes of the polar deserts, including climatology, geology, hydrology,
soils, biology and the indigenous inhabitants. Additional information presents costs
imposed by environmental stress; resource development past, present and future;
communications and transportation; health and sanitation; and the design of habitats
for man in the harsh environment of the polar desert.

28 **Arctic and Antarctic; a modern geographical synthesis.**
David Sugden. Oxford: Basil Blackwell, 1982. 472p. maps. bibliog.
This is a well-researched study of both polar regions by a professional field worker.
The first half of the book makes an attempt to synthesize polar regional geography by
relating the various natural systems to each other, rather than describing them in
isolated compartments. These systems include plate tectonics, climate, glaciers,
periglacial features and the marine system. The second half of the book deals with
human systems, including the early history of man in the Arctic, and with problems
relating to the present-day inhabitants of Greenland, Arctic Canada, Alaska and the
Soviet North, comparing and contrasting the human spatial pattern of their respective
peoples, settlements and communication networks. Northern Scandinavia is, by
definition, excluded.

29 **Soils of the polar landscapes.**
John C. F. Tedrow. New Brunswick, New Jersey: Rutgers University
Press, 1977. 638p. maps. bibliog.
Tedrow's is a comprehensive text on the soils of the Arctic (and Antarctic) regions.
Essential background material is contained in chapters on climate, biotic factors,
permafrost, weathering, cryogenic processes and patterned ground. A substantial
portion of the book is devoted to soils of specific polar regions – Alaska, Canada,
Greenland, northern Europe, Asiatic Russia and Kamchatka.

30 **Picture atlas of the Arctic.**
R. Thoren. Amsterdam: Elsevier, 1969. 449p.

The author, a specialist and lecturer in photographic interpretation, has selected a remarkable collection of photographs – obliques and ground photographs, close-ups and long distance shots – to illustrate this review of the Arctic regions. In addition to chapters covering the Arctic Ocean and Soviet drifting stations, there are sections, of varying detail and coverage, on Alaska, the Canadian Arctic, Greenland, Iceland, Jan Mayen, Svalbard, Scandinavia and the Soviet Arctic, the latter being the most comprehensive.

31 **The arctic circle; aspects of the North from the circumpolar nations.**
Edited by William C. Wonders. Don Mills, Ontario: Longmans Canada, 1976. 142p. bibliog.

These are the papers resulting from a panel discussion on 'Distinctive features of northern development in the circumpolar lands', held at the 22nd International Geographical Congress in Montreal, August 1972, in which geographers from several polar countries presented interpretations from their national viewpoints. In this volume these papers have been expanded and include ten contributions from Alaska, Canada, Finland, Greenland, Iceland, Norway, Sweden and the USSR.

32 **Arctic and Alpine Research.**
Boulder, Colorado: Institute of Arctic and Alpine Research, 1969- . quarterly.

This is essentially a scientific journal, containing original research papers, resulting correspondence and short notes dealing with aspects of Arctic and alpine environments and correlative topics on the subarctic and subalpine zones and on related paleoenvironments. The emphasis is on the inter-disciplinary appeal. Book reviews are included.

33 **Norsk Polarinstitutt Skrifter.**
Oslo: Norskpolarinstitutt, 1927- . irregular.

A series of specialised monographs dealing with different aspects of the Arctic, published by the Norwegian Polar Institute in English and Norwegian.

34 **Polar Geography and Geology.**
Silver Spring, Maryland: V. H. Winston, 1977- . quarterly.

The general coverage of this journal is the Arctic and Antarctic with papers covering a wide variety of topics including glaciology, glacial geology, former climates and marine geology. The journal specializes in translation, from Russian language publications and occasionally from Japanese and other foreign language literature.

35 **Polar Research.**
Oslo: Norsk Polarinstitutt (Norwegian Polar Institute), 1982- . twice- or three times yearly.

English language scientific papers in such disciplines as biology, geology, glaciology, meteorology, oceanography and geophysics, as they relate to the polar regions, appear in this publication.

36 **Problems of the Arctic and the Antarctic.**
New Delhi, Calcutta: Oxonian Press PVT, 1968- . irregular.
Offers translations of the contents of the scientific papers in the Soviet journal *Problemy arktiki i antarktiki*, published by the Arctic and Antarctic Institute, Leningrad. The papers are mostly devoted to scientific discussions in the fields of oceanography, meteorology and ice navigation.

Geology

37 **Arctic geology and geophysics. Proceedings of the third international symposium on arctic geology.**
Edited by Ashton F. Embry, Hugh R. Balkwill. Calgary, Alberta: Canadian Society of Petroleum Geologists, 1982. 552p. maps. bibliog. (Memoir 8).
Presents over 100 papers in the field of arctic geology, the environment, geophysics and development, based on the theme of 'Arctic resources, exploration and exploitation'. Topics discussed include the hydrocarbon resources of Canada, the geology of Greenland and the coal resources of Svalbard.

38 **Geophysics of the polar regions.**
Edited by E. S. Husebye, G. L. Johnson, Y. Kristoffersen. Amsterdam: Elsevier, 1985. 470p. bibliog.
Proceedings of a symposium on the geophysics of the polar regions, held in Hamburg, 1983, with papers on a multiplicity of topics presented by twenty-three scientists from eleven countries. The first seven papers are concerned with the Arctic Ocean basin and surrounding areas. The second section, of four papers, concentrates on the tectonic development of Svalbard (Spitsbergen) and the Barents Sea area. The remainder of the papers focus on the Antarctic.

Snow, ice and permafrost

39 **Illustrated glossary of snow and ice.**
Terence Armstrong, Brian Roberts, Charles Swithinbank. Cambridge, England: Scott Polar Research Institute, 1969. 2nd ed. 60p. bibliog. (Special Publication, no. 4).
The object of this glossary is to cover the minimum number of terms required by anyone working in a polar environment. It covers snow, floating ice, land ice and ice in the atmosphere. Also included are linguistic equivalents of terms used in eight languages. Every term is accompanied by an appropriate illustrative photograph.

Geography. Snow, ice and permafrost

40 **The world of ice.**
James L. Dyson. New York: Alfred A. Knopf, 1962. 305p. map.
bibliog.
A popular account of snow and ice worldwide, in the polar regions and on mountains,
covering its influence on man and its economic effects. Also included are chapters on
the history of ice ages, the land beneath the glaciers, ice and climate and life on ice.

41 **Avalanches and snow safety.**
Colin Fraser. London: John Murray, 1978. 269p. bibliog.
A partly scientific, partly descriptive handbook on avalanches. It includes chapters on
such topics as the forms of avalanches, their build-up and release, survival, rescue
organizations and methods and protection against avalanches.

42 **Handbook of snow; principles, processes, management & use.**
Edited by D. M. Gray, D. H. Male. Toronto: Pergamon, 1981. 776p.
bibliog.
Sections by expert contributors are arranged under four sections: (1) Snow and the
environment; (2) Snowfall and snowcover; (3) Snow and engineering; and (4) Snow
and recreation. Thus, part one deals with the human and animal aspects of snow; part
two with the formation and distribution of snow, including avalanches; part three with
travel over snow, snow and building, methods of control and removal; and part four
with the practical aspects and mechanisms of skiing.

43 **Remote sensing ice and snow.**
D. K. Hall, J. Martinec. London: Chapman & Hall, 1985. 189p. map.
bibliog.
This book concerns environmental remote sensing, the observation and measurement
of the earth from space. This is now a recognized discipline, here concentrating on
snow and ice. The Arctic (and Antarctic) naturally figure prominently. Thus, chapters
three and four examine the seasonal snow cover of both polar regions as well as of
more temperate mountainous regions. Chapter five deals with the remote sensing of
lake and river ice. Permafrost is discussed in chapter six. The final two chapters
examine terrestrial ice, including glaciers, ice caps, ice sheets and sea ice, including
icebergs.

44 **The permafrost environment.**
S. A. Harris. London: Croom Helm, 1986. 276p. maps. bibliog.
A course book, aimed at advanced undergraduates and interested professionals,
covering the use of permafrost with an account of the nature and processes of the
environment and the engineering implications. One-third of the book deals with the
history of permafrost research, identification, nature and processes, and the
distribution and stability of permafrost. The remaining two-thirds are devoted to the
engineering implications of permafrost, including foundations, roads and railways,
airfields, oil and gas, mining, water and electricity, agriculture and forestry.

45 **Icebergs: a bibliography relevant to eastern Canadian waters.**
Edited by L. M. Howard. Calgary, Alberta: Arctic Institute of North
America, 1986. 277p. (Environmental Studies Revolving Funds Report
030).
A bibliography of over 1,100 annotated citations listed by subject, geographic, title and
serial indexes. The area covered is the east coast of Canada and the west coast of
Greenland, including all waters from Baffin Bay south to the Grand Banks and out
into the North Atlantic. Also included are works relevant to iceberg towing, remote
sensing, survey and measuring techniques.

46 **The ice age past and present.**
Brian S. John. London: Collins, 1977. 254p. bibliog.
A useful popular introduction to present day snow and ice conditions and to former ice
ages. The author discusses not only the movement of glaciers and the effects on the
landscape and the rise and fall of sea level, but also how ice has affected animal and
plant life, and how the Eskimos have learned to cope with the problems of their arctic
world which is dominated by ice.

47 **Snow.**
Ruth Kirk. New York: William Morrow, 1977. 320p. bibliog.
A popular account of snow as it affects the land and human beings, which includes
chapters on climate, the Arctic, shelter and clothing, blizzards and avalanches, human
adaptations to snow, sledge dogs and reindeer and skiing.

48 **Ice atlas: Canadian Arctic waterways.**
W. E. Markham. Ottawa: Environment Canada, 1981. 35p.
A presentation of 315 charts depicting regional concentrations and distributions over a
period of twenty-five years, beginning in the 1950s. The atlas also contains useful
background information on monthly and seasonal air temperatures, wind speed and
direction, melting and freezing degree days, measured ice thickness and sea level
pressure. The atlas is based chiefly on material obtained on routine ice reconnaissance
flights, supplemented by some satellite data, and was designed primarily to support
arctic shipping. A supplement was published in 1984.

49 **Snow structures and ski fields; being an account of snow and ice forms
met in nature and a study on avalanches and snowcraft.**
Gerald Seligman. Cambridge, England: International Glaciological
Society, 1980. 2nd ed. 555p.
A classic account of snow and ice forms encountered by the amateur mountain-goer.
Part one consists of descriptive chapters on snow and snow forms, and snow drifting.
Parts two and three deal with avalanches and their classification, safety in mountains
and winter and spring skiing conditions.

50 **Sea ice.**
Vernon A. Squire. *Science Progress*, vol. 69 (1984), p. 19-43. bibliog.
A review of the current state of knowledge of the sea ice of the polar and marginal seas
is outlined and discussed with reference to recent interest shown in the Arctic by the
offshore engineering industry.

51 **The geophysics of sea ice.**
Edited by N. Untersteiner. New York: Plenum, 1986. 1196p. (NATO ASI series B, 146).

This volume is based on the proceedings of the NATO Advanced Study Institute on Air-Sea-Ice Interaction, Acquafredda di Maratea, Italy, 28 September–10 October 1981. Each chapter, contributed by an expert, forms a complete treatise in its own selected field, taking the novice from first principles to research level. The main body of the book is devoted to the behaviour and characteristics of sea ice in its different forms, together with detailed accounts of associated oceanographic and meteorological phenomena.

52 **Annals of Glaciology.**
Cambridge, England: International Glaciological Society, 1980- . annual.

Each volume in this series is devoted to publishing the proceedings of a specialized symposium on some aspect of snow and ice studies. Themes include use of icebergs, remote sensing, glacier mapping and surveying, snow and ice chemistry, and others.

53 **Bibliography on Cold Regions Science and Technology.**
Springfield, Virginia: National Technical Information Service, 1951- . annual.

This bibliography covers all aspects of snow, ice and permafrost research in the polar regions. Publications, many with full abstracts, are listed numerically, a second volume contains author and subject indexes. The annual volumes are compiled from monthly current awareness listings entitled *Current literature cold regions. Science and technology*. The bibliography is prepared by the US Library of Congress, Science and Technology Division for the US Army Corps of Engineers, Cold Regions Research and Engineering Laboratory, Hanover, New Hampshire. The references are also available on an online version entitled COLD.

54 **Cold Regions Science and Technology.**
Amsterdam: Elsevier, 1979- . three times yearly.

An international journal dealing with the scientific and technical problems of cold environments. The journal is primarily concerned with problems related to the freezing of water, and especially with the many forms of ice, snow and frozen ground. Emphasis is given to applied science with a broad coverage of the physics, chemistry and mechanics of ice. The technology content stresses research, development and professional practice in engineering.

55 **Journal of Glaciology.**
Cambridge, England: International Glaciological Society, 1947- . three times yearly.

A professional journal publishing articles of high scientific and practical interest on all aspects of snow and ice study.

56 **Report of the International Ice Patrol in the North Atlantic. Bulletin.**
Washington, DC: United States Coast Guard, [1914]- . annual.

The International Ice Patrol came into being as a result of the sinking of the *Titanic* in 1912 and has been carried out ever since by the United States on behalf of other maritime powers subscribing to the original convention of 1913. Originally reports were made by US Coast Guard vessels during the ice season. Today, the work is largely carried out by aircraft in the region of the Grand Banks. Facsimile broadcasting stations provide special forecasts.

Weather and climate

57 **Arctic climate.**
Roger G. Barry, Kenneth F. Hare.   In: *Arctic and alpine environments.*
Edited by J. D. Ives, R. G. Barry.   London: Methuen, 1974, p. 17-54.
maps. bibliog.

Offers a general review of arctic climate.

58 **The ocean-atmosphere system.**
A. H. Perry, J. M. Walker.   London: Longman, 160p. maps. bibliog.

This book is about the interactions between the atmosphere and the oceans, and the interdependence of atmospheric and oceanic circulations. There are sections dealing with the Arctic Ocean and the programmes of international scientific cooperation covering this region, such as POLEX (North) 1973-83 and Arctic Ice Dynamics Joint Experiment (AIDJEX).

59 **Climate of the Arctic.**
Edited by Gunter Weller, Sue Ann Bowling.   Fairbanks, Alaska:
Geophysical Institute, 1975. 436p. maps. bibliog.

Papers read at the 24th Alaska Science Conference, 15-17 August, 1973. Topics discussed are arranged under the following headings. Part one: The changing climate: evidence of past climate, climatic fluctuations in the 20th century, theories of climatic changes, numerical models of climatic change. Part two: The current climate: atmospheric circulation, physical processes and climate, descriptive climatology, man-modified climates, the hydrological cycle, the frozen oceans, moving towards a systematic study of the arctic climate.

Aurora

60   **The northern light: from mythology to space research.**
Asgeir Brekke, Alv Egeland.   Berlin: Springer-Verlag, 1983. 170p.
bibliog.

An historical study of beliefs and research on the northern lights, or aurora borealis. It begins with references to the phenomenon in the works of the Greek philosophers and proceeds to discuss the different explanations given in the mythology, literature and early science of Scandinavia. There is also a discussion of early scientific theories as well as the treatment of the aurora borealis in poetry and imaginative writing and in art.

61   **Majestic lights; the aurora in science, history, and the arts.**
Robert H. Eather.   Washington, DC: American Geophysical Union,
1980. 323p. bibliog.

An authoritative and well-illustrated book, covering all aspects of the aurora from early history, including the beginning of scientific enquiry, legends and folklore, poetry and literature and modern scientific understanding.

62   **Aurora.**
Alister Vallance Jones.   Dordrecht, Netherlands: D. Riedel, 1974.
301p. bibliog.

This monograph is directed principally at students and scientists of optical studies of aurora. It provides an introduction to the science of the subject with an emphasis on relatively simple physical interpretations and models. A very comprehensive list of references is appended.

Flora and Fauna

General

63 **Tundra ecosystems; a comparative analysis.**
Edited by L. C. Bliss, O. W. Heal, J. J. Moore.   Cambridge, England:
Cambridge University Press, 1981. 813p. bibliog.
Contains specialist papers, presenting the results of international research on tundra
and related ecosystems, covering flora, fauna and the utilization and conservation of
tundra by man.

64 **The life of the far north.**
William A. Fuller, John C. Holmes.   New York: McGraw-Hill in
cooperation with World Book Encyclopaedia, 1972. 232p. bibliog. (Our
Living World of Nature).
A well-illustrated account of arctic wildlife, and ecology in general, written by
professional ecologists for the younger reader. The appendixes include a list of arctic
national parks.

65 **Temperature and animal life.**
Richard N. Hardy.   London: Edward Arnold, 1979, 2nd ed. 84p.
bibliog.
This book reviews the various ways in which temperature imposes itself upon the
biology of animals, and demonstrates in particular the special advantages possessed by
animals which regulate their deep body temperature. Chapter seven is concerned with
adaptation to cold environments.

66 **Arctic life of birds and mammals including man.**
Laurence Irving.   Berlin: Springer-Verlag, 1972. 192p. maps. bibliog.
A study of the adaptive processes to a cold environment, by animals and man, which is
based on the author's experience as a professional zoologist in Alaska. After

introductory chapters dealing with the arctic environment and its animal and human populations, Irving goes on to consider the migration of arctic birds and the way in which they maintain their populations. This is followed by a consideration of the maintenance of arctic populations of mammals. The temperature of birds and mammals and its maintenance is discussed, together with the metabolic supply of heat. Finally, the insulation of man is considered from the viewpoint of clothing and physiological adjustment.

67 **The Arctic and its wildlife.**
    Bryan Sage, with specialist contributions from Hugh Danks, Eric Haber, Peter G. Kevan, Thomas G. Smith.   London: Croom Helm, 1986.
    190p. maps. bibliog.

A book about the ecology and resources of the Arctic for the general reader written by recognised experts in this field. Sage's contribution includes five chapters dealing with definitions, topography, climate, marine environment and terrestrial environment. Six additional chapters by individual specialists cover plant and animal adaptation, flora. insects, breeding birds, terrestrial mammals and marine mammals. Two appendixes tabulate the distributions of the 183 species of breeding birds and the forty-eight terrestrial mammals of the Arctic.

68 **Wildlife and wilderness: an artist's world.**
    Keith Shackleton.   London: Clive Holloway, 1986. 120p.

An account of the artist's fifteen years of travel as naturalist aboard *Lindblad Explorer*, an Arctic and Antarctic tourist ship. The book is illustrated with the author's own sketches.

69 **Biological Papers of the University of Alaska.**
    Fairbanks, Alaska: Institute of Arctic Biology, 1957- . occasional.

This series offers a forum for the publication of original works on any aspect of circumpolar arctic or subarctic life sciences.

70 **Polar Biology.**
    Berlin, Heidelberg: Springer-Verlag, 1982- . six times yearly.

This scientific journal publishes papers on plants, animals and micro-organisms in the polar and subpolar regions.

Flora

71 **The Arctic and Antarctic; their division into geobotanical areas.**
    V. D. Aleksandrova.   Translated by Doris Löve. Cambridge, England: Cambridge University Press, 1980. bibliog. (29 Komarov Lecture presented 14 Oct. 1974).

A classification of arctic and antarctic vegetation, produced by one of the world's leading ecologists. The Arctic is here divided into two provinces – tundra and polar desert – and further subdivided into subarctic with shrubby *Betula* (birch) and true arctic tundra without *Betula*. The book includes a full list of references and a glossary of Latin plant names.

72 **The boreal ecosystem.**
James A. Larsen. New York: Academic Press, 1980. 500p. map. bibliog.

A summary of current knowledge on the boreal forest of North America, with some reference to the boreal regions of Eurasia, written for students and graduate researchers.

73 **Cytotaxonomical atlas of the arctic flora.**
Askell Löve, Doris Löve. Vaduz, Liechtenstein: J. Cramer, 1975. 598p.

A complete checklist of families, genera, species and subspecies of vascular plants native to the northlands, giving outline details of their distribution, together with a critical review of characteristic chromosome numbers.

74 **Circumpolar arctic flora.**
Nicholas Polunin. Oxford: Clarendon Press, 1959. 514p. map. bibliog.

A systematic key to the arctic vascular flora which is based on the author's fieldwork in Svalbard, Greenland, arctic Canada and Alaska. Each species described is accompanied by a black-and-white sketch. There is a glossary and an index to plant names.

Fauna

General

75 **Encounters with arctic animals.**
Fred Bruemmer. Toronto: McGraw-Hill Ryerson, 1972. 254p. bibliog.

The author, a professional photographer, has spent many years in the Arctic. This is an account of his personal experiences with arctic animals, detailing how they live, how they are hunted, how they have been affected by the coming of European man and what measures have been taken to protect them. The book is illustrated by some outstanding colour plates.

76 **Arctic animal ecology.**
Hermann Remmert. Berlin: Springer-Verlag, 1980. 250p. maps. bibliog.

Based on the author's ecological and physiological research work in the Arctic – mostly in Svalbard – this book deals with diurnal rhythm and its relation to temperature conditions, common characteristics of arctic animals, types of arctic climates, and case studies from northern Scandinavia. It concludes with a comparison with the Antarctic in order to illustrate the vast difference between the two regions.

77 **Animals of the Arctic; the ecology of the far north.**
Bernard Stonehouse. London: Ward Lock, 1971. 172p. maps. bibliog.
The purpose of this book, by a leading arctic zoologist, is to show the simple relationships which exist between plants and animals in the arctic environment. The book opens with a definition of what is meant by 'Arctic' and 'Subarctic' followed by an account, in outline, of arctic life. Further chapters deal with the climate of the Arctic past and present, the chain of life in the arctic marine environment, sea birds of the Arctic, the invertebrate and vertebrate animals of the arctic tundra and, finally, the native populations of the Arctic and the exploitation of arctic resources by man. A glossary of terms is appended.

Birds

78 **Status and conservation of the world's seabirds.**
Edited by J. P. Croxall, P. G. H. Evans, R. W. Schreiber. Cambridge, England: International Council for Bird Preservation, 1984. 778p. maps. bibliog. (ICB Technical Publication, no. 2).
Includes forty-seven papers presented to the ICBP Seabird Conservation Symposium, Cambridge, August 1982, four of which relate to arctic regions.

79 **Swimmers and sea birds.**
Robin Minion. Edmonton, Alberta: University of Alberta, Boreal Institute for Northern Studies, 1984. 79p. (BINS Bibliographic Series, no. 12).
A bibliography of 201 references, many with short indicative notes on contents, relating to the birds of the Arctic. Indexes relate to author, region, title and species.

80 **The Snow Bunting.**
Desmond Nethersole-Thompson. Edinburgh; London: Oliver & Boyd, 1966. 316p. bibliog.
A study in the Cairngorms, Scotland, of *Plectrophenax nivalis*, a common arctic bird, dealing with courtship, territorial behaviour, voice, nesting, incubation, young, breeding, predators and distribution in Scotland.

81 **The arctic skua; a study of the ecology and evolution of a seabird.**
Peter O'Donald. Cambridge, England: Cambridge University Press, 1983. 323p. bibliog.
An eleven-year study of the arctic skua (or parasitic jaeger) *Stercorarius parasiticus* in Fair Isle. The study was undertaken with the aim of explaining how natural and sexual selection act to maintain the three forms of skua in its populations. A chapter on feeding ecology is also included giving a complete account of the population ecology and sociobiology of a single species of bird.

Land animals

82 **Arctic mammals; a celebration of survival.**
Fred Bruemmer.   Toronto: McClelland & Stewart, 1986. 159p. bibliog.
The author has spent at least six months in every year, over a period of twenty years, travelling in the arctic regions of Canada, Alaska, Greenland, Siberia and Lapland, usually in the company of scientists. This account of arctic wildlife is beautifully illustrated with the author's own colour and black-and-white photographs.

83 **Caribou and the barren lands.**
George Calef.   Ottawa: Canadian Arctic Resources Committee; Toronto: Firefly, 1981. 176p. maps. bibliog.
An account of the seasonal life-cycle of *Rangifer tarandus* in the arctic tundra together with discussions on animal ecology. The author, a professional biologist, has illustrated the volume with his own splendid photographs.

84 **Proceedings of the third international theriological congress Helsinki 15-20 August 1982. VII. Third international reindeer/caribou symposium Saariselkä 23-26 August, 1982.**
Edited by Erkki Pulliainen.   *Acta Zoologica Fennica*, no. 175 (1983), p. 1-187. maps. bibliog.
Comprises eighty papers presented on all aspects of reindeer/caribou, *Rangifer tarandus*, in Finland, Svalbard, Greenland, arctic Canada, and Alaska. The first symposium was held in Fairbanks, Alaska in 1972 and the second in Norway in 1979.

85 **Muskox bibliography.**
Julia H. Triplehorn, Lee E. Johnson.   Fairbanks, Alaska: University of Alaska, Institute of Arctic Biology, 1980. 216p.
A comprehensive reference source on musk-oxen, *Ovibos moschatus*, for the biological researcher which includes books, periodicals and newspapers. There are no annotations.

Marine mammals

86 **Seals and man; a study of interactions.**
W. Nigel Bonner.   Seattle, Washington: University of Washington Press, 1982. 170p.
A series of nine lectures on seals of the world which lays special emphasis on their interaction with man and the problems of their conservation.

87 **The life of the harp seal.**
Fred Bruemmer.   Newton Abbot, England: David & Charles, 1978.
173p. bibliog.
This first-hand account of the controversial harp seal fishery off the coast of
Newfoundland and Labrador is illustrated with the author's colour photographs.

88 **The encyclopedia of sea mammals.**
David J. Coffey.   London: Hart-Davis, MacGibbon, 1977. 223p.
A well-illustrated popular account of whales, seals, sirenia and sea otters by a
veterinary clinician specializing in animal behaviour.

89 **Lords of the Arctic; a journey among the polar bears.**
Richard C. Davids.   London: Sidgwick & Jackson, 1982. 140p. bibliog.
A personal journey into the world of the polar bear (*Ursus maritimus*), this is a
mixture of personal observations and first-rate photographs. The observations were
made in Canada and Alaska between 1977 and 1981.

90 **The book of whales.**
Richard Ellis.   New York: Alfred A. Knopf, 1982. 202p. bibliog.
A well-illustrated guide to the principle cetacean species, with reference to the past
literature. The author is a marine artist.

91 **Marine mammals of eastern North Pacific and Arctic waters.**
Edited by Delphine Haley.   Seattle: Pacific Search Press, 1978. 256p.
maps. bibliog.
An account, by twenty-one specialist authors, of the sea lions, walruses, dolphins,
whales, polar bears and sea otters, with special regard to their adaptations, biology,
behaviour and conservation.

92 **Marine mammals.**
Richard J. Harrison, Judith E. King.   London: Hutchinson University
Library, 1965. 192p. bibliog.
A general account, by two senior British zoologists, of marine mammals, including
whales, dolphins and porpoises, seals, sea lions and walruses, manatees and dugongs.

93 **The world of the polar bear.**
Thor Larsen.   London: Hamlyn, 1978. 96p. bibliog.
The author, a scientist employed by the Norwegian Polar Institute in Oslo, describes
the life-cycle, physical characteristics and distribution of the polar bear (*Ursus
maritimus*) together with an account of the measures taken for its protection.

94 **Whales, dolphins and porpoises of the eastern North Pacific and adjacent Arctic waters. A guide to their identification.**
Stephen Leatherwood, Randall R. Reeves, William F. Perrin, William E. Evans.   Seattle, Washington: National Oceanic and Atmospheric Administration, National Marine Fisheries Service, 1982. 245p.
An identification guide, well-illustrated with photographs, for cetacean identification off North American coasts.

95 **The world of the walrus.**
Richard Perry.   London: Cassell, 1967. 162p. map. bibliog.
This book provides a popular account of the life histories of the Atlantic and Pacific walrus, with chapters on the walrus industry and on the geographical range of the species.

96 **Polar bears; proceedings of the eighth working meeting of the IUCN/SSC polar bear specialist group January 1981.**
Gland, Switzerland: International Union for Conservation of Nature and Natural Resources, 1985. 151p.
A conference on polar bear research and management. Papers presented discuss current knowledge of the species (*Ursus maritimus*) from Denmark, Greenland, Svalbard (Spitsbergen), Canada, Alaska and the USSR.

97 **Handbook of marine mammals; Volume 1, the walrus, sea lions, fur seals and sea otter. Volume 2, seals.**
Edited by Sam E. Ridgway, Richard J. Harrison.   London: Academic Press, 1981. bibliog.
A guide to marine mammal types for use in the field and laboratory. It offers practical aid to identification, and provides useful basic information. Individual chapters are written by subject specialists.

98 **Research and management of polar bears *Ursus maritimus*.**
Ian Stirling.   *Polar Record*, vol. 23, no. 143 (May 1986), p. 167-76. bibliog.
In 1973 an international agreement on the conservation of polar bears and their habitats was signed in Oslo, Norway. This paper describes some of the research and management undertaken in the years leading up to the agreement and initiatives that are continuing because of this, 'an international success story in conservation'. The bibliography is especially useful.

99 **Sea mammals of the world.**
Bernard Stonehouse.   Harmondsworth, England: Penguin, 1985. 159p. maps. bibliog.
The purpose of this book is to serve as an identification manual for the general reader, to aid identification of species of sea mammals, to provide basic information on their background, numbers and way of life, and to summarize what is interesting about them. The author is a seasoned biologist and writer of numerous books and articles in this field.

100   **Whales of the world; a handbook and field guide to all the living species of whales, dolphins and porpoises.**
Lyall Watson.   London: Hutchinson, 1985. 2nd ed. 303p. maps. bibliog.
Seventy-six species of cetaceans are described in this book. Details include a summary of all known information on their appearance, distribution and habits in the wild, much of this information being published here for the first time.

Prehistory and Archaeology

101 **Eskimo prehistory.**
Hans-Georg Bandi. Translated by Ann E. Keep. London: Methuen, 1967. 226p. bibliog.
First published in 1964 as *Urgeschichte der Eskimo* (Stuttgart: Gustav Fischer-Verlag) this was written as an introduction to the subject for non-specialists. The book opens with an account of early population movements of the Eskimos and the development of theories on their prehistory. This is followed by a description of sites which spread from the eastern tip of Siberia through Alaska and arctic Canada to Greenland.

102 **The Arctic and Subarctic.**
Henry B. Collins. In: *Prehistoric man in the New World.* Edited by Jesse D. Jennings, Edward Norbeck. Chicago: University of Chicago Press for William Marsh Rice University, 1965, p. 85–114. map. bibliog.
A review of the evidence for Thule culture sites in Alaska and the Aleutian Islands and Dorset people sites in the central and eastern Arctic.

103 **Arctic archaeology; a bibliography and history.**
Albert A. Dekin, Jr. New York: Garland, 1978. 279p.
An historical review of arctic archaeological research and publications concluding with some reflections on current trends and problems. The bibliography, which this review prefaces, was compiled by the author between 1965 and 1977 as a by-product of his research. It includes a list of libraries specializing in arctic literature, a list of relevant museums and a list of serial publications with significant content on arctic archaeology.

104 **Prehistoric maritime adaptations of the circumpolar zone.**
Edited by William Fitzhugh. The Hague: Mouton, 1975. 405p. maps.
bibliog.

A collection of specialist contributions relating to the archaeological and historical
adaptations of the human species and to the complex of environments in circumpolar
Arctic, and questioning the diffusionist theories associated with Gutorm Gjessing's
circumpolar stone age concept.

105 **The discovery of a Norse settlement in America; excavations at L'Anse
aux Meadows, Newfoundland 1961–1968.**
Anne Stine Ingstad. Oslo: Universitetsforlaget, 1977. 430p. maps.
bibliog.

This, volume one, presents the results of the excavations of a settlement discovered by
the Norwegian archaeologist, Helge Ingstad, in 1960, on the northern point of
Newfoundland, Canada, together with an archaeological assessment of the finds,
comprising house-sites and other archaeological material. A number of archaeological
features are of a type suggesting that this must have been a Norse settlement. Volume
two appears not to have been published.

106 **The first Americans: origins, affinities, and adaptations.**
Edited by William S. Laughlin. Stuttgart: Albert B. Harper, 1979.
340p. maps. bibliog.

A number of specialized contributions by an internationally selected body of
anthropologists, which review the past and present research into the origins, affinities
and adaptations of the 'first Americans', such as Indians, Eskimos and Aleuts,
providing good evidence that any sample of the human species is capable of any
intellectual achievement.

107 **Prehistory of the eastern Arctic.**
Moreau S. Maxwell. London: Academic Press, 1985. 327p. maps.
bibliog. (New World Archaeological Record).

'An attempt to arrange in sequence descriptions of the adaptive technologies, tactics
and strategies devised by the prehistoric eastern Arctic Eskimo over a nearly 4,000-
year period'. Chapters describe the geographical setting, the origins of migrations, the
earliest palaeoeskimo cultures, the pre-Dorset and the Dorset cultures, the Thule
whale hunters and the period dividing the Thule culture from the first historic contact.

108 **Bibliografi over Nord-Norges arkeologi; tillegg for årene 1964-1975.**
(Bibliography of north Norwegian archaeology 1964-1975).
Poul Simonsen. Tromsø, Norway: Tromsø Museum, 1975, 51p. (*Acta
Borealia, B. Humaniora*, no. 14).

An archaeological bibliography for north Norway and Svalbard (Spitsbergen) covering
the period 1964 to 1975, supplementing an earlier bibliography of this subject up to,
and including, 1963, and published in the same series (no. 8, 1964).

109 **Reindeer and caribou hunters; an archaeological study.**
Arthur E. Spiess.   New York: Academic Press, 1979. 312p. maps.
bibliog.

A study of Arctic caribou (*Rangifer tarandus*) and its hunters, their adaptations, band structure and functioning, subsistence and settlement strategies and material culture usage. The book concludes with an analogous behavioural study of the Upper Paleolithic abri-dwellers of southeastern Europe.

History

General

110 **Russia in Pacific waters in 1715-1825; a survey of the origins of Russia's naval presence in the North and South Pacific.**
Glynn R. Barratt. Vancouver: University of British Columbia Press, 1981. 300p. bibliog. (University of British Columbia Press Pacific Maritime Studies 1).
Based on original Russian and British archival sources, this book is the first study in Russian or western literature of the rise and fall of Russian naval influence in the North Pacific Ocean from the time of Peter the Great to Tsar Nicholas I. The author explores the inherent tension between Russian naval and mercantile interests and the origins of international rivalry in the North Pacific at large.

111 **A chronological history of voyages into the arctic regions (1818). Undertaken chiefly for the purpose of discovering a North-East, North-West or polar passage between the Atlantic and Pacific.**
John Barrow. Introduction by Christopher Lloyd. Newton Abbot, England: David & Charles Reprints, 1971. 427p.
A reprint of the edition of 1818 (London: John Murray). The author of this history was Second Secretary of the British Admiralty and responsible for initiating the search for a Northwest Passage which characterized British naval activity during the first half of the 19th century. The book constitutes a review of British arctic exploration from the earliest times to 1818, when two Royal Navy expeditions – one to seek a Northwest Passage, one towards Spitsbergen and the North Pole – were despatched at Barrow's suggestion. A brief account of the fitting out of these expeditions constitutes the final chapter. After his retirement in 1845 Barrow (now Sir John) published a supplementary volume entitled *Voyages of discovery and research within the arctic regions from the year 1818 to the present time . . .* (London: John Murray, 530p.) which continued the history up to the loss of Sir John Franklin.

112 **Search for the Northwest Passage; an annotated bibliography.**
Alan Edwin Day. New York, London: Garland Publishing. 632p.
An historical approach to the gradual unveiling of this northern sea route linking the Atlantic with the Pacific Ocean which exercised the imagination of geographers and navigators from the earliest times. This listing, arranged by historic periods, traces the search from the late 15th-century voyages of the Cabots to that of Henry Larsen on the *St. Roch* in 1940-42. It includes all categories of printed material.

113 **The discoverers; an encyclopedia of explorers and exploration.**
Edited by Helen Delpar. New York: McGraw-Hill, 1980. 471p. maps.
A valuable compedium of background information for all students of the history of the polar regions. The articles contained in it are of two kinds: biographical articles relating to the careers of pre-eminent explorers, and articles dealing with the principal geographical regions. The latter cover a variety of topics such as cartography and oceanography. Articles particularly relevant to the Arctic include those dealing with the search for a Northwest and Northeast Passage, the efforts to penetrate the Arctic, and Norse maritime discoveries. The contributors are all recognized experts in their special fields.

114 **An evaluation of British Royal Naval arctic exploration techniques: 1818-1876.**
R. D. Ellis. Cambridge, England: Scott Polar Research Institute, 1986. 120p. maps. bibliog. (Thesis submitted for the M. Phil. in Polar Studies, University of Cambridge).
The British Royal Navy arctic expeditions of the 19th century have been criticized as being rigid in approach, refusing to adapt to native technologies of survival in polar conditions. This thesis is a review of the methods of sailors, including Sir John Ross, Sir William Edward Parry, Sir John Franklin and Sir Leopold McClintock. The author concludes that though 'heavy in basic approach, [the Navy] nevertheless showed a remarkable capacity for adaptation to indigenous survival techniques given the rigid system under which it operated'.

115 **The white road; a survey of polar exploration.**
L. P. Kirwan. London: Hollis & Carter, 1959. 374p. maps. bibliog.
Written by a former Director and Secretary of the Royal Geographical Society this text still remains the best succinct and critical history of polar exploration in print. It is divided approximately equally between the Arctic and Antarctic. A subsequent edition was later published in paperback under the title *History of polar exploration* (Harmondsworth, England: Penguin, 1962).

116 **To the Arctic! The story of northern exploration from earliest times to the present.**
Jeannette Mirsky. Introduction by Vilhjalmur Stefansson. Chicago: University of Chicago Press, 1970. 352p. bibliog.
An updated version of the author's *To the north*, published in 1934 and reprinted in 1948 under the present title. The late Dr Vilhjalmur Stefansson, in his introduction to this edition, describes the book as 'the best history of northern exploration so far written'. Beginning with a description of the circumpolar arctic regions the author then outlines the earliest recorded northern voyages by Greeks and Vikings, following with

an account of the pre-Columban voyages up to the rediscovery of Greenland by John Davis. Subsequent chapters deal with the Dutch voyages to the Arctic and the Spitsbergen whaling industry, the discoveries of Henry Hudson, Russian exploration in the Arctic and the British attack on the Arctic in the early 19th century. An account of the tragic last voyage of Sir John Franklin and the series of search voyages that resulted then follows. The second half of the 19th century was characterized by expeditions towards the North Pole, the exploration of Greenland, the discovery of the Northeast and Northwest Passages and Peary's achievement of the North Pole. A chapter on the early arctic flights and the first use of a submarine under the polar ice by Sir Hubert Wilkins concludes this invaluable handbook. Among the appendixes is a useful chronology of northern exploration.

117 **A history of polar exploration.**
David Mountfield.   London: Book Club Associates, 1974. 208p. bibliog.

A popular, well-illustrated history of arctic and antarctic exploration.

118 **The polar passion; the quest for the North Pole with selections from arctic journals.**
Farley Mowat.   Toronto: McClelland & Stewart, 1967. 303p. maps. bibliog.

The history of the quest for the North Pole, told through extracts from selected contemporary accounts, each prefaced by an analysis by Farley Mowat. The selection ranges from the Norse saga of Thorgish Orrabeinsfostri (c. 997 AD) to the controversy surrounding Frederick Cook and Robert Peary in 1907-8.

119 **In northern mists. Arctic exploration in early times.**
Fridtjof Nansen.   London: Heinemann, 1911. 2 vols.

These two volumes by the famous Norwegian oceanographer and arctic explorer represent a seminal work in the field of polar history. They cover the Norse voyages and settlements, and the discoveries by the Portuguese and John Cabot in Newfoundland and southern Labrador.

120 **To the ends of the earth; four expeditions to the Arctic, the Congo, the Gobi and Siberia.**
John Perkins.   New York: Pantheon, 1981. 184p.

An account, largely in the explorers' own words, of four expeditions (two to the Arctic) in the early years of this century, mounted by the American Museum of Natural History. Of the two polar expeditions, one, under the leadership of Robert E. Peary, was the first to achieve the North Pole on 6 April, 1909, and is described in Peary's book *The North Pole* (q.v.). The second expedition, sponsored by Morris K. Jessup (known as the Jessup North Pacific Expedition) and led by the great anthropologist Franz Boas, visited the native peoples on both sides of Bering Strait to see if they were related and to deduce how and when people might have passed between the two continents. Much of the field work was carried out in eastern Siberia between 1899 and 1902, by two assistant anthropologists, Waldemar Jochelson and Waldemar Bogaras, working among the Koryak, Chukchi and Yukagir peoples. Additional field work was carried out on the northwest coast of America and in southeast Siberia. The book is illustrated with numerous contemporary photographs.

121 **The white ribbon; a medallic record of British polar exploration.**
Neville Poulsom.   London: B. A. Seaby, 1968. 216p.

An account of those arctic and antarctic expeditions between 1818 and 1961, whose members received the award of the Arctic or Polar Medal. A description is given of each expedition from 1818, together with details of the medals themselves and the names of all the men to whom an award has been made for polar exploration and scientific research, up to the end of 1966.

122 **Unveiling the Arctic.**
Edited by Louis Rey, Claudette Reed Upton, Marvin Falk.   Calgary, Alberta: Arctic Institute of North America; Monaco; Comité Arctique International; Fairbanks, Alaska: University of Alaska Press, 1984. 613p. bibliog.

Represents a volume of papers presented at a conference held in Rome in 1981, entitled 'The history of the discovery of the arctic regions as seen through the descriptions of travellers and the work of cartographers from early antiquity to the 18th century', and organized by the Comité Arctique International. The twenty-eight contributions, all by internationally recognized experts, deal primarily with the early history of arctic exploration and cartography, but are also concerned with native peoples, law of the sea, missionary activity, the whaling industry and fisheries.

123 **An account of the Arctic regions with a history and description of the northern whale-fishery. Volume 1: The Arctic. Volume 2: The whale-fishery.**
William Scoresby.   Newton Abbot, England: David & Charles, 1969. 2 vols.

A reprint of the original edition (Edinburgh: Archibald Constable, 1820) with an introduction by the late Sir Alister Hardy. The first volume is virtually a textbook of arctic geography which includes a discourse on the supposed sea communication between the Atlantic and Pacific Oceans, a description of Spitsbergen and Jan Mayen Island, a hydrographical survey of the Greenland Sea and an account of polar sea ice, meteorology and zoology including a definitive account of the Greenland whale. The second volume, in Hardy's opinion, is 'the finest account of the arctic whale fishery ever written . . . an excellent early history, a detailed account of the methods used and a study of the economics of the industry at the end of the eighteenth and the beginning of the nineteenth centuries . . . here we find some of the most striking passages in literature . . . which stand comparison with *Moby Dick*'.

124 **The polar ice (1815); The North Pole (1828).**
William Scoresby.   Whitby, England: Caedmon of Whitby, 1980. [100]p.

William Scoresby, Jr. F.R.S. (1789-1857) was remarkable not only as an arctic whaler and navigator, but as an astute observer and scientist. This book consists of reprints of two of his early learned papers. The first, whose full title is *On the Greenland or polar ice*, was first published in the *Memoirs* of the Wernerian Society, (vol. II, (1815), p. 328-36). It constitutes one of the first attempts to classify and describe floating ice, concluding with remarks on the possibility of achieving the North Pole by travelling over the frozen sea. The second paper, *On the probability of reaching the North Pole*, first published in the *Edinburgh New Philosophical Journal* (July, 1828), p. 1-20), continues the theme with special reference to Captain William Edward Parry's attempt to reach the North Pole from Spitsbergen in 1827.

125 **Icebound; journeys to the northwest sea.**
J. M. Scott. London: Gordon & Cremonesi, 1977. 156p. maps.
A short history, by a seasoned arctic explorer, of the disovery of the Northwest Passage from Cabot to Franklin.

126 **The private life of polar exploration.**
J. M. Scott. Edinburgh: William Blackwood, 1982. 177p. maps.
The author, himself an experienced arctic explorer, has selected, from the annals of polar history, tales of the discomforts, obstacles and dangers encountered by explorers over the centuries, including the rescue of the survivors from the *Italia* disaster of 1928, the incredible flights of Lincoln Ellsworth, the death of the German explorer and scientist Dr Alfred Wegener on the Greenland ice sheet in 1929, the tragic and mysterious death of the American explorer Charles Francis Hall in north Greenland in 1871 and Jane Franklin's efforts to solve the mystery of the loss of her husband Sir John Franklin.

127 **William Scoresby; arctic scientist.**
Tom Stamp, Cordelia Stamp. Whitby, England: Caedmon of Whitby Press, 1976. 253p.
A life of the famous Yorkshireman, William Scoresby (1789-1857), who in turn was Greenland whaler, Anglican clergyman, and scientist. This biography is based on the Scoresby papers belonging to the Whitby Literary and Philosophical Society.

128 **British parliamentary papers on exploration in the Canadian north.**
Andrew Taylor. In: *Arctic bibliography*. Edited by Marie
Tremaine. Washington, DC: Department of Defense, 1959, vol. 8, p. 317-52.
Items 45212-45257 describe and detail the contents of documents concerning the British government expeditions in the North American Arctic in the 19th century. Most of these papers originated in the Admiralty and were presented to one or both Houses of Parliament in connection with an inquiry and were published as Sessional Papers. Most deal with the mid-century search for Sir John Franklin; others concern the abortive expedition towards the North Pole under the leadership of Sir George Nares, 1875-76.

129 **Polar exploration.**
Terence Wise. London: Almark, 1973. 167p.
A brief summary history of arctic and antarctic exploration with a final chapter dealing with polar transportation.

130 **Fram: Journal of Polar Studies.**
Bangor, Maine: Polaris, 1984- . twice-yearly.
A journal devoted to aspects of arctic and antarctic history and including reprints of rare pamphlets and other documents.

Voyages and expeditions

Early voyages

131 **The Norse discoverers of America; the Wineland sagas.**
G. M. Gathorne-Hardy. Introduction by Gwyn Jones. Oxford:
Clarendon, 1970. 304p. bibliog.
A reprint of the 1921 edition, with a new introduction by Professor Gwyn Jones. The
first part of the book is a translation of the Icelandic sagas relating to Eric the Red and
his son Leif, covering also the colonization of Greenland, together with early voyages
to 'Wineland' (Vinland). Part two discusses the historical significance of the sagas.

132 **The Norse-Atlantic saga; being the Norse voyages of discovery and
settlement to Iceland, Greenland, America.**
Gwyn Jones. London: Oxford University Press, 1986. 2nd ed. 337p.
maps. bibliog.
The theme of this book is the Norsemen's search for new land westward across the
North Atlantic from their homes in Scandinavia. It deals with voyages of discovery and
exploration to Iceland and Greenland and to the west coast of North America, and the
attempts of the Norsemen to colonize all three. Part one of the book is a narrative
account of the history of these events. Part two contains the sagas which constitute the
source material for the history. Additional sagas are reviewed and summarized in the
appendices.

133 **The Vinland sagas; the Norse discovery of America. Graelendinga saga
and Erik's saga.**
Translated by Magnus Magnusson, Hermann Palsson. Harmondsworth,
England: Penguin, 1968. 124p. maps.
An annotated translation of two mediaeval Icelandic sagas telling of the founding of a
colony on the west coast of Greenland by Eric the Red and of subsequent voyages to
the shores of the New World.

134 **The conquest of the North Atlantic.**
G. J. Marcus. Woodbridge, England: Boydell, 1980. 224p. maps.
bibliog.
The first section of this book is devoted to a scholarly assessment of the voyages made
in the northwest Atlantic by Irish monks from the 6th century AD onwards, leading to
the first discovery of Iceland sometime in the 8th century. The second section deals
with Norse expansion leading to the settlement of Greenland. The third section is
concerned with the history of English trafficking with Iceland and Greenland and with
the voyages of John Cabot. Throughout the book considerable emphasis is laid on
contemporary naval technology and seamanship.

135 **Early voyages and northern approaches 1000-1632.**
Tryggvi J. Oleson. Toronto: McClelland & Stewart; London: Oxford University Press, 1964. 211p. map. bibliog.

A history of pre-Columban voyages to North America which submits evidence of some cultural intermixing of peoples from Iceland with the peoples of Dorset in what is now the Canadian Arctic.

136 **Atlantic crossings before Columbus.**
Frederick J. Pohl. New York: W. W. Norton, 1961. 315p. bibliog.

An investigation of the early Irish and Viking voyages to North America, the highly speculative voyage made by the Venetian brothers Nicolo and Antonio Zeno to Iceland and Greenland in 1380-87, and the Kensington runestone, the supposed relic of a 14th-century Scandinavian expedition to North America.

137 **The Cabot voyages and Bristol discovery under Henry VII.**
James A. Williamson. Cambridge, England: Cambridge University Press for the Hakluyt Society, 1962. 332p. maps. bibliog. (Hakluyt Society Second Series, no. 120).

Of particular interest in this well-documented study of the Cabot voyages is the appraisal of Sebastian Cabot's voyage in 1508-09, intended for the discovery of the Northwest Passage, the evidence for which is fragmentary. An important category of the evidence is the maps reproduced here and explained by the late R. A. Skelton of the British Museum Map Room.

138 **The problem of Pytheas' Thule.**
Ian Whitaker. *Classical Journal*, vol. 77, no. 2 (Dec. 1981/Jan. 1982), p. 148-64.

A scholarly analysis of a voyage made by Pytheas of Massilia (modern Marseilles) sometime during the 4th century BC, which passed through the Pillars of Hercules and into the Atlantic Ocean, then circumnavigated Great Britain and finally achieved 'Ultima Thule' on the Arctic Circle – possibly Iceland.

16th to 18th centuries

139 **The three voyages of William Barents to the arctic regions (1594, 1595 and 1596).**
Gerrit de Veer. 1st ed. edited by Charles T. Beeke, 2nd ed. introduction by Lieutenant Koolemans Beynen. New York: Burt Franklin, (n.d.). 290p. (Reprint of Hakluyt Society Publication First Series, no. 54, 1876).

Gerrit de Veer participated in William Barents' three voyages of 1594, 1595 and 1596, on the last of which Bear Island (Bjørnøya) and the northwest coast of Spitsbergen were discovered. The ship was wrecked on the coast of Novaya Zemlya, where the expedition spent two winters. Barents was later rescued by Russians but died of scurvy.

The second edition of the Hakluyt Society's translation contains much information on the relics brought back to England in 1871. The maps published in the original edition are lacking in this reprint.

140 **The possibility of approaching the North Pole asserted by the Hon. D. Barrington. A new edition with an appendix containing papers on the same subject and on a North West Passage by Colonel Beaufoy, F.R.S.**
Daines Barrington, Mark Beaufoy. London: T. & J. Allman, 1818. 2nd ed. 258p. map.

A collection of tracts or documents relating to the records of early navigators concerning the navigability of the Arctic Ocean and the best season for open water, including the evidence of whaling and fishing captains. It was Barrington who proposed the voyage undertaken by Constantine Phipps, described in *A voyage towards the North Pole . . .*, in 1773 (q.v.). This second edition of his book, first published in 1775, has some additional papers by Colonel Beaufoy relating to the practicability of reaching the North Pole in winter from Spitsbergen by sledge travel over the sea ice. Publication coincided with the imminent departure of the Arctic expeditions led by John Ross and David Buchan, which Ross described in his book *A voyage of discovery . . . in His Majesty's ships Isabella and Alexander* (q.v.).

141 **A voyage towards the North Pole undertaken by His Majesty's Command.**
Constantine John Phipps. London: J. Nourse, 1774. 253p.

At the instigation of the Honourable Daines Barrington, a lawyer and keen naturalist, an expedition under Captain the Honourable Constantine John Phipps (later 2nd Lord Mulgrave) was despatched by the British Admiralty in 1773 to the North Pole by way of Spitsbergen. Phipps commanded the *Racehorse* accompanied by the *Carcass* under Commander Skeffington Lutwidge with the young Horatio Nelson aboard. Neither vessel succeeded in getting anywhere near the North Pole, but Hudson Bay and Spitsbergen waters were explored. This volume was reprinted in part (p. 1-76) by Caedmon Press, Whitby, England in 1978, but without the scientific appendixes.

142 **The voyage of the *Resolution* and *Discovery* 1776-1780.**
Edited by J. C. Beaglehole. Cambridge, England: Cambridge University Press for the Hakluyt Society, 1967. 2 vols. maps. bibliog. (Hakluyt Society, Extra Series, 36).

This, the last of Captain James Cook's three great voyages of discovery, had as its objective the discovery of 'a Northern Passage by sea from the Pacific to the Atlantic Ocean' – the long-sought Northwest Passage. This remarkable voyage led northward along the west coast of Canada and Alaska, through Bering Strait, to a farthest north of latitute 70°44'. Returning to Hawaii, Cook was murdered by the natives. Under the command of Lieutenant Gore and Commander Clerke the ships returned north to visit Kamchatka and Bering Strait, but achieved little. These volumes contain not only a scrupulously edited text of Cook's holograph journals, but also those of many other ships' officers. In addition there are appendixes of documents and correspondence together with reproductions of drawings and paintings by the expedition's artist John Webber.

19th century

143 **A voyage of discovery towards the North Pole, performed in His Majesty's ships Dorothea and Trent, under the command of Captain David Buchan, R.N., 1818; to which is added, a summary of all the early attempts to reach the Pacific by way of the Pole.**
F. W. Beechey. London: Richard Bentley, 1843. 351p. map.
The author, later Sir Frederick William Beechey, arctic explorer of renown, took part in this voyage under Captain John Franklin in command of *Trent*. In part one Beechey describes the voyage, ice conditions and surveying in northwestern Spitsbergen. Part two is a review of earlier voyages to discover a Northeast Passage in this region.

144 **A voyage round the world 1826-1829. Vol. 1. To Russian America and Siberia.**
Frederick Litke. Edited by Richard A. Pierce. Kingston, Ontario: Limestone, 1987. 230p. maps.
An account of the voyage of the Russian sloop-of-war *Seniavin* under the command of Captain Fedor Petrovich Litke, from 1826-28. Visits were made to Sitka and to St. Matthew Island, Alaska, in 1827. In 1828 the east coast of Kamchatka was surveyed and the shores of the Chukotka Peninsula, northern Bering Sea, described. This edition is a translation of the French edition of 1835. An appendix (p. 121-89) contains an English translation of an account of the journey by the expedition's ornithologist, Friederich Heinrich, Baron von Kittlitz, originally published in German in 1858.

145 **Narrative of a voyage to the polar sea during 1875-76 in H.M. Ships 'Alert' and 'Discovery' . . .**
Sir G. S. Nares. London: Sampson, Low, Marston, Searle & Rivington, 1878. 2nd ed, 2 vols. map.
The official narrative, by its commanding officer, of a British naval expedition whose principle objective was the achievement of the highest possible northern latitude, if possible the North Pole, by way of Smith Sound. While *Discovery* wintered in Lady Franklin Bay, Ellesmere Island, northern Canada, *Alert* achieved what was then the highest northern latitude of 82°27'N and then wintered at Floeberg Beach on the east coast of Ellesmere Island. In the spring and summer of 1876 parties from *Alert* sledged towards the North Pole, achieving latitutde 83°20'26", but unfortunately a severe outbreak of scurvy prevented further progress and prompted the premature return of the expedition to England in the autumn of 1876. Though primarily a voyage of geographical discovery, the geology and biology of the regions were investigated, and notes on these by the naturalist H. W. Feilden are appended.

146 **The voyage of the Jeannette; the ship and ice journals of George W. De Long.**
George W. De Long. Edited by Emma De Long. Boston, Massachusetts: 1884. 2 vols. maps.
This ill-fated expedition left San Francisco in July 1879 bound for the North Pole. On board were thirty-three explorers commanded by Lieutenant George Washington De

Long, USN. Financed by publisher J. Gordon Bennett and supported by the US Navy the crew were, nevertheless, inexperienced in arctic navigation. Clearing Bering Strait *Jeannette* eventually went adrift in the ice off Herald Island in November 1879. She then drifted north and west for nine months and was finally crushed by ice and sank northeast of the New Siberian Islands, latitude 77°14′N. Only twenty-five men survived to eventually reach the delta of the Lena River in Siberia where De Long and eleven others perished. This account is based on De Long's private papers and other material.

147   **Icebound; the Jeannette expedition's quest for the North Pole.**
Leonard F. Guttridge.   Shrewsbury, England: Airlife, 1988. 357p.
maps. bibliog.
The story of George Washington De Long's North Pole expedition of 1879 concluding with an account of the naval enquiry concerning the loss of the ship *Jeannette* together with De Long and eleven companions.

148   **The first International Polar Year, 1882-83.**
F. W. G. Baker.   *Polar Record*, vol. 21, no. 132 (Sept. 1982),
p. 275-85, bibliog.
The idea of a coordinated programme of scientific research in the polar regions was developed by the Austrian Karl Weyprecht in 1875 and put into operation with the first International Polar Year (IPY) 1882-83. This article traces the origins of the idea in the 18th century, describes its subsequent development and outlines the organizational plans of the IPY when eleven nations established circumpolar stations in the Arctic. There follows an outline account of the several expeditions involved, and there is also a summary of the second IPY (1932-33) and its successor, the International Geophysical Year (IGY) of 1957-58.

149   **The expeditions of the first International Polar Year 1882-83.**
W. Barr.   Calgary, Alberta: Arctic Institute of North America, 1985.
222p. map. bibliog.
A concise, expert and comprehensive account of the American, Austrian, British, Danish, Dutch, Finnish, German, Norwegian, Russian and Swedish expeditions to the Arctic contributing to the first truly international exercise in polar scientific cooperation.

150   **'Farthest north'; being the record of a voyage of exploration of the ship**
Fram 1893-96 and of a fifteen months' sleigh journey by Dr. Nansen and
Lieut. Johansen with an appendix by Otto Sverdrup captain of the
Fram.
Fridtjof Nansen.   London: Archibald Constable, 1897. 2 vols. maps.
A translation of the Norwegian edition *Fram over polhavet* . . . (Kristiania: H. Aschehoug, 1897). This is an account of an expedition led by the famous Norwegian arctic explorer Fridtjof Nansen with the object of investigating the hydrology of the central arctic basin by drifting in the ice in the region of the North Pole. *Fram* was purpose-built to withstand the pressure of the polar pack. The narrative tells of the *Fram's* voyage from northern Norway, across the Kara Sea to the New Siberian Islands (Novosibirskiye Ostrova), and the subsequent drift across the Arctic Ocean from September 1893 to March 1895, including the sledge journey made by Nansen and

F. H. Johansen towards the North Pole, their wintering on Franz Josef Land (Zemlya Frantsa-Iosifa) and their meeting with the Jackson–Harmsworth expedition. led by Frederick G. Jackson, who described it in *A thousand days in the Arctic* (q.v.). Finally their voyage home on *Windward* is described. This classic expedition not only conclusively disproved the prevalent theory of an open polar sea around the North Pole, but brought back scientific data that was to prove seminal to our understanding of the circulation of currents in the arctic basin.

151 **The arctic diary of Russell Williams Porter.**
Russell Williams Porter. Edited by Herman R. Friis. Charlottesville, Virginia: University of Virginia Press, 1976. 172p. maps. bibliog.
Born in 1871 Porter took part in ten arctic expeditions between 1894 and 1912 as surveyor, cartographer, astronomer and artist. This book is an edited version of his *Arctic diary* based on his field notes and sketches, and is illustrated with many of his own illustrations. The main expeditions described are the Baldwin-Ziegler expedition to Franz Josef Land, 1901-02 and the Fiala-Ziegler expedition of 1903-05.

152 **On the 'Polar Star' in the Arctic Sea . . . with the statements of Commander U. Cagni upon the sledge expedition to 86° North, and of Dr A. Cavalli Molinelli upon his return to the Bay of Teplitz.**
Luigi Amedeo of Savoy. Translated by William Le Queux. London: Hutchinson, 1903. 2 vols. maps.
Offers a translation of the Italian *La 'Stella Polare' nel mare Artico, 1899-1900.* This is the official narrative by the leader, Luigi Duke of the Abruzzi, of an expedition to Rudolph Island, Franz Josef Land, from whence sledge journeys were undertaken in an attempt to reach the North Pole. The narrative of this latter journey is taken from Commander Cagni's journal.

153 **The Andrée diaries, being the diaries and records of S. A. Andrée, Nils Strindberg and Knut Fraenkel written during their balloon expedition to the North Pole in 1897 and discovered on White Island in 1930, together with a complete record of the expedition and discovery.**
S. A. Andrée, Nils Strindberg, Knut Fraenkel. Translated by Edward Adams-Ray. London: John Lane, Bodley Head, 1931. 471p. maps.
In 1897 Salomon August Andrée, a Swedish scientist, influenced by Fridtjof Nansen's drift on the *Fram*, described in Nansen's book (q.v.) made the first attempt to reach the North Pole by balloon. Accompanied by Strindberg and Fraenkel, Andrée left Danes Island, Spitsbergen in the balloon *Örnen* (*Eagle*) on 11 July but the steering failed, gas was lost, and on 14 July a forced landing was made on the ice in latitude 82°56′N, longitude 29°56′E, 327 miles having been travelled. The stranded men made camp on the ice and attempted to make for Franz Josef Land. The drifting ice frustrated their efforts and by October had carried them to White Island, off the North East coast of Spitsbergen. The fate of the three men remained a mystery until, by a miraculous chance, the bodies and journals together with undeveloped photographs were found by Dr Gunnar Horn in 1930. Thus the almost complete story of this historic journey was made public. This edition is translated from the original Swedish *Med Örnen mot Polen.* (Stockholm: Albert Bonniers Forlag.)

20th century

154 **My life as an explorer.**
Roald Amundsen. London: William Heinemann, 1927. 283p.
The autobiography of the great Norwegian explorer who first achieved fame for his navigation of the Northwest Passage in *Gjøa*, 1903-06. In 1911 he reached the South Pole ahead of Captain Scott. His career culminated with a flight over the North Pole with Lincoln Ellsworth in 1926.

155 **Nearest the Pole; a narrative of the polar expedition of the Peary Arctic Club in the S.S. Roosevelt, 1905-1906.**
R. E. Peary. New York: Doubleday, Page, 1907. 411p. maps.
After gaining his early arctic travel experience in Greenland from 1886 onwards, Robert Peary (later to become Admiral Robert Peary, USN) made his first assault on the North Pole in the years 1898-1902 with the ship *Windward* achieving latitutde 84°17'N on the Arctic Ocean ice. This book is an account of his second attempt in 1905-06 when Peary pushed north as far as latitude 86°34'N from his base in northern Ellesmere Island. The support vessel, *Roosevelt*, was designed by Peary to withstand ice pressure.

156 **The North Pole.**
Robert E. Peary. London: Hodder & Stoughton, 1910. 326p. map.
In July 1908 Peary started on his eighth and last arctic expedition of which this is the classic narrative. Sailing north on the SS *Roosevelt* he established his base camp at Cape Sheridan, northern Ellesmere Island. Peary's plan to achieve the North Pole by a sequence of four supporting dog sledging parties proved finally successful. On 6 April 1909 Peary reached the Pole, accompanied by a negro, Matthew Henson, and four Eskimos.

157 **My attainment of the Pole; being the record of the expedition that first reached the boreal center 1907-1909, with the final summary of the polar controversy.**
Frederick A. Cook. New York: Polar; London: Arlen, 1911. 604p. map.
The official narrative of Frederick Cook's sledge journey with Eskimo companions across Ellesmere Island to Axel Heiberg Island, Northwest Territories of Canada, and thence, as he claimed, to the North Pole, reached on 21 April 1908. The book concludes with a discussion of the validity of his claim, which is also considered by William R. Hunt (q.v.).

158 **To stand at the Pole; the Dr Cook-Admiral Peary North Pole controversy.**
William R. Hunt. New York: Stein & Day, 1981. 288p. bibliog.
A scholarly appraisal by a senior polar historian of the evidence for and against Dr Frederick Cook's claim to have reached the North Pole in 1908, a year before Robert E. Peary. The book does not claim to be a definitive analysis of evidence either for or

against Cook's polar claim or his claim to be the first to climb Mount McKinley, Alaska's highest mountain. Rather, it focuses on the people who believed or doubted Cook, and thereby gives perspective to the whole complex issue.

159 Peary at the North Pole; fact or fiction?

Dennis Rawlins.   Washington, DC; New York: Robert B. Luce, 1973, 320p. bibliog.

The achievement of the North Pole is usually attributed to Robert Edwin Peary. At the time, however, this claim was bitterly contested by Dr Frederick Cook who asserted that he had reached the Pole on 21 April, 1908. Subsequently, because of other deceptions, Cook's story was discredited. In this book Dr Rawlins attempts to demonstrate that Peary's claims to have achieved the Pole are also questionable and maintains that the first explorers to properly make this claim were Roald Amundsen and Lincoln Ellsworth in the airship *Norge* in 1926, who describe their journey in *The first flight across the polar sea* (q.v.). The first completely verified achievement of the North Pole by surface travel was the United States–Canadian expedition under the leadership of Ralph Plaisted in 1968.

160 The first flight across the polar sea.

Roald Amundsen, Lincoln Ellsworth.   London: Hutchinson, [1927], 274p. map.

The official narrative of the Norwegian Roald Amundsen's flight, with the US aviator Lincoln Ellsworth and pilot Umberto Nobile in the Italian airship *Norge*, over the North Pole in 1926. The airship flew from King's Bay, Spitsbergen, over the Pole to Teller, Alaska. This was the first polar expedition to use an airship. The book includes biographical information on the expedition members and some specialist contributions concerning such topics as navigation and weather conditions.

161 Skyward.

Richard Evelyn Byrd.   New York: Knickerbocker Press, 1928. 359p.

An autobiographical account by America's leading air explorer in the 1920s and 1930s which includes the narrative of the first flight to the North Pole by Byrd and Floyd Bennett in the Fokker trimotor *Josephine Ford*, 9 May, 1926.

162 With the 'Italia' to the North Pole.

Umberto Nobile.   English translation by Frank Fleetwood. London: George Allen & Unwin, 1930. 353p. maps.

Commanded by Nobile and supported by the Italian government, this expedition, with the dirigible *Italia*, left Europe on 5 May 1928, and flew to West Spitsbergen then to Severnaya Zemlya, returning to West Spitsbergen on 18 May. A flight to the North Pole via Greenland on 23 May was accomplished, but on the return voyage *Italia* crashed on 25 May on the sea ice north of West Spitsbergen. The men in the pilot's cabin were spilled out on to the ice, mostly with only minor injuries. The gondola, still attached to the gas bag, with six men in it disappeared forever. A number of relief expeditions were sent out to search for the survivors. Nobile himself was rescued by the Swedish aviator Lundborg; the remainder, after many attempts, were eventually taken off the ice by the Russian icebreaker *Krassin*. It was on one of these search expeditions that the famous polar explorer Roald Amundsen was lost with his aircraft.

163   **Under the North Pole; the Wilkins-Ellsworth submarine expedition.**
Sir Hubert Wilkins.   [New York]: Brewer, Warren & Putnam, [1931].
347p. map.
An account of the first attempt to navigate under the Arctic Ocean ice to the North
Pole, by submarine *Nautilus*. Accompanied by the Norwegian oceanographer Professor
Harald Sverdrup, Wilkins set out from Longyearbyen, Spitsbergen, in August 1931;
but *Nautilus* suffered damage to the diving gear and achieved only latitude 82°15'N.
Not until 1958 did Commander W. R. Anderson USN in another *Nautilus*, this time
atomic-powered, achieve the first submarine trans-polar crossing, a voyage he
describes in *Nautilus 90 North* (q.v.).

164   **Nautilus 90 North.**
William R. Anderson, Clay Blair, Jr.   London: Hodder & Stoughton,
1959. 190p.
An account, by her captain, of the voyage of the United States Navy atomic-powered
submarine *Nautilus* from Pearl Harbour, Hawaii, by way of Bering Strait and under
the North Pole to Iceland and England in 1958. The submarine was under the ice pack
for ninety-six hours, covering a distance of 1,830 miles as a depth of 400 feet. This was
the first successful submarine voyage under the arctic ice and fulfilled the dream of Sir
Hubert Wilkins, whose attempt to achieve this himself is told in *Under the North Pole
. . .* (q.v.).

165   **Surface at the Pole; the story of USS *Skate*.**
James Calvert.   London: Hutchinson, 1961. 220p. maps.
This United States submarine expedition of 1959 achieved fame by being the first to
actually surface at the North Pole where a cairn was built and the ashes of Sir Hubert
Wilkins, the pioneer subarctic mariner, were scattered.

166   **On skis toward the North Pole.**
Bjørn O. Staib.   Translated by Christopher Nordman. Garden City,
New York: Doubleday, 1965. 178p. map.
The official narrative by the leader of an eleven-man Norwegian expedition which set
out in 1964 with husky dogs to retrace Robert E. Peary's route to the North Pole of
1909. Appalling weather conditions finally defeated Bjørn Staib's party and the
attempt had to be abandoned 200 miles from the Pole at latitude 86°31'N, but some
valuable research was carried out on the physiology of arctic survival.

167   **To the top of the world; the adventures and misadventures of the
Plaisted Polar Expedition, March 28-May 4, 1967.**
Charles Kuralt.   New York: Holt, Rinehart & Winston, 1968. 193p.
Describes a twelve-man American expedition to the North Pole, under the leadership
of Ralph Plaisted, the first attempt to achieve 'the top of the world' by an overland
motorized vehicle ('snowmobile'). The expedition was, in fact, a failure, achieving only
latitude 83°36'N before being lifted off the ice by airplane.

168 **Across the top of the world; the British Trans-Arctic Expedition.**
Wally Herbert. London: Longmans, 1969. 209p. map.

The leader's account of a record-making journey which took him and his three companions, with thirty-four husky dogs and sledges, from Point Barrow, Alaska, across the Arctic Ocean and via the North Pole to Spitsbergen, covering a distance of some 3,600 miles. Compelled to winter among the ice floes, the journey took Herbert from 21 February 1968 to 29 May 1969 to complete.

169 **Due north.**
Myrtle Simpson. London: Victor Gollancz, 1970. 191p.

An attempt to achieve the North Pole with sledge and skis by Dr Hugh Simpson, his wife Myrtle and Roger Tufft, from February to April, 1969. The expedition turned back at latitude 84°42′N, thus frustrating Myrtle Simpson's ambition to be the first woman to reach the North Pole.

170 **Hell on ice.**
Ranulph Fiennes. London: Hodder & Stoughton, 1979. 256p. maps.

The leader's narrative of an expedition consisting of four men and two women over the arctic sea ice towards the North Pole in the winter of 1976-77. The expedition set out from Alert in northern Ellesmere Island, arctic Canada, with sledges and motor skidoos and assisted by air re-supply. The party failed to reach the North Pole but attained latitude 87°11.5′N. The expedition constituted an exercise prior to setting off on the Transglobe Expedition in September 1979, which is detailed by Fiennes in *To the ends of the earth* (q.v.).

171 **Icebreaker voyage to the North Pole, 1977.**
Polar Record, vol. 19, no. 118 (Jan. 1978), p. 67-68, map.

A short account summarized from reports in the Soviet journals *Pravda* and *Vodnyy Transport* of the successful voyage to the North Pole made in August 1977 by the Soviet nuclear-powered icebreaker *Arktika*, the first surface vessel ever to accomplish this feat.

172 **Solo to the Pole.**
Naomi Uemura. *National Geographic*, vol. 154, no. 3 (Sept. 1978), p. 298-325, map.

The story of the first solo expedition to the North Pole in 1978 by the Japanese explorer Naomi Uemura. From Cape Columbia, northern Ellesmere Island, using sledge dogs, Uemura covered 500 miles of ice-covered ocean in eight weeks. From the Pole he was airlifted to northern Greenland were he began an attempt to cross the inland icesheet.

173 **To the ends of the earth.**
Ranulph Fiennes. London: Hodder & Stoughton, 1983. 320p. maps. bibliog.

Described by its patron Prince Charles as 'a mad and splendidly British enterprise' the Transglobe Expedition, 1979-83, was planned to travel round the world from Greenwich, London, and back to Greenwich along the zero meridian. After a preliminary limbering-up operation in Greenland and the Arctic Ocean described by

Sir Ranulph Fiennes in *Hell on ice* (q.v.) the expedition, under Fiennes' leadership, set sail for Antarctica and the South Pole in September 1979. Having successfully traversed the Southern Continent the expedition returned to the Arctic where the Northwest Passage was navigated and, with the aid of motor skidoos, the pressure ridges and melt pools of the Arctic Ocean negotiated, the North Pole finally being reached on 10 April, 1982. Subsequently, the pole party was rescued from a drifing ice floe by the expedition ship, *Benjamin Bowring*, returning to London by the following August. An outline of the scientific work achieved is included in the appendixes, together with a chronological listing of previous arctic expeditions.

174 **Ymer-80: a Swedish expedition to the Arctic Ocean.**
Walter Schytt. *Geographical Journal*, vol. 149, no. 1 (March 1983), p. 22-28. map.

A description, by its scientific director, of an international expedition under the auspices of the Swedish Royal Academy of Sciences to follow in the tracks of A. E. Nordenskiöld's great voyage on the ship *Vega* through the Northeast Passage of 1878-79. The expedition sailed on the icebreaker *Ymer* in June 1980 with 119 scientists and technicians aboard to carry out programmes in atmospheric pollution, marine biology (with emphasis on the evolution of species in the Arctic Ocean), and marine geology. A review of this work off Spitsbergen and northeast Greenland concludes the article.

175 **Northern Light; its epic Arctic-Antarctic sailing voyage.**
Rolf Bjelke, Deborah Shapiro. London: Macdonald, Queen Anne Press, 1986. 116p. maps.

An account of a voyage made in [1982-84] in a French-built twelve-metre, fourteen-ton steel ketch which covered a distance of 33,000 miles, coasting Norway and penetrating the Arctic just north of Spitsbergen (Svalbard) at latitude 80°N. From here the ketch was sailed southwestwards through Denmark Strait to Labrador and thence via the Panama Canal to Polynesia, Chile and the Antarctic Peninsula. The book is well-illustrated with the author's photographs.

176 **Skiing alone to the Pole.**
Jean-Louis Etienne. *National Geographic*, vol. 170, no. 3 (Sept. 1986), p. 318-23.

Offers a short account of a solo trek to the North Pole on skis. Etienne, a Frenchman, left Ward Hunt Island, Canadian Arctic, on 9 March 1986 and reached the Pole on 11 May. During the journey he was resupplied by airplane. Etienne claims to be the first traveller to achieve the Pole under his own power. A map and an account of Etienne's meeting with Will Steger's party are offered by B. C. Imbert (q.v.).

177 **Solo man-hauling journey to the North Pole.**
B. C. Imbert. *Polar Record*, vol. 23, no. 144 (Sept. 1986), p. 340.

A brief report of Dr Jean-Louis Etienne's solo man-hauling skiing and sledging journey to the geographical North Pole, achieved on 11 May 1986. He carried a specially-built beacon which enabled the CNES space centre in Toulouse, France, to compute Etienne's navigational accuracy at the Pole as latitude 89°.999 – the best ever achieved.

178 **On skis to North Pole.**
Vladimir Nikolayevich Snegirev.   Translated from the Russian by
George Watts. New York: Sphinx, 1985. 240p. map.
An account of an expedition to the North Pole by dog sledge in 1986.

179 **North to the Pole.**
Will Steger, Paul Schurke.   London: Macmillan, 1987. 339p. maps.
An account by the leader of an American expedition whose aim was to become the
first to reach the North Pole without resupply since Robert Peary's historic journey in
1909. The expedition members consisted of seven men, one woman and forty-nine
dogs. They set out from the north coast of Ellesmere Island, northern Canada, on 8
March 1986 and after fifty-five days and 1,000 miles of travel across the frozen Arctic
Ocean, with temperatures as low as −70°F, six members of the team reached the Pole
by 1 May, from where they were airlifted back to base. Appendixes include accounts of
rations, dogs, equipment, and psychological and medical profiles. A shorter account of
the expedition was published in *National Geographic*, (vol. 170, no. 3 (Sept. 1986),
p. 288-323).

Aviation history

180 **Lifelines through the Arctic.**
William S. Carlson.   New York: Duell, Sloan & Pearce, 1962. 271p.
map. bibliog.
A history of United States air transport routes in the Arctic during World War II,
including an account of 'Operation Alsib' in which some 7,000 US aircraft were ferried
by Soviet pilots from Fairbanks, Alaska, to the USSR. The book concludes with a
description of the establishment of the arctic DEW (Distant Early Warning) system
designed to provide detection of any ballistic missiles launched from Siberia.

181 **Polar flight.**
Basil Clarke.   London: Ian Allen, 1964. 187p. map. bibliog.
Presents a history of Arctic and Antarctic aviation, from the first and disastrous
attempt of S. A. Andrée to achieve the North Pole by balloon in 1897 to the opening
up of the trans-polar route between Europe and North America by Scandinavian
Airlines system (SAS) in the 1950s. A separate chapter is devoted to the problems of
air navigation in Polar regions.

182 **Polar aviation.**
Edited by C. V. Glines.   New York: Franklin Watts, 1964. 287p.
maps.
This anthology of polar aviation history was selected mostly from published first-hand
accounts, ranging from Andrée's balloon flight of 1897 to a non-stop flight from
Moscow to San Francisco across the North Pole in 1935 by Mikhail Gromov. Other
chapters cover air warfare in World War II, flying the Alaska bush country, and some
postwar developments in arctic aviation.

183 **Heroes of the polar skies.**
John Grierson. London: Heinemann, 1967. 179p. maps. bibliog.
A popular general history of arctic and antarctic aviation by a seasoned polar aviator
with chapters on Andrée and Wellman, Amundsen, Byrd, Nobile, Ellsworth and
Wilkins, covered elsewhere in this section in more detail.

184 **Challenge to the poles; highlights of arctic and antarctic aviation.**
John Grierson. London: G. T. Foulis, 1964. 695p. maps. bibliog.
The author, a professional pilot with experience in the Arctic and Antarctic, was well
qualified to research what, even now, is probably still the definitive history of polar
flight. The appendixes include a 'Summary of flights and air expeditions to Arctic and
Antarctic from 1896-1954'.

185 **Aviation in arctic North America and Greenland.**
Trevor Lloyd. *Polar Record*, vol. 5, nos. 35/36 (Jan/July 1948),
p. 163-71, map.
A summary history of air routes across the North American Arctic during and shortly
after World War II when, in 1947, Thule air base was established as a weather station
in Slidre Fjord, northwest Greenland. Shortly after a similar station was set up at
Resolute Bay, Cornwallis Island, Northwest Territories, Canada.

186 **Oceans, poles and airmen; the first flights over wide waters and desolate
ice.**
Richard Montague. New York: Random House, 1971. 307p.
A journalist's view of some famous polar aviators and their accomplishments in the
1920s and 1930s which questions Admiral Richard E. Byrd's claim to have flown over
the North Pole in 1926, put forward by Byrd in his book *Skyward* (q.v.).

187 **Arctic airmen; the RAF in Spitsbergen and north Russia in 1942.**
Ernest Schofield, Roy Conyers Nesbit. London: William Kimber,
1987. 253p. maps. bibliog.
An account by the navigator of a Royal Air Force Catalina flying boat selected to carry
out a series of highly secret operations in the Arctic in the spring of 1942, associated
with a Norwegian expedition from Britain to Spitsbergen to deny the use of vital
weather stations to the occupying Germans. These flights, frequently over twenty-four
hours in length, and carried out in conditions of extreme cold, included an attempt to
achieve the North Pole. Later, the Catalina squadron was detached to north Russia to
provide cover for the convoys taking vital supplies to the Eastern Front. Appendixes
include notes on polar air navigation, a list of decorations, official correspondence and
other topics.

188 **Target Arctic; men in the skies at the top of the world.**
George Simmons. Philadelphia: Chilton, 1965. 420p. maps. bibliog.
Offers a history of the pioneers of Arctic aviation. Appendixes include: 'Aircraft used
in pioneer Arctic flying'; 'Greenland-Iceland transatlantic air route' and 'Purpose of
drifting stations in the Arctic Ocean'.

Naval history

189 **Naval and maritime history; an annotated bibliography.**
Robert Greenhalgh Albion. Newton Abbot, England: David &
Charles, 1973. 4th ed. 370p.

Some 5,000 items are covered in this revised and expanded edition of a work
first issued in 1951. A most comprehensive listing in its field, it ranges over the whole
of the relevant English language material, including dissertations as well as published
works. World War I, 1914-18, is covered by p. 270-76 and World War II, 1939-45, by
p. 281-302.

190 **Allied convoys to Murmansk and Arkhangel'sk, 1941-45.**
Polar Record, vol. 5, no. 39 (Jan. 1950), p. 427-36.

An account of the convoys to Murmansk and Archangel, north Russia, that followed
upon the Three-power Conference on Aid to Russia (1941), and covering the year
1941-45. The article concludes with a summary of convoys, casualties, military and civil
supplies, and their value.

191 **Operation 'Wunderland'; *Admiral Scheer*; in the Kara Sea, August 1942.**
William Barr. *Polar Record*, vol. 17, no. 110 (May 1975), p. 461-72.
map. bibliog.

Considers a little-known episode in World War II involving an attempt by the
Germans, largely with U-boats, to disrupt the alleged movement of 'lend-lease'
supplies from the Pacific coasts of Canada and the USA along the Northern Sea Route
for the relief of the Russian front. In addition to attacking Allied convoys the Germans
planned to attack the Kara Sea port of Anderma.

192 **The Kola run; a record of arctic convoys 1941-1945.**
Sir Ian Campbell, Donald Macintyre. London: Frederick Muller,
1958. 254p. map.

The story of the Royal Navy convoys which fought their way to north Russia
throughout four years of World War II. Both the authors held naval commands during
these operations and their exploits and experiences are included in this book. A typical
convoy route would include Iceland, Bear Island, Jan Mayen, Norway's North Cape
and finally the Kola Inlet; the convoy would be continuously at high risk from German
based naval squadrons and aircraft operating from occupied Norway.

193 **Submarines in arctic waters.**
I. Kolyshkin. Translated by David Skvirsky. Moscow: Progress
Publishers, 1966. 253p.

Offers a translation of the memoirs of Rear-Admiral Kolyshkin, Soviet northern fleet
submarine commander in World War II.

194 **History of United States naval operations in World War II.**
Samuel Eliot Morison. Boston, Massachusetts: Little, Brown,
1947-62. 15 vols. maps. bibliog.
The definitive history of the work of the United States Navy in World War II. The
following volumes are of special relevance to operations in arctic waters: Volume I,
'Greenland patrol', 'Denmark Strait patrol', 'North Russia run (December 1941-July
1942)'; Volume IV, 'The Aleutians (June 1942-August 1943)'; Volume X, 'Northern
trans-Atlantic convoys (April-May 1943)', 'Arctic waters (May-December 1943; 1944-
45)'.

195 **73 North; the battle of the Barents Sea.**
Dudley Pope. London: Weidenfeld & Nicolson, 1958. 320p.
The story of an attack on 31 December 1942 by the German pocket battleship *Lutzöw*
and the heavy cruiser *Hipper* and six destroyers on a small convoy of four British and
ten American merchantmen bound for Russia via arctic waters. The German attack
was beaten off and not one allied merchant vessel lost. The author sees this failure as
the reason for Hitler's subsequent decision to do away with the German high seas fleet.
Although the author claims to 'have been more than fortunate with (his) sources' these
are, in fact, not listed.

196 **The war at sea 1939-1945.**
S. W. Roskill. Series editor, J. R. M. Butler. London: HM Stationery
Office, 1954-61. 4 vols. maps. bibliog. (History of the Second World
War United Kingdom Military Series).
The official British history of World War II naval operations, which is based on British
and German official records. Volume I includes an account of the British arctic
convoys, June-December 1941 and the campaign in Norway. Volume II covers the
British arctic convoys to north Russia, January 1942-May 1943. Volume III covers
arctic operations from June 1943 to August 1945.

197 **The Russian convoys.**
B. B. Schofield. London: Batsford, 1964. 224p. maps. bibliog.
The story of how German attempts to interfere with the carrying of war material to
Russia were thwarted despite the advantage to the Germans of their occupation of
Norway. It is also the story of the convoys themselves and the sea battles waged to
protect them in the worst natural conditions to be found anywhere in the world.

198 **Arctic victory; the story of Convoy PQ 18.**
Peter C. Smith. London: William Kimber, 1975. 238p. maps. bibliog.
A detailed operational description of this Allied arctic convoy of forty merchant ships
protected by some ninety British warships of all types, and its voyage to Murmansk,
northern Russia, in September 1942 and in the face of formidable German opposition
from sea and air. Appendixes include a listing of the composition of PQ 18 and its
escort, radio call signs, a summary of aircraft sorties and a list of German naval units.

199 **Ice is where you find it.**
Charles W. Thomas. Indianapolis, Indiana: Bobbs-Merrill, 1951.
378p. maps.
An account of a United States Coast Guard captain of coast guard activities against
German radio stations in Greenland and Jan Mayen during World War II. The book
includes chapters on the Bering Sea Patrol cruise in 1948 which gave logistic support to
various coast guard stations on the Aleutian Islands and the Pribilof Islands, and
Alaska as far north as Point Barrow.

Military history

200 **German meteorological activities in the Arctic, 1940-45.**
J. D. M. Blyth. *Polar Record*, vol. 6, no. 42 (July 1951), p. 185-226.
map.
A detailed account, based on British and German sources, of German naval
expeditions to Arctic locations, including Jan Mayen, east Greenland, Svalbard
(Spitsbergen) and Franz Josef Land to obtain regular synoptic weather reports, the
international exchange of which practically ceased in 1939. J. G. Elbo also covers this
subject in *The war in Svalbard, 1939-45* (q.v.).

201 **The war in arctic Europe, 1941-45.**
J. D. M. Blyth. *Polar Record*, vol. 7, no. 49 (Jan. 1955), map.
bibliog.
This article, based on German sources, describes the military operations in arctic
Europe which followed the German invasion of the Soviet Union in 1941, ending with
the German surrender in 1945. It describes the events leading to the capitulation of
Finland in September 1944, the German retreat through northern Norway and Finland,
and the accompanying 'scorched earth' policy.

202 **Allied intervention in Russia.**
John Bradley. London: Weidenfeld & Nicolson, 1968. 251p. maps.
bibliog.
The attempts by the Western powers to intervene in Russia after the Bolshevik *coup
d'état* of 1917 is a subject much neglected by historians. The author, a university
teacher, has here consulted British, French and other archives in an effort to provide
much new material on the subject.

203 **Arctic travel and warfare in the sixteenth century.**
M. P. Charlesworth. *Polar Record*, vol. 4, no. 25 (Jan. 1943),
p. 52-60.
Presents translated extracts from Olaus Magnus's treatise *Historia de gentibus
septentionalibus* . . . (History of the northern peoples . . .) (Rome: 1555). This volume
of over 800 pages, written in Latin, contains an extraordinary collection of stories,

folklore, marvels, customs, and so on, relating to the lands bordering the Baltic, and is illustrated with some interesting woodcuts. The extracts translated here describe techniques of travel and warfare in northern lands.

204 **The campaign in Norway.**
T. K. Derry. London: HM Stationery Office, 1952. 289p. maps. bibliog.
This fully-documented account of British operations against the Germans in arctic Norway from 8 April-8 June 1940 includes the capture and final evacuation of Narvik.

205 **The war in Jan Mayen, 1940-45.**
J. G. Elbo. *Polar Record*, vol. 6, no. 46 (July 1953), p. 735-39. bibliog.
An account of the re-opening of the Norwegian weather station on Jan Mayen, looking at its manning and supply during the war years, and measures to forestall any German attempt to occupy the island.

206 **The war in Svalbard, 1939-45.**
J. G. Elbo. *Polar Record*, vol. 6, no. 44 (July 1952), p. 484-95. bibliog.
This is a year-by-year account of the Allied activities in Svalbard (Spitsbergen), German operations being referred to in detail only when they directly affect the narrative. A short note on German wartime meteorological expeditions to Svalbard is appended. For a fuller account see J. D. M. Blyth's article *German meteorological activities in the Arctic, 1940-45* (q.v.).

207 **The ignorant armies; the Anglo-American Archangel expedition: 1918-1919.**
E. M. Halliday. London: Weidenfeld & Nicolson, 1961. 232p. maps. bibliog.
A non-academic attempt to give a clear account of the United States expedition to north Russia in 1918-19.

208 **The sledge patrol.**
David Howarth. London: Collins, 1957. 255p. maps.
A balanced and factual account of an obscure and minuscule campaign of World War II which took place on the northeast coast of Greenland. Here the Greenland dog-sledge patrol, consisting of six Danes, three Norwegians and six Eskimo sledge drivers, had to counter a German invading force of nineteen men in 1942. The Germans were well-armed but unskilled in polar travel. Neither side felt able to shoot at the other. This is a study of human motives as much as of military history, and is based on evidence from both sides.

209 **Archangel 1918-1919.**
Sir Edmund Ironside. London: Constable, 1953. 220p. maps.
General Ironside's personal account of the north Russian campaign of 1918-19, based on his journals, shows how Allied forces came to be at Archangel and illustrates the problems of waging war in Arctic conditions.

210 **At war with the Bolsheviks; the Allied intervention into Russia 1917-20.**
Robert Jackson. London: Tom Stacey, 1972. 251p. maps. bibliog.
This is a popular history of the Allied war of intervention against the Russian
Bolshevik régime following the separate peace treaty between Germany and the Soviet
government at Brest-Litovsk in March 1918. Fought on several fronts, it proved to be
utterly disastrous. The story told is from the point of view of those who took part
rather than that of the politicians.

211 **Finland, Germany, and the Soviet Union, 1940-1941. The Petsamo
dispute.**
H. Peter Krosby. Madison, Wisconsin: University of Wisconsin Press,
1968. 276p. bibliog.
A scholarly and well-documented account of how Finland, nervous at the prospect of
possible Soviet intervention, sought an alliance with Nazi Germany to jointly exploit
the nickel deposits at Petsamo (Pechenga) in a vain attempt to retain its neutrality. In
June 1941 a co-ordinated Finnish-German attack across the Soviet frontier followed.
Subsequently the mines, by then in the middle of a war zone, continued to produce ore
for the German war effort. The Red Army's counter-attack of 1944 witnessed the
demolition of the mines.

212 **The third front; the strange story of the secret war in the Arctic.**
Douglas Liverside. London: Souvenir, 1960. 219p.
A popular account of the German expeditions to arctic waters during World War II to
set up automatic and other weather stations that were essential to the planning
operations further south, and of the counter-measures taken by the Danish sledge
patrol in east Greenland alongside the United States Coast Guard. The British and
Norwegians concentrated their energies on Jan Mayen and Svalbard (Spitsbergen)
while the Russians monitored Franz Josef Land.

213 **Arctic meteorological operations and counter-operation during World
War II.**
Franz Selinger, Alexander R. Glen. *Polar Record*, vol. 21, no. 135
(Sept. 1983), p. 559-67. maps.
Part one of this article, 'German activities', describes in detail German efforts to
establish meteorological stations in east Greenland and Svalbard (Spitsbergen) during
World War II, 1939-45, and is written from the German viewpoint. Part two, 'British
activities', is again written by one who participated and describes how Allied raiding
groups succeeded in destroying enemy installations and generally made life difficult for
the Germans.

Biographies of Arctic Explorers

214 Mr Barrow of the Admiralty; a life of Sir John Barrow 1764-1848.
Christopher Lloyd.   London: Collins, 1970. 224p. maps. bibliog.
Sir John Barrow, who lent his name to places as remote as Barrow Strait and Point Barrow in Alaska, served as Secretary to the British Admiralty from 1804 to 1845 and was the prime mover in the great renaissance of polar exploration achieved by the expeditions of Sir John Ross, Sir William Edward Parry and Sir John Franklin.

215 Bartlett, the great Canadian explorer.
Harold Horwood.   Garden City, New York: Doubleday, 1977. 194p. maps. bibliog.
A life of Captain Robert Bartlett, a Newfoundlander born in 1875, who spent over fifty years of his life charting arctic waters and was leader of over twenty expeditions. Bartlett was in command of the ship *Roosevelt* on Robert E. Peary's North Pole expeditions of 1905-06 and 1908-09, and was subsequently on Vilhjalmur Stefansson's Canadian Arctic Expedition of 1913-18 as captain of the ill-fated *Karluk* (1913-14) helping to save the lives of most of its stranded participants. In later years 'Bob' Bartlett led many scientific expeditions to the Canadian Arctic, Greenland and Siberia.

216 Winner lose all. Dr Cook and the theft of the North Pole.
Hugh Eames.   Boston; Toronto: Little, Brown, 1973. 346p. bibliog.
A biography of Dr Frederick Cook which seeks to prove that this 'prince of losers' beat Robert E. Peary to the North Pole in 1908.

217 The life of Captain James Cook.
J. G. Beaglehole.   London: Hakluyt Society, 1974. 760p. bibliog.
(Hakluyt Society Extra Series, no. 37. The Journals Of Captain James Cook On His Voyages Of Discovery, vol. 4).
The definitive account of the life of this famous explorer-seaman whose third voyage of discovery in 1776-79 took him in *Resolution* up the north west coast of America to Bering Strait and beyond until he was stopped by the ice.

Biographies of Arctic Explorers.

218 **The man on the ice cap; the life of August Courtauld.**
Nicholas Wollaston. London: Constable, 1980. 260p.
August Courtauld, though not a major figure in arctic exploration, is remembered as
the man who, on the British Arctic Air Route Expedition of 1930-31, elected to winter
alone in a meteorological station on the Greenland icesheet. Here he remained
virtually buried alive under snow and ice until dug out by his companions after 150
days, by which time he was down to his last cupful of paraffin and a scrap of
pemmican.

219 **To Greenland's icy mountains; the story of Hans Egede explorer,
colonist, missionary.**
Eve Garnett. London: Heinemann, 1968. 190p. maps.
Written for a junior audience, this book serves as an introduction to the life of the
Norwegian Lutheran priest who left for Greenland in 1708 to look for the descendants
of the 10th-century Christians who once had a flourishing settlement there.

220 **The fate of Franklin.**
Roderic Owen. London: Hutchinson, 1978. 471p. maps. bibliog.
A life of the Arctic explorer Sir John Franklin which investigates, with the use of
contemporary sources, the story of his last expedition of 1845 in search of a Northwest
Passage, an expedition on which both he and his ships, *Erebus* and *Terror* disappeared
with their crews in the Canadian Arctic, thereby triggering a series of search
expeditions whose combined discoveries resulted in the final charting of the passage.

221 **Arctic adventure; my life in the frozen north.**
Peter Freuchen. London: William Heinemann, 1936. 405p. map.
An autobiographical account of the travels of the Danish arctic explorer, adventurer
and writer, Peter Freuchen (1886-1957). His work was carried out largely in Greenland
where he gave support to Amundsen's *Maud* expedition in 1919 and took part in Knud
Rasmussen's Fifth Thule Expedition in 1921-24, acting as cartographer and biologist. It
was on this expedition that Freuchen lost his left foot from frostbite.

222 **Samuel Hearne and the Northwest Passage.**
Gordon Speck. Caldwell, Idaho: Caxton Printers, 1963. 337p. maps.
An account of the major steps taken in the search for the Northwest Passage and an
attempt to show how Hearne's work was the culmination of this search.

223 **Doctor Kane of the arctic seas.**
George W. Corner. Philadelphia: Temple University Press, 1972.
306p. maps. bibliog.
A life of the United States polar explorer Elisha Kent Kane (1820-57) who, as doctor
and naval surgeon, accompanied the first Grinnell expedition under E. J. De Haven in
1850-51. In 1853-55 Kane commanded the second Grinnell expedition to the Arctic.

Biographies of Arctic Explorers.

224 **An arctic man; sixty-five years in Canada's north.**
Ernie Lyall. Edmonton, Alberta: Hurtig, 1979. 239p. map.
This is the autobiography of a former employee of the Hudson's Bay Company who
had lived for almost half a century above the Arctic Circle working for the Eskimos
and living their life.

225 **Alexander Mackenzie, explorer; the hero who failed.**
James K. Smith. Toronto: McGraw-Hill Ryerson, 1973. 190p. maps.
bibliog.
An account of the first man to have reached the Pacific Ocean coast overland north of
Mexico. In 1789, while searching for a trade route to the Pacific, Mackenzie discovered
the river that now bears his name at its mouth at the Arctic Ocean. However, he was
essentially a fur trader and, in this respect, so the author argues, was a failure in so far
as none of his trade routes proved practicable.

226 **Nansen the explorer.**
Edward Shackleton. London: H. F. & G. Witherby, 1959. 209p.
A short biography of the great Norwegian explorer Fridtjof Nansen (1861-1930)
concentrating on his arctic expeditions, first to Greenland in 1888, where he
successfully crossed the inland icesheet. Subsequently, in 1893-96, he took his ice-
strengthened vessel *Fram* into the Arctic Ocean to drift in the vicinity of the North
Pole, and made an incredible journey over the polar ice with a single companion,
F. H. Johansen, to Franz Josef Land, where he met the English explorer F. G.
Jackson.

227 **North-east passage; Adolf Erik Nordenskiöld, his life and times.**
George Kish. Amsterdam: Nico Israel, 1973. 283p.
This is the first account in English, other than a contemporary very partial biography,
of this brilliant Swedish-Finnish explorer who voyaged in the Arctic between 1853 and
1883. Nordenskiöld organised eight expeditions to Spitsbergen, Greenland and
northern Siberia, the best known being his traverse of the Northeast Passage in the
ship *Vega* and his return to Sweden via the Suez Canal, in 1878-79. This scholarly life is
based principally on the Nordenskiöld papers in the library of the Royal Swedish
Academy of Sciences.

228 **Parry of the Arctic; the life story of Admiral Sir Edward Parry**
1790-1855.
Ann Parry. London: Chatto & Windus, 1963. 240p. maps. bibliog.
A life of the British arctic explorer Admiral Sir William Edward Parry (1790-1855) by a
great-great-grandaughter, which is based on his original journals and correspondence.

229 **Peary the explorer and the man. Based on his personal papers.**
John Edward Weems. London: Eyre & Spottiswoode, 1967. 362p.
map. bibliog.
This is a well-documented biography of the first man to achieve the North Pole. The
book is divided into five periods of the explorer's life and work: (1) Peary's youth,
education and naval commission; (2) his early experience and first visit to Greenland;

Biographies of Arctic Explorers.

(3) the Greenland expeditions, (1891-97); (4) 'nearing the goal' – preparatory expeditions and the final achievement of the Pole (1898-1909); and (5) 'aftermath', the Cook controversy, aviation and military preparedness, and death.

230 **Dr John Rae.**
R. L. Richards. Whitby, England: Caedmon of Whitby, 1985. 231p. maps. bibliog.

A full and scholarly biography of this Scottish Hudson's Bay Company surgeon who explored the mainland coast of arctic Canada between 1846 and 1854. It is based in part on Rae's incomplete autobiography, now in the archives of the Scott Polar Research Institute, Cambridge, England, and other source material. An introductory chapter establishes the historical background to Rae's expeditions and there is a concluding assessment of Rae's refinement of native American techniques of living and travelling in arctic regions.

231 **Sir John Richardson; arctic explorer, natural historian, naval surgeon.**
Robert W. Johnson. London: Taylor & Francis, 1976. 209p. maps. bibliog.

Johnson's is the first full-length biography of this Royal Navy surgeon, arctic explorer and founder of arctic biology. The book is divided into five alphabetical sections: (A) is concerned with Richardson's childhood and medical education; (B) concerns his career as a naval surgeon in the Napoleonic wars; (C) deals with his experiences in the Canadian Arctic on John Franklin's first and second overland expeditions to the polar sea; (D) discusses Richardson's career as a medical administrator and his work as a natural historian with John Rae during the Franklin search expeditions of 1848-55; and (E) assesses his character and his place in the development of natural history. In addition to several appendixes there is a definitive bibliography of Richardson's published and unpublished papers.

232 **The polar Rosses; John and James Clark Ross and their explorations.**
Ernest S. Dodge. London: Faber & Faber, 1973. 260p. maps. bibliog.

Sir John Ross (1777-1856) and his nephew Sir James Clark Ross (1800-62) were both eminent in the field of polar exploration. Sir John Ross commanded two arctic expeditions and in his old age took part in the Franklin search expeditions. His nephew accompanied his uncle on his first arctic voyage, served with Sir William Parry on four arctic expeditions, and, on his uncle's second arctic expedition (1829-34), determined the position of the North Magnetic Pole.

233 **Vilhjalmur Stefansson and the development of arctic terrestrial science.**
Edited by G. Edgar Folk, Jr., Mary A. Folk. Iowa City: University of Iowa, 1984. 240p. bibliog.

Presents the proceedings of the Vilhjalmur Stefansson centennial symposium, held at the University of Iowa, May, 1980. Part one of the symposium was devoted to reminiscences by his wife and colleagues. Part two featured specialist papers covering aspects of Stefansson's scientific interests, namely dietetics, the Eskimo peoples and their habitat, and oil, gas and mineral exploration on the arctic islands.

234 **Stefansson and the Canadian Arctic.**
Richard J. Diubaldo.   Montreal: McGill-Queen's University Press,
1978. 274p. maps. bibliog.

A study of Vilhjalmur Stefansson, Canada's greatest Arctic explorer, during the period
1906 to 1926 when he was most active in Canada. For the first quarter of the present
century Stefansson's ideas and discoveries in the Arctic captured the imagination of all
Canadians, but by the 1920s he had become *persona non grata*. This book examines
Stefansson's career in the light of much new evidence and attempts to find out why his
reputation attracted criticism.

235 **Stef; a biography of Vilhjalmur Stefansson Canadian Arctic explorer.**
William R. Hunt.   Vancouver: University of British Columbia Press,
1986. 317p. maps. bibliog.

Based largely on previously unpublished material this scholarly biography, the first to
examine all Stefansson's varied careers, gives a new and balanced perspective to his
complex and diversified life. Having had access to the explorer's large private
correspondence the author examines the major interpersonal conflicts in Stefansson's
career and evaluates his relationship with the Canadian government and with the
scientists of the Canadian Arctic expedition of 1913-18.

236 **Georg Wilhelm Steller; the pioneer of Alaskan natural history.**
Leonhard Stejneger.   Cambridge, Massachusetts: Harvard University
Press, 1936. 623p. maps. bibliog.

A definitive biography, based on all available sources, of one of the greatest of the
early naturalist explorers, who accompanied Vitus Bering on his second expedition
(1741-42). Steller was not only the first European to set foot on Alaskan soil but the
first naturalist to collect, study and describe Alaskan plants and animals.

Philately

237 **Greenland postal history. Vol. 1. Parcel-cards.**
Torben Hjørne. Århus, Denmark: The Author, 1982. 196p. maps.
A specialist volume for philatelists offering detailed information on the history of postal rates and statistics of parcel-cards to and from Greenland, amongst other things.

238 **Ice Cap News.**
El Paso, Texas: American Society of Polar Philatelists, 1956- .
bi-monthly.
This journal tends to specialize in arctic and antarctic polar history, short notes and book reviews. The editor hopes to meet in the future the needs of thematic stamp collecting.

239 **Polar Post.**
Cottingham, Yorkshire: Polar Postal History Society of Great Britain, 1958- . quarterly.
A society journal devoted to arctic and antarctic philately with such features as historical and thematic material, covers, new issues and book reviews.

Arctic Peoples

General

240　Circumpolar problems; habitat, economy, and social relations in the
　　　Arctic. A symposium for anthropological research in the North,
　　　September 1969.
　　　Edited by Gösta Berg.　Oxford: Pergamon, 1973. 194p. maps. bibliog.
　　　(Wenner-Gren Center International Symposium Series, vol. 21).
A collection of specialist papers dealing with the archaeology and ethnology of
northern Scandinavia, Greenland, Siberia, arctic Canada and Alaska, many of which
are concerned with problems relating to the integration of native peoples into modern
economy and public life.

241　**Peoples of the earth. Vol. 16. The Arctic.**
　　　Hugh Brody, consultant.　[London]: Robert B. Clarke, Danbury,
　　　1973. maps.
A popular illustrated introduction to the peoples of the circumpolar Arctic consisting
of individual chapters by contributing specialists.

242　**Children of the North.**
　　　Fred Bruemmer.　Montreal, Toronto: Optimum, 1979. 159p.
Lavishly-illustrated with the author's own photographs this book is a commentary,
based on Fred Bruemmer's own travels, on Eskimo children in the past and in the
modern world, with comment on the problems of acculturation facing Eskimo youth
today.

243 **The ethnography of northern North America: a guide to recent research.**
Ernest S. Burch, Jr. *Arctic Anthropology*, vol. 16, no. 1 (1979),
p. 62-146. map. bibliog.

A comprehensive overview of recent ethnographic research in northern North America
combined with an attempt to relate recent work to earlier studies. Topics discussed
include the demographic aspects of northern research, northern research organizations,
ethnographic publications in general and specific studies of Eskimos, Aleuts, and other
northern ethnic groups, including Athapaskans and Algonquians. The bibliography is
especially valuable.

244 **Handbook of North American Indians. Vol. 5. Arctic.**
Edited by D. Damas. Washington, DC: Smithsonian Institution, 1985.
862p. map. bibliog.

An encyclopaedic summary of our current knowledge of the prehistory, history and
cultures of the aboriginal peoples of North America, including the Eskimos. This
volume, which is prefaced by a history of research before 1945, covers, in a general
section, the history of arctic ethnology and archaeology, physical environment,
languages, human biology and prehistory. The regional sections that follow deal with
the western Arctic, Canadian Arctic and Greenland. The volume concludes with the
period 1950 to 1980.

245 **Comparative studies of North American Indians.**
Harold E. Driver, William C. Massey. Philadelphia: American
Philosophical Society, 1957. 456p. maps. bibliog. (Transactions of the
American Philosophical Society, vol. 47, part 2).

Makes an attempt at integrating anthropological data on North American Indian
(including Eskimo) cultures. The aim of the work is to offer a series of broad
generalizations about these cultures together with the data on which they are based.
Most of the data presented are on a series of schematic maps on which individual tribal
territories are differentiated by means of boundary lines. The monograph is divided
into the following sections: (A) Subsistence; (B) Material culture; (C) Economics; and
(D) Social organization.

246 **An ore body of note: theses and dissertations on Indians, Metis and Inuit
at the University of Alberta.**
Aldrich J. Dyer. *Canadian Journal of Education*, vol. 13, no. 2
(1986), p. 40-51.

A description and listing of theses on North American indigenous peoples, held by the
University of Alberta library, Edmonton, Alberta.

247 **The native races of America; a copious selection of passages for the study
of social anthropology from the manuscript notebooks of Sir James
George Frazer.**
Edited by Robert Angus Downie. London: Percy Lund Humphries,
1939. 351p. maps. (Anthologia Anthropologica).

A selection from the notebooks of the famous anthropologist, arranged geographically.
Book one (p. 1-177) includes sections concerned with the Eskimos of North America
and Greenland in addition to the Indians of the North American Subarctic.

248 **Circumpolar peoples: an anthropological perspective.**
Nelson H. H. Graburn, B. Stephen Strong.   Pacific Palisades,
California: Goodyear, 1973. 236p. bibliog.

Offers an introduction to northern peoples in both Eurasia and America, including
Lapps, Yakuts, Tungus, Chukchi, Indians, Aleuts and Eskimos. The book contains
some general ethnographic sketches as well as such specific anthropological problems
as kinship, ecology and culture history.

249 **The fourth world: the heritage of the Arctic and its destruction.**
Sam Hall.   London: Bodley Head, 1987. 240p. bibliog.

An evocation of the traditional life styles of the arctic peoples, discussing the erosion
of their culture and making a plea to save the Arctic from further despoliation. The
author describes the strategic importance of arctic regions today and warns against the
dangers of the kind of pollution in the Arctic caused by the Chernobyl disaster, stating
that only international collaboration can save 'the fourth world' from destruction.

250 **Handbook of North American Indians. Vol. 6. Subarctic.**
Edited by June Helm.   Washington, DC: Smithsonian Institution,
1981. 837p. maps. bibliog.

The subarctic culture area as delimited in this volume encompasses approximately
2,000,000 square miles and extends from the coast of Labrador on the Atlantic to Cook
Inlet, Alaska, on the Pacific. The culture area subdivisions correspond to the Subarctic
portion of the Canadian Shield and associated Hudson Bay Lowlands and Mackenzie
Borderlands, the Cordillera, the Alaska Plateau and the region south of the Alaska
Range. Articles relating to the cultural history of the peoples in these four regions
(including the Eskimos) are preceded by an introductory set of articles dealing with
general topics such as the environment, prehistory, languages and the history of
research. The volume concludes with a section on native settlements and another on
special topics.

251 **The meaning of political development in the North.**
Thomas A. Morehouse.   *Polar Record*, vol. 23, no. 145 (Jan. 1987),
p. 405-10. bibliog.

Modern political development in the North – Alaska, Canada, Greenland, northern
Scandinavia and the Soviet North – has occurred largely in response to incursions from
the South. These incursions, particularly for the exploitation of the North's natural
resources, have precipitated a series of political conflicts between 'the paramount
power and its northern subjects'. This article discusses problems of native autonomy in
the circumpolar countries with special reference to Alaska.

252 **Consequences of economic change in circumpolar regions.**
Edited by Ludger Müller-Wille, Pertti J. Pelto, Linna Müller-Wille,
Regna Darnell.   Edmonton, Alberta: University of Alberta, Boreal
Institute for Northern Studies, 1978. 269p. bibliog.

Consists of a collection of papers presented to a symposium on the unexpected
consequences of economic change in circumpolar regions at the 34th annual meeting of
the Society for Applied Anthropology in Amsterdam, 21-22 March, 1975. The papers

range over a wide range of topics including native peoples economy, ecological and human aspects of hydroelectric projects, acculturation problems, adaptations to urban life and land-use conflicts.

253 **Political expressions on the northern fourth world; Inuit, Cree, Sami.**
Ludger Müller-Wille, Pertti J. Pelto. *Inuit Studies*, vol. 3, no. 2 (1979), p. 3-72. bibliog.

These five papers were communicated to a session entitled: 'Politics of indigenous groups', organized as part of the 7th Annual Congress of the Canadian Ethnology Society, Montreal, 1980. The aim of the session was to look at recent political changes and socio-political developments among indigenous populations in the western circumpolar North. The 'Fourth World' referred to includes the ethnic minority groups of Alaska, northern Canada, Greenland and northern Scandinavia.

254 **Ethnographic bibliography of North America.**
George Peter Murdock. New Haven, Connecticut: Human Relations Area Files, 1960. 3rd ed. 393p. maps.

Books and journal article references are listed under regions and subdivided by tribal groups in this bibliography. Relevant sections for those interested in the Arctic are: (1) Arctic coast (including west Greenland); (2) Mackenzie-Yukon; and (3) Northwest coast.

255 **Native studies; American and Canadian Indians.**
John A. Price. Toronto: McGraw-Hill Ryerson, 1978. 309p. maps. bibliog.

An introductory textbook on United States and Canadian Indians, including Eskimos (Inuit). The first chapter reviews the rise of native peoples studies as a new interdisciplinary academic subject in the USA and Canada. Other chapters cover such topics as 'Genesis and traditional heritage', 'Indian urbanization and institutionalization', and 'Modern problems and their solutions'. The last chapter examines the need to bring science and humanism together in future native studies.

256 **Human adaptation: health and disease.**
Otto Schaefer. *Transactions of the Royal Society of Canada*, vol. XX, 4th series (1982), p. 417-27.

The author suggests that certain characteristics of Eskimo physiological evolution which enable them to adapt to their environment turn out to be disadvantageous in times of cultural change, leading to feelings of frustration, anger and hostility. Alcohol, which Eskimos and Indians metabolize less efficiently than Caucasians, often acts as an unmasking agent for these emotions, leading to suicide and crimes of violence.

257 **Indian-Eskimo relations: an introduction.**
Edited by James G. E. Smith. *Arctic Anthropology*, vol. 16, no. 2 (1979), p. 1-195.

Twelve papers presented at an American Anthropological Association symposium, dealing with questions relating to the conditions under which peace, trade or hostilities between North American Eskimos and Indians occurred. These papers take a broad historical approach including a consideration of environmental conditions, consequences of the fur trade, and increasing contact with Europeans. Relationships between Eskimos and Indians from the Atlantic to the Pacific are considered.

258 **Economic development of American Indians and Eskimos, 1930 through 1967; a bibliography.**
Marjorie P. Snodgrass. Washington, DC: US Department of the Interior, Bureau of Indian Affairs, 1968. 263p.
Economic development is defined here as meaning individual and collective efforts on and off the reservations that are directed to the production of tangible income. A useful guide to official publications and unpublished material, such as theses, the bibliography is arranged by subject areas and is subdivided by authors.

259 **Acta Borealia: a Norwegian Journal of Circumpolar Societies.**
Tromsø, Norway: Novus Forlag A/S, 1952- . twice-yearly.
A journal which is devoted to the history, social anthropology, language, and so on, of northern Scandinavian peoples. Articles not in the English language are accompanied by English abstracts.

260 **Anthropological Papers of the University of Alaska.**
Fairbanks, Alaska: University of Alaska, Department of Anthropology, 1952- . irregular.
A series of specialised articles which are concerned with all phases of arctic and subarctic anthropology.

261 **Arctic Anthropology.**
Madison, Wisconsin: University of Wisconsin Press, 1962- .
twice-yearly.
This international journal is devoted to the study of northern cultures and peoples, past and present, in the Old and New Worlds. The fields represented include archaeology, ethnology, ethnohistory, linguistics, human biology and related areas.

262 **Folk.**
Copenhagen: National Museum of Denmark, Department of Ethnography, 1959- . annual.
Folk is published by the Danish Ethnographic Society and presents articles on social and cultural anthropology over a broad geographical field; it is an especially useful source on Greenland Eskimos.

Eskimos

263 The term 'Eskimo'.
Terence Armstrong, Hugh Brody. *Polar Record*, vol. 19, no. 119
(May 1978), p. 177-80. bibliog.
There is no generally agreed term in use among the Eskimos of Alaska, northern
Canada, Greenland and the USSR to take the place of the European 'Eskimo'. Thus,
Canadian Eskimos prefer 'Inuit', in Greenland 'Grønlaender' is accepted, and so on.
This note discusses these differences and lays down a policy for the journal *Polar
Record.*

264 The Eskimos.
Kaj Birket-Smith. London: Methuen, 1959. 262p. map. bibliog.
A translation of the Danish original, published under the title *Eskimoerne*
(Copenhagen, Gyldendal, 1927). Based on the author's extensive work as an
ethnologist among the Eskimos of northern Canada and Greenland in the 1920s, this
work has become a classic standard text. Chapter headings include the country,
language, the struggle for food, fighting the cold, the community, view of life, origin
and development of the Eskimo culture and Eskimo rites. Appendixes include a
summary of Eskimo tribal groups and rules of pronunciation.

265 The number of Eskimos: an Arctic enigma.
Robert M. Bone. *Polar Record*, vol. 16, no. 103 (Jan. 1973),
p. 553-57.
A short article which attempts to indicate the number of Eskimos inhabiting arctic
lands at this date and at various times in the past.

266 The origins and antiquity of the Eskimo.
Henry B. Collins. Washington, DC: Smithsonian Institution, 1951.
p. 423-67. bibliog. (*Smithsonian Report*, 1950. Publication 4041).
After a brief summary of archaeological discoveries to date and their implications, the
author attempts an overall interpretation of the available evidence relating to the
origins and affinities of the Eskimo race type and culture.

267 Social anthropology of the central Eskimos.
David Damas. *Canadian Review of Sociology and Anthropology*,
vol. 12, no. 3 (1975), p. 252-66. bibliog.
A review of recent work on the sociology of the central Eskimos, these being Copper,
Netsilik, Iglulik, Caribou and Baffin Land Eskimos, under the headings of 'Kinship
systems'; 'The kindred'; 'Family strucure'; 'Authority structure'; 'Alliance mechanisms'; 'Local organization'; 'Cultural ecology'; and 'Social change'.

268 **Bibliography of bibliographies on the Inuit.**
Edited by Sylvie Devers, Inge Kleivan. In: *Arctica 1978 . . . 7th Northern Libraries Colloquy 19-23 September 1978.* Edited by Sylvie Devers. Paris: Éditions du Centre National de la Recherche Scientifique, 1982, p. 39-41.
This bibliography lists approximately eighty bibliographies specializing in Eskimo studies as well as some works which include comprehensive bibliographies.

269 **Peter Freuchen's book of the Eskimo.**
Edited by Dagmar Freuchen. London: Arthur Barker, 1962. 441p. map.
Peter Freuchen first became acquainted with the Eskimos in 1906 when he accompanied a Danish expedition to Greenland. Subsequently, he founded a trading station at Thule, northwest Greenland, where he remained until 1919, travelling, hunting and living among the Eskimos. In later years he travelled extensively throughout the Arctic. This account of the Eskimos is based on Freuchen's diaries and notes. Part two 'Adventures with the Eskimos' is principally anecdotal and autobiographical.

270 **Give me my father's body; the life of Minik, the New York Eskimo.**
Kenn Harper. Frobisher Bay, Northwest Territories: Blackhead Books, 1986. 275p. bibliog.
The story of Minik Wallace, an Eskimo from northwest Greenland, taken to New York in 1897 by the American explorer Robert E. Peary. During his twelve years in the USA Minik's adoptive family went from riches to rags, and Minik experienced the trauma of discovering his own father's skeleton on display in the American Museum of Natural History. Sent back to Greenland in 1909, Minik had to relearn his own language and his old hunting skills. Later he became interpreter and guide on Donald MacMillan's Crocker Land expedition, 1913-15.

271 **Eskimos.**
Wally Herbert. Glasgow: Franklin Watts, 1976. 128p. maps. bibliog.
A popular, well-illustrated introduction to the Eskimo people, considering their prehistory, culture, life-cycle, techniques for survival and present-day problems of acculturation. A final chapter describes the Thule Eskimos of northwest Greenland, of whom the author has much personal knowledge.

272 **Eskimo acculturation; a selected, annotated bibliography of Alaskan and other Eskimo acculturation studies.**
Arthur E. Hippler. Fairbanks, Alaska: University of Alaska, 1970. 209p.
This bibliography has been compiled primarily as a research tool for students and researchers. The entries, which have been carefully selected to include early 'base line' materials, include entries for northwest Alaska, Canada ånd some for Siberia. Annotations, in many cases, contain value judgements. Entries are cross-indexed under various headings.

273 **Adaptation to frigid zones by arctic peoples.**
Helge Larsen. *Folk*, vol. 23 (1981), p. 113-38. map.
The Eskimos appear to excel, in comparison with the other indigenous peoples of northernmost Eurasia, in ability to survive under and adapt to severe climatic conditions. Here the author considers aspects of the Eskimo material culture, including hunting and fishing, equipment and technique, methods of travel, clothing and dwellings.

274 **Oil and amulets; Inuit: a people united at the top of the world.**
Philip Lauritzen. [Anchorage, Alaska]: Breakwater Books, 1983. 278p. bibliog. (Arctic and Northern Life Series).
This volume was originally published in Danish as *Olie og amuletter* (Cogenhagen: Informations Forlag, 1979). The author, a journalist who has travelled extensively throughout Greenland, Canada and Alaska, here reviews the changed position of the Eskimos (Inuit) since the Danish anthropologist, Knud Rasmussen, studied their way of life in the 1920s. The book allows the Eskimos to speak for themselves and to express their concern for the threat to animals and the environment brought about by technological development, and for the future of their culture. The book concludes with the text of the Inuit Circumpolar Conference charter.

275 **Inuit; essai de bibliographie thematique selective (a selected thematic bibliography on the Inuit).**
Jean Malaurie. In: *Arctica 1978 . . . 7th Northern Libraries Colloquy 19-23 September 1978.* Edited by Sylvie Devers. Paris: Editions du Centre National de la Recherche Scientifique, 1982, p. 43-82.
A bibliography of 1374 references to the circumpolar Eskimos with entries arranged under subject headings.

276 **Eskimos and explorers.**
Wendell H. Oswalt. Novato, California: Chandler & Sharp, 1970. 349p. maps. bibliog.
The author's purpose is to trace the emergence of Eskimos from the era when Europeans thought of them as more legendary than real, to the time when the last of Eskimo country was explored. The narrative begins in Greenland about AD 1000, then moves to Canada and reaches northern Alaska in the 1800s, with a retrospective coverage of Russian penetration into Alaska. The final chapter deals with the life of the Eskimos after discovery, their material culture and trade, missionaries, health conditions, economic development and political domination.

277 **A matter of life and death; an investigation into the practice of female infanticide in the Arctic.**
Carmel Schrire, William Lee Steiger. *Man*, vol. 9, new series, no. 2 (June 1974), p. 161-81, bibliog.
The purpose of this article is to examine an assertion made by the anthropologist Knud Rasmussen in 1931 that some eighty per cent of girls among the Netsilik tribe of Eskimos were killed at birth. Firstly, this analysis reviews the enthnographic data in order to find out just how systematically female infanticide was practised, and secondly

to employ a computer programme to study the extent to which this method of population control may be practised before a group becomes unable to maintain a normal growth rate. The practise is, of course, no longer current.

278 **Arctic policy. Papers presented at the Arctic Policy Conference September 19-21, 1985, Centre for Northern Studies and Research, in conjunction with the Inuit Circumpolar Conference and the Eben Hopson chair.**
Edited by M. A. Stenbaek.   Montreal: McGill University, Centre for Northern Studies and Research, 1987. 312p. bibliog.
Twenty-six papers presented at the first Arctic Policy Conference designed to help in the implementation of the policies of the Inuit Circumpolar Conference, an international association of the circumpolar Inuit (Eskimos). Founded by Eben Hopson, Mayor of North Slope Borough, Alaska, the ICC is concerned with protecting the Eskimo way of life and environment from the dangers of industrial and commercial development. The papers in this volume stem from the six workshops set up to discuss issues relating to the arctic economy and environment, social problems, educational, cultural and communications problems, together with a special workshop on the Sami (Lapps) in the circumpolar world. A series of specially prepared papers on the present state of Canadian, American, Danish and Soviet arctic policy were delivered by experts. Appended are: (1) The Greenland Home Rule Act and (2) The United States Research and Policy Act of 1984.

279 **Inuit Studies/Etudes Inuit.**
Québec: Université Laval, Département d'anthropologie, 1977- .
twice-yearly.
Articles in English and French relating to the Inuit (Eskimo) peoples of the circumpolar Arctic appear in this publication.

Indians

280 **Indians of North America.**
Harold E. Driver.   Chicago; London: University of Chicago Press, 1970. 2nd ed. 632p. maps. bibliog.
An essential handbook for the study of the North American Indian from the Arctic to Panama, covering all aspects of their anthropology – origin and prehistory, culture areas, language, subsistence patterns, horticulture, art, trade, the family, kin groups, government, war, social class, ceremonies, education, religion, personality and culture. The five terminal chapters have been re-written for this edition to meet the demand for information on Indian activities in the 20th century.

281 **Problems in the prehistory of the North American Subarctic: the
Athapaskan question.**
Edited by J. W. Helmer, S. van Dyke, F. J. Kense. Calgary, Alberta:
Department of Archaeology, Archaeological Association, 1977. 258p.
maps. bibliog.

A selection of contributions to a symposium held at Calgary in 1976, discussing various
aspects of the prehistoric culture of the Athabaskan Indians, a widely diffused family
of peoples throughout the interior of Alaska, northern Canada and British Columbia.
There is a very full thirty-five-page bibliography.

282 **Indians, animals and the fur trade; a critique of** *Keepers of the game.*
Edited by Shepard Krech III. Athens, Georgia: University of Georgia
Press, 1981. 207p. bibliog.

In this volume seven anthropologists respond to the thesis presented by Calvin Martin
in *Keepers of the game: Indian-animal relationships and the fur trade* (Berkeley,
California: University of California Press, 1978). The thesis suggests that the
Athapaskan Indians of North America's eastern subarctic were motivated to overkill
game resources, in part because they believed that the animals were responsible for the
epidemics that decimated their ranks. Once 'despiritualization' of the Indians occurred
traditional sanctions against wildlife were lifted.

Languages

283 **Eskimo languages; their present-day conditions: 'Majority language influence on Eskimo minority languages'.**
Edited by Bjarne Basse, Kirsten Jensen.   Aarhus, Denmark: Arkona, 1979. 200p.

A collection of papers given at a symposium on 'Majority language influence on Eskimo minority languages', which was held at the University of Aarhus, Institute of Linguistics, Department of Greenlandic. The symposium dealt with the Eskimos themselves as well as the Aleuts, and with aspects of the changes their languages have experienced and the influence of the majority on the minority languages.

284 **An introduction to the Uralic languages.**
Björn Collinder.   Berkeley, Los Angeles, California: University of California Press, 1965. 167p. bibliog.

Offers an introduction for the general reader to the Uralic (Finno-Ugrian) family of languages. These include Hungarian (Magyar), Vogul (Mansi), Ostyak (Chanti), Zyryan (Komi), Votyak (Udmurt), Cheremis (Mari), Mordvin, the Finnic languages (Finnish, Carelian, Estonian, Livonian and Lapp) and, lastly, the Samoyed languages (Nenets, Enets, or Yenisei Samoyed), Nganasan and Selkup. Chapters include an introduction to the Uralic peoples and languages, the structure of the languages and etymological phonology.

285 **Finno-Ugrian languages and peoples.**
Péter Hajdú.   Translated and adapted by G. F. Cushing. London: André Deutsch, 1975. 254p. maps. bibliog. (Language Library).

A translation from the Hungarian original, published in 1963, this book is a concise introduction to each of the peoples in their turn, their geographical background, their dialects and their cultural background.

Languages

286 **Some linguistic problems in the Arctic.**
Louis L. Hammerich. *Acta Arctica*, fasc. 12 (1960), p. 83-89.

The author discusses the existence of a former Eskimo-Aleut community, possibly in Asia, and points to the need for more cooperation between linguists, archaeologists and ethnologists in identifying ancient cultures.

Religion

287 Tôrnârssuk, an Eskimo deity.
Erik Holtved. *Folk*, vol. 5 (1963), p. 157-72. bibliog.
A discussion of this 'master of assistant spirits' who occupied a prominent position in the religious ideas of the Greenlanders and other Eskimo cultures, with reference to the variants and origins of the myth.

288 Man, God and magic.
Ivar Lissner. Translated from the German by J. Maxwell Brownjohn. London: Jonathan Cape, 1961. 344p. bibliog.
A survey of the culture, and especially the religious beliefs and practices, of prehistoric man, comparing these with the cultural practices and religious beliefs of still-existent primitive peoples. The author's theory is that early man believed in one supreme god. There is anthropological evidence that early man in several different areas of the world worshipped God in the same way. It is possible that man's original concept of God was monotheistic with polytheism representing a step backwards. This book contains accounts of worship among primitive tribes, including those inhabiting the circumpolar arctic regions.

289 A comparative survey of Eskimo-Aleut religion.
Gordon H. Marsh. *Anthropological Papers of the University of Alaska*, vol. 3, no. 1 (Dec. 1954), p. 21-36. bibliog.
A study of the basic beliefs of the Eskimos under the following categories: (1) charms, amulets, talismans and magic formulas; (2) the immortal and perpetually reincarnated souls of men and animals; (3) the 'persons' of creatures; (4) the demonic spirits of the earth and air; and (5) the 'persons' or spirit-powers directing the universe and forces of nature. The study concludes with a consideration of the private rituals, or rules of life, in relation to the spirit-powers of the world.

Religion

290 **Religions of the circumpolar north.**
Compiled by Robin Minion. Edmonton, Alberta: University of
Alberta, Boreal Institute for Northern Studies, 1985. 92p. (BINS
Bibliographic Series no. 15).
A listing of 260 references, some with brief indicative notes, which includes author,
geographic and title indexes.

291 **Die religionen Nordeurasiens und der amerikanischen Arktis** (The
religions of North America and the American Arctic.)
Ivar Paulson, Åke Hultkrantz, Karl Jettmar. Stuttgart: W.
Kohlhammer, 1962. 425p. maps. bibliog. (Die Religionen der
Menschheit Bd. 3).
Offers a comprehensive account of the religious beliefs of the northern peoples of
Siberia, the Finns, Lapps, Eskimos (including the Greenland Eskimos), and Aleuts.

Social Services, Health, Welfare and Medicine

292 **Greenland medical bibliography.**
Søren Andersen.   Oulu, Finland: Nordic Council for Arctic Medical
Research, 1981. 137p. (Report 29/81).

A computerized version of a bibliography compiled by a former medical officer in
Angmagssalik district, Greenland, concerning all aspects of health conditions,
including veterinary medicine, in the country from the 18th century to the 1970s. A
supplement containing a further 1,200 entries was published by Grønlandsmedicinsk
Selskab, Copenhagen, 1983.

293 **The history of scurvy and vitamin C.**
C. Carpenter.   Cambridge, England: Cambridge University Press,
1986. 288p. bibliog.

A comprehensive account of one of the diseases which has had the most significant
effect on the history of travel and exploration. The information is investigated on an
historical basis, beginning in the Middle Ages and finishing with a discussion of 'mega
vitamins'. One chapter concentrates on the subject of scurvy in polar regions.

294 **Polar human biology; the proceeding of the SCAR/IUPS/IUBS**
symposium on human biology and medicine in the Antarctic.
Edited by O. G. Edholm, E. K. E. Gunderson.   London: William
Heinemann, Medical Books, 1973. 443p. bibliog.

These papers were read at a conference organized under the auspices of the Scientific
Committee on Antarctic Research (SCAR), the International Union of Physiological
Sciences (IUPS), and the International Union of Biological Sciences (IUBS), held in
Cambridge, England, in 1972. The contents of the volume reflect the multidisciplinary
aspects of the work carried out in both antarctic and arctic regions, covering clinical,
virological, physiological and psychological studies.

295 **Food and emergency food in the circumpolar area.**
Kerstin Eidlitz. Uppsala, Sweden: Uppsala Universitet, 1969. 175p.
map. bibliog. (Studia Ethnographica Upsaliensia XXXII).

This monograph describes and analyses the basic foodstuffs and patterns of consumption among the circumpolar peoples in order to demonstrate the existence of varying types of consumption associated with the differing types of economy. This study is also concerned with other nutritional topics, including the relationships between normal and emergency foods, the factors affecting the annual food cycle and social aspects of diet.

296 **Tuberculosis in western Alaska 1900-1950.**
N. E. Flanders. *Polar Record*, vol. 23, no. 145 (Jan. 1987), p. 383-96.
maps. bibliog.

Tuberculosis was the major cause of death among Alaska native peoples during the first half of the 20th century. Little is known of the impact of the disease on the people. This paper reviews published articles, unpublished reports by government teachers, hospital records, and other material from several native villages.

297 **Circumpolar health 84. Proceedings of the Sixth International Symposium on Circumpolar Health.**
Edited by Robert Fortuine. Seattle; London: University of Washington Press, 1985. 484p. bibliog.

A selection of the papers and addresses presented at this polar health conference held in Anchorage, Alaska, in May 1984 and attended by scientists, administrators and health workers from twenty-one countries, and concerned with the health and welfare of all peoples living in the circumpolar North. Papers presented are arranged by subject under the following headings: (1) Introductory statements and general surveys; (2) physiology and pathology of cold climates; (3) Demography, morbidity and mortality; (4) Infectious disease; (5) Non-infectious and chronic disease; (6) Acculturation, mental health, and substance abuse; (7) Health programmes and manpower; and (8) Progress in self determination (among indigenous populations).

298 **Work in the north: physiological aspects.**
Richard R. Gonzalez. *Arctic Medical Research* no. 44 (1986), p. 7-17.
bibliog.

This review discusses general physiological responses during physical exertion in normal thermal environments with implications for responses in cold extremes.

299 **Health and disease among the Lapps.**
Sixten R. S. Haraldson. *Polar Record*, vol. 21, no. 133 (Jan. 1983), p. 345-57. map. bibliog.

A study, by an experienced northern doctor, of the minority tenth of those north Scandinavian peoples calling themselves Lapps, being the 'Mountain Lapps' living from reindeer herding. Aspects covered include vital statistics and ethnic features, economy and nutrition, hereditary and congenital diseases, life expectations, illness and death, and health services.

300 **Bibliography on Arctic medical research in the USSR.**
V. P. Kaznacheev, V. Ju. Kulikov, E. Soini, J. Leppäluoto, F.
Stenbäck. *Arctic Medical Research*, no. 39 (1985), 143p.
A computer-based bibliography of 818 references arranged according to the US
National Library of Medicine classification scheme. The entries are arranged
alphabetically under classes.

301 **Cold and frost injuries – rewarming damages; biological, angiological and clinical aspects.**
Hans Killian, T. Graf-Baumann. Berlin: Springer-Verlag, 1981. 250p.
bibliog.
An updated monograph based on the author's personal experiences gained in winter
warfare in northern Russia, 1941-43, and using data from the latest Himalayan
expeditions. The main topics covered are clinical descriptions of local cold injuries,
pathology, complications of cold injuries and prophylaxis, and treatment of localized
cold damage.

302 **Man in the cold.**
Jacques Le Blanc. Springfield, Illinois: Charles C. Thomas, 1975.
195p. bibliog.
The author, a professor of physiology, relates existing data based on laboratory studies
of animals to that obtained from various human populations in field or laboratory
conditions, and presents a summary of our present understanding of human functional
responses to cold exposure.

303 **The human biology of circumpolar populations.**
Edited by F. A. Milan. Cambridge, England: Cambridge University
Press, 1980. 381p. bibliog.
One of a series of volumes summarizing the work of the International Biological
Programme (IBP) 1967-74. This volume contains twelve specialized papers elucidating
the biological and behavioural processes responsible for the successful perpetuation of
circumpolar human populations, and their adaptation to the environment and its
resources as well as to each other.

304 **Cancer incidence in Greenland.**
Nils Højgaard Nielsen. *Arctic Medical Research*, no. 43 (1986), 168p.
This epidemiological study charts the incidence of cancer among Greenlanders during
the period 1950-74, a period of radical social changes. It attempts to illustrate the
cancer pattern during the first half of the 20th century.

305 **Polar biological research; an assessment.**
Polar Research Board. Washington, DC: National Academy Press,
1982. 2 vols.
An examination of current knowledge of the medical aspects of life in polar regions
and of polar biomedical research needs. Volume two is an appendix containing a
literature review of polar medicine.

306 **Problems of family health in circumpolar regions. Report on a WHO/NCAMR working group, Ilulissat, Jakobshavn, Greenland, April 20-22, 1985.**
Arctic Medical Research, no. 40 (1985), 99p. bibliog.
The papers offered here were presented to a World Health Organization/Nordic Council for Arctic Medical Research working group. Family health problems identified in the circumpolar regions include acculturation, education, suicide, violence, mortality, family health, families with absent fathers, amongst others.

307 **Arctic underwater operation: medical and operational aspects of diving activities in arctic conditions.**
Edited by Louis Rey. London: Graham & Trotman, 1985. 356p.
Twenty-nine papers presented to the International Conference ICEDIVE 84 in Stockholm, dealing with medical and technical problems and related underwater activities in arctic conditions. The volume is divided into three parts: (1) Medical and physical problems; (2) Diving and operational management; and (3) Underwater operations including arctic ice conditions and submarine navigation under ice.

308 **Nutrition of Indian and Eskimo children. Report of the second Canadian Ross conference on paediatric research.**
Ross Laboratories. Montreal: The Author, 1975. 193p.
This volume comprises the proceedings of a conference of experts held in Toronto, November 1974. Topics covered included nutrition surveys, specific nutritional problems and nutritional basis of disease. The proceedings closed with a general discussion and recommendations.

309 **Arctic medical bibliography.**
Esa Soini, Juhani Leppäluoto. Oulu, Finland: Nordic Council for Arctic Medical Research, 1982. 129p. (Nordic Council for Arctic Medical Research, report 34).
This is a computerized bibliography of 839 references to published literature on polar medicine and public health in Nordic libraries, with keyword and author indexes.

310 **Symposium on women diseases in northern sparsely populated areas. Umeå, Sweden, November 23-24, 1982.**
Arctic Medical Research, no. 36 (1983), 60p. bibliog.
Fourteen papers presented by medical experts from Denmark, Finland, Iceland, Norway and Sweden, covering a broad range of topics from infertility to breast cancer.

311 **Proceedings symposia on arctic biology and medicine IV. Frostbite.**
Edited by Eleanor G. Viereck. College, Alaska: University of Alaska, Geophysical Institute, 1964. 457p.
A presentation of fourteen papers dealing with the prevention and treatment of frostbite.

312   **The WHO programme in circumpolar health.**
      Hannu Vuori.   *Arctic Medical Research* no. 37 (1984), p. 5-9, bibliog.
In the expectation that the circumpolar regions will become the focus of increasing
attention in future years, with consequent health hazards for migrants and native
peoples alike, the World Health Organization (WHO) has launched a special
programme in circumpolar health.

313   **Starving sailors: the influence of nutrition upon naval and maritime**
      history.
      Edited by J. Watt, E. J. Freeman, W. F. Bynum.   London: National
      Maritime Museum, 1981. 212p.
A review, by maritime historians, nutrition scientists and medical specialists, of past
maritime expeditions in the light of present-day knowledge of nutrition. The object
was to evaluate the role of nutrition, not only in relation to the physical performance
of seafarers in the past three centuries, but particularly in relation to decision-making
by naval and expedition commanders. One chapter deals specifically with nutritional
aspects of British arctic expeditions.

314   **Symposium on psychiatric epidemiology and suicidology among children**
      and adults in the far north.
      Oulu, Finland: Nordic Council for Arctic Medical Research, 1981.
      116p. (Nordic Council for Arctic Medical Research, report 27).
Presents papers read at an international symposium, with contributions relating to
mental problems encountered in Alaska, Greenland, the Faroes, Canada, northern
Scandinavia and Iceland.

315   **Alaska Medicine.**
      Anchorage, Alaska: Alaska State Medical Association, 1968- .
      twice-monthly.
This journal covers all aspects of public health and medicine in the State of Alaska.

316   **Arctic Medical Research.**
      Aapistie, Finland: Nordic Council for Arctic Medical Research, 1972- .
      quarterly.
Originally published in a report series, the new title dates from vol. 46, issue no. 1,
1987. Papers contributed (in the English language) cover all aspects of health and
medicine in the circumpolar Arctic and include letters to the editor.

The Arctic as a Strategic Military Area

317 **Northern waters: security and resource issues.**
   C. Archer, P. Scrivener.   London: Croom Helm, 1986. 240p. map.
   bibliog.

This book consists of fifteen contributions from the USA, Canada, Norway, Denmark and the United Kingdom. The focus is on the sea area between 60° to 80°N and 90°W to 40°E. These northern waters are important, firstly, because they cover the regular sea lanes between North America and Europe; secondly, they are rich in fish and petroleum resources; thirdly, they have a strategic importance as they lie between the two super powers, the USA and the USSR. The book has two main parts. The first considers themes within the area as a whole, such as natural resources, transport, strategy and military technology. The second part deals with the natural resources and the strategic perspectives of individual nations.

318 **Greenland and the Artic [*sic*] region – resources and security policy.**
   H. C. Bach, Jørgen Taagholt.   Copenhagen: Information and Welfare
   Service of the Danish Defence, 1982. 79p. maps. bibliog.

This booklet contains chapters on the history, geography and climate of Greenland, resources, law of the sea, fisheries and environment, weapon technology, strategy and defence policies and defence tasks.

319 **Soviet oil and security interests in the Barents Sea.**
   Helge Ole Bergesen, Arild Moe, Willy Østreng.   London: Frances
   Pinter, 1987. 144p. maps.

The Barents Sea, which harbours the Soviet northern fleet, has been marked by military activity and East–West tension since the end of World War II. In the early 1980s exploration for oil in the Norwegian and Soviet sectors of the Barents Sea introduced a new factor of commercial as well as strategic importance. This book constitutes a professional analysis of Soviet energy policy, military interests and needs in the region. Two appendixes cover the organization of Barents Sea offshore research, planning exploration and development.

320 **The new central front.**
Timothy E. Deschenau. *United States Naval Institute Proceedings*,
vol. 103, no. 9 (Sept. 1977), p. 38-46.
Makes consideration of the Arctic as a strategic region between the United States and
the USSR and the problems of military operations in the North.

321 **Custos borealis: the military in the Canadian north.**
Kenneth Charles Eyre. London: University of London, King's
College, Department of War Studies, 1981. 313p map. bibliog. (Thesis
submitted for PhD degree).
An examination of the historic involvement of military forces in the Canadian Arctic
between 1898 and 1975 by an ex-officer of the Canadian Airborne Regiment with polar
experience. The study seeks to answer two main questions. Firstly, what effect has the
Canadian north had on the defence policy of Canada and, to a lesser extent, of the
United States? Secondly, what effect has the presence of Canadian and American
military forces had on the Canadian north? Military activity and programmes in the
north relating to this focus are analysed in terms of national defence, national
sovereignty, and national development.

322 **European security, nuclear weapons and public confidence.**
Edited by William Gutteridge, Marian Dobrosielski, Jorma
Miettinen. London, Basingstoke: Macmillan, 1982. 236p. maps.
bibliog.
Relevant chapters (p. 107-74) cover regional defence problems in the Baltic and the
Arctic Ocean, strategic balance, arms control and the energy politics of the Arctic, and
non-living natural resources of the Arctic Ocean.

323 **Europe's northern cap and the Soviet Union.**
Nils Ørvik. Cambridge, Massachusetts, Center for International
Affairs, Harvard University, 1963. 64p. (Occasional Papers in
International Affairs, no. 6).
The author see the 'northern cap' as the northern flank of the NATO alliance most
vulnerable to Soviet attack. As defined in this paper the 'cap', for purposes of
discussion, includes those parts of Norway, Sweden, Finland and the Soviet Union
north of latitude 66°N, and extending from the Norwegian Sea on the west to the
White Sea on the east. It also includes the ocean areas and islands (such as
Spitsbergen) between the coasts of these countries and the North Pole. This paper
explores Soviet strategy and the response of Norway asking whether she will choose
semi-neturality or to contribute to Nordic stability by full and active participation in
the Western Alliance?

324 **The Soviet Union in arctic waters; security implications for the northern
flank of NATO.**
Willy Østreng. Oslo: Fridtjof Nansen Institute, 1982. 116p. maps.
(Studie: R.013/2).
The central theme of the author's paper is that a major change is taking place in the
strategy of the Soviet northern fleet, namely that the strategic centre of gravity in the

Norwegian Sea is tending to move towards the Arctic and not southwards as is assumed by some analysts. Chapters include an interpretation of the northern fleet and Norwegian security operating conditions for submarines in the Arctic; the Soviet 'strait' problem; the strategic significance of the Arctic Basin; and the Arctic as a nuclear-free zone.

325 **The economic and strategic importance of the Norwegian and Barents Seas.**
Finn Sollie.   Oslo: Fridtjof Nansen Foundation at Polhøgda, 1978.
19p. maps.

A discussion from the Norwegian viewpoint of (1) the future economic role of the Norwegian and Barents Seas to Norway and the USSR; (2) the importance of the Arctic Ocean in providing the main access to maritime routes in this region, as well as sailings to and from Soviet ports in the North and future transpolar routes; and (3) the strategic role of these seas together with the White Sea and Kara Sea, in the age of submarine-based, long-range nuclear weapon systems.

326 **The DEW Line.**
Michael Stephenson.   *Beaver*, outfit 314, no. 3 (winter 1983), p. 14-19.

A brief history of the Distant Early Warning (DEW) Line constructed jointly by the USA and Canada between 1954-57 and extending across the northernmost continental limits north of the Arctic Circle. Today it consists of thirty-one stations extending from Alaska to Greenland. The article concludes with a forecast of updating plans to 1988.

The Arctic in International Law

327 **The law of Soviet territorial waters; a case study of maritime legislation and practice.**
William E. Butler.   New York: Frederick A. Praeger, 1967. 192p. bibliog.

This book, written by an international lawyer, is intended as a resource volume for those professionally interested in specific aspects of Soviet maritime or international law. It describes the existing legal régime of Soviet territorial waters, outlines its pattern of development in Soviet legislation and treaty practice, and surveys its philosophical and legal foundations as they have been conceived by Soviet publicists.

328 **The Soviet Union and the law of the sea.**
William E. Butler.   Baltimore, Maryland; London: Johns Hopkins University Press, 1971. 245p. maps. bibliog.

This book examines the salient aspects of the Soviet approach to the international law of the sea with special attention accorded to both the doctrine and practice of the Tsarist and Soviet periods. The principal divisions of the text are: legal régime of territorial waters; internal sea waters; legal régime of the continental shelf; legal régime of the sea bed; and legal régime of the high seas. A table of treaties is appended.

329 **The Arctic in question.**
Edited by E. J. Dosman.   Toronto: Oxford University Press, 1976. 206p.

A number of contributions by academic specialists, outlining and exploring northern sovereignty as an issue in Canadian foreign policy. Problems discussed include the current legal status of arctic lands and waters; challenges to Canadian sovereignty in the North and the direction from which these challenges come; whether Canada is equipped to deal vigorously with its rivals; and the stakes in maintaining a Canadian (rather then a North American) Arctic.

330 The law of international spaces.

John Kish.   Leiden, Netherlands: A. W. Sijthoff, 1973. 236p. bibliog.

This monograph concerns problems arising from the delimitation of international spaces, including the Arctic. It analyses the rule prohibiting territorial sovereignty over international spaces together with the rule of the jurisdiction of the flag state in international space. Finally, the author considers the problems arising from the use of force in international spaces.

331 Innocent passage in the Arctic.

A. Donat Pharand. *Canadian Yearbook of International Law*, (1968), p. 3-60.

A review of the principles of international law relating to innocent passage in general and an enquiry into the right of innocent passage through the Northwest Passage, with a similar enquiry for the Northeast Passage.

332 The law of the sea of the Arctic with special reference to Canada.

A. Donat Pharand.   Ottawa: University of Ottawa Press, 1973. 367p. maps. bibliog. (Collection des Travaux de la Faculté de Droit de l'Université d'Ottawa. Monographies Juridiques, no. 7).

This monograph, by the professor of international law at the University of Ottawa, was occasioned by the Third Law of the Sea Conference in 1974 and addresses itself to the problems of legal ownership of the seabed following the discovery of vast oil reserves in the arctic regions. Seven major questions are studied. These are: (1) the applicability of the right of innocent passage to the Northwest and Northeast Passages; (2) the status of the waters of the Canadian arctic archipelago; (3) the possibility of claiming an historic title to some of the arctic waters; (4) the applicability of the principle of 'the freedom of the seas' to the Arctic Ocean; (5) the status of ice shelves and ice islands; (6) the international validity of the Canadian Arctic pollution prevention legislation; and (7) the state boundaries of the arctic continental shelf and seabed.

333 The Northwest Passage: arctic straits.

A. Donat Pharand, L. H. Leghault.   Dordrecht, Netherlands: Martinus Nijhoff, 1984. 199p. maps. bibliog. (International Straits of the World).

Dr Pharand, a professor of international law specializing in arctic application, here provides a general description of the Northwest Passage and outlines the history of its discovery. He includes a complete list of transits and surveys of actual and possible commercial development. The author concludes that the Northwest Passage does not qualify as an international strait in law, but may become one. In this event Canada would still be able, legally, to enforce pollution prevention regulations under the 'Arctic Clause' of the Law of the Sea Convention of 1982. Attention is also paid to the effect of a functioning Northwest Passage on the way of life of the indigenous Eskimos and on the national security of Canada.

334　**The evolution of the law of the sea; a study of resources and strategy with special regard to the polar regions.**
Bo Johnson Theutenberg.　Dublin: Tycooly International, 1984. 261p. maps. bibliog. (Natural Resources and the Environment Series, vol. 17).

This book is a gloss on the Law of the Sea Convention of 1982 together with its full text. Chapter four is devoted to the effects of this law on the Arctic from the strategic and military points of view, with comments on sovereignty, the sector principle, Soviet claims, the legal status of the northern circumpolar seas, innocent passage, the new Arctic maritime zones, the areas in the Barents Sea disputed by Norway and the USSR, and the problem of Svalbard (Spitsbergen). The chapter closes with a section on scientific research in the Arctic and international cooperation and resource exploitation.

Economic Resources and Development

335 **Land use in northern Canada and Alaska.**
Compiled by Robin Minion. Edmonton, Alberta: University of
Alberta, Boreal Institute for Northern Studies, 1984. 67p. (BINS
Bibliographic Series no. 2).

A bibliography of 163 references, many with brief contents notes, covering aspects c
land use in northern North America including, for example, settlement studies
resource use and subsistence, economic and cultural impact of oil and gas programme
and legal aspects. Appended are author, geographic and title indexes.

336 **Offshore development in northern Canada and Alaska.**
Compiled by Robin Minion. Edmonton, Alberta: University of
Alberta, Boreal Institute for Northern Studies, 1985. 83p. (BINS
Bibliographic Series, no. 14).

A bibliography of 201 references, some with brief indicative contents notes, relating to
hydro-carbon exploration and related topics such as sea-ice hazards, environmental
impact statements and socio-economic impact statements.

337 **Hydroelectric developments in northern regions.**
Compiled by Robin Minion. Edmonton, Alberta: Boreal Institute for
Northern Studies, 1985. 78p. (BINS Bibliographic Series, no. 21).

A listing of publications compiled from the Institute's computerized library data base,
arranged by authors with geographic and author indexes. Material covered includes
monographs, theses, government documents, atlases, microfilms and periodicals.

338 **Northern ecology and resource management; memorial essay honouring Don Gill.**

Edited by Rod Olson, Ross Hastings, Frank Geddes. Edmonton, Alberta: University of Alberta Press, 1984. 438p. bibliog.

A collection of specialist papers dealing with issues relating to arctic ecology and resource management. The book is divided into the following sections: (1) Abiotic components – soils, climate, snow cover; (2) Animal communities – ecology of various arctic animals, e.g. caribou; (3) Plant communities; and (4) Land use – energy development, tourism, nature conservation, a case history of Aklavik town.

339 **Arctic energy resources: proceeding of the Comité Arctique international conference on arctic energy resources held at the Veritas Centre, Oslo, Norway, September 22-24, 1982.**

Edited by Louis Rey. Amsterdam: Elsevier, 1983. 366p. maps. bibliog. (Energy Research, vol. 2).

The editor describes the arctic regions as 'the modern Eldorado'. The contributions to this international conference of experts cover the broad range of arctic energy resources including, for example, petroleum and coal; the technological and economic aspects of exploration; and the exploitation of arctic energy resources. The conference concluded with a review of the environmental and social impact of industrial development; the effects of pollution on the biota; and the impact of development on northern peoples.

340 **Arctic environment and resources.**

John E. Sater, A. G. Ronhovde, L. C. van Allen. Washington, DC: Arctic Institute of North America, 1971. 310p. bibliog.

This volume was compiled as a comprehensive presentation of arctic environmental conditions as they might be expected to affect resources development in northern areas. It is divided into two parts. Part one describes the arctic environment, covering, for example, geophysics, atmospherics, sea ice, ocean, climate and terrain. Part two analyses arctic resources of the United States, Canada, USSR and Scandinavia, and considers the future significance of these. For the period 1970-2000, oil and gas were judged to be the arctic resources of greatest economic and strategic concern.

341 **US arctic interests: the 1980s and 1990s.**

Edited by W. E. Westermeyer, K. M. Shusterich. New York: Springer-Verlag, 1984. 369p.

A volume of sixteen papers relating to United States interests in the Arctic. Contributors include academics, representatives of native groups, industrialists and environmentalists. The main theme stresses resource exploitation and its effects, and the related issues of jurisdiction and policy making. One paper covers military security problems.

342 **The age of the Arctic.**

Oran R. Young. *Oceanus*, vol. 29, no. 1 (1986), p. 9-17.

An outline of the present stategic policy and the state of economic development around the Arctic basin.

343 **Arctic News-Record.**
Bergen, Norway, 1982- . irregular.

A journal which is devoted to current oil, gas and mineral development in the Soviet Arctic, Barents Sea–Svalbard region, northern Canada, and elsewhere in the North.

Fisheries

Whaling

History

344   **American whalers in the western Arctic, the final epoch of the great American sailing whaling fleet; watercolors and drawings by William Gilkerson.**
John R. Bockstoce.   Fairhaven, Massachusetts: Edward J. Lefkowicz, 1983. 48p.

A history of the early arctic whaling industry illustrated by watercolours and drawings.

345   **Whales, ice and men; the history of whaling in the western Arctic.**
John R. Bockstoce.   Seattle, London: University of Washington Press in association with the New Bedford Whaling Museum, Massachusetts, 1986. 400p. bibliog.

Since 500 BC the native peoples of Siberia regularly hunted marine mammals from shore bases, including the largest creature of all, the bowhead whale. By 1000 AD the industry was being pursued across Bering Strait by the Eskimos of northern Alaska, Canada and Greenland. In 1848 American whalers sailed through Bering Strait and discovered the bowhead whales. A major profit-making industry developed. This monograph covers the history of commercial whaling in the western Arctic by an American scholar who also knows the shores and waters of the region from personal exploration, and has made a close study of the historical records and archaeological sites. This beautifully-illustrated volume contains several useful appendixes, including a chronology of major events, a statistical graph, a gazetteer of whalers' place-names and a glossary of terms.

346 Whaling industry of New London.
Robert Owen Decker.   York, Pennsylvania: Liberty Cap, 1973. 202p. bibliog.

A specialist study of the whaling industry of New London, Connecticut, which dates from the mid-17th century. It achieved its peak in 1845, being second only in importance to that of New Bedford. Based on an exhaustive search of the primary sources, this monograph traces the history of the industry which sought the sperm whale in both arctic and antarctic waters.

347 The whale.
Leonard Harrison Matthews.   London: Allen & Unwin, 1968. 287p. maps. bibliog.

A well-illustrated history of whales and the whaling industry by one of the world's leading experts in the field, with added contributions by various experts.

348 An arctic whaling diary: the journal of Captain George Comer in Hudson Bay 1903-05.
Edited by W. Gillies Ross.   Toronto: University of Toronto Press, 1984. 271p.

Captain George Comer was probably the best known of the arctic whaling masters who sailed in both arctic and antarctic waters and who kept careful and detailed records of natural phenomena and native cultures. He collected early sound recordings for the American Museum of Natural History. His 1903-05 journal of a voyage in the ship *Era* describes operations at the start of the last decade of Hudson Bay bowhead whaling. Of special interest are his descriptions of the mutually beneficial socio-economic relationships which developed between the whaling crews and the Eskimos who provided labour and skin clothing for the whalers in return for ammunition and food.

349 Arctic whalers, icy seas; narratives of the Davis Strait whale fishery.
W. Gillies Ross.   Toronto: Irwin, 1985. 263p. map. bibliog.

First-hand accounts by fifteen whaleman, mostly from British ports, relate their dramatic experiences in the eastern Arctic between 1824 and 1817. The accounts are edited and introduced by a leading scholar in the field of whaling history.

350 Whaling logbooks and journals 1613-1927; an inventory of manuscript records in public collections.
Stuart C. Sherman. Revised and edited by Judith M. Downey, Virginia M. Adams, Howard Pasternack.   New York: Garland Publishing, 1986. 469p. map.

A listing of 5,108 manuscript logbooks and journals, held in eighty-two public collections throughout the world, from sailing vessels employed on whaling voyages.

351 **Harpooned; the story of whaling.**
Bill Spence. London: Conway Maritime Press, 1980. 192p. bibliog.
This is a popular well-illustrated account of arctic and antarctic whaling. Chapters cover topics including the Dutch, British and American Arctic whale fisheries, leading to the decline of the Dutch and British fisheries and the 19th-century American expansion, and the birth of modern whaling.

352 **Greenland voyager.**
Tom Stamp, Cordelia Stamp. Whitby, England: Caedmon of Whitby, 1983. 191p.
A selection of extracts from the logbooks and journals of the great whaling captain and naturalist William Scoresby (1789-1857). These extracts throw much light on life aboard an arctic whaler in the early 19th century as well as on the hazards of the whale hunt. The book concludes with a list of Scoresby's ships and crews.

353 **The history of modern whaling.**
J. N. Tønnessen, A. O. Johnsen. London: Hurst; Canberra: Australian National University Press, 1982. 798p. map. bibliog.
Offers a translation of the much more comprehensive Norwegian edition *Der moderne hvalfangste historie; opprimelse og utvikling.* (Vol. 1. A. O. Johnsen. Oslo: H. Aschehoug, 1959. Vols. 2-4. J. N. Tønnessen. Sandefjord, Norway: Norges Hvalfangstforbund, 1967, 1969, 1970). The translation omits the source list and general references contained in the original work, but includes a comprehensive bibliography.

354 **The ice-bound whalers; the story of the *Dee* and the *Grenville Bay* 1836-37.**
Edited by James A. Troup. Stromness, Scotland: Orkney Press in association with Stromness Museum, 1987. 129p. maps.
An account of the Orkney and arctic whaling industry in the 19th century, with contemporary accounts of the whale ships *Dee* and *Grenville Bay* which were icebound in Davis Straits, 1836-37, with consequent suffering and loss of life.

355 **Early European exploration of the northern Atlantic 800-1700, February 1981.**
University of Groningen, Arctic Centre. Groningen, Netherlands: The Author, 1981. 229p. maps. bibliog.
Presents the proceedings of an international symposium held at the Arctic Centre, University of Groningen, February 1981. The papers published here deal with different aspects of arctic whaling during the 16th and 17th centuries with emphasis on the Dutch whaling stations on Spitsbergen, and the rise and fall of the industry.

Modern whaling

356 **Conservation and management of whales.**
K. Radway Allen. Seattle: University of Washington Press; London: Butterworths, 1980. 107p. bibliog.
This book, based on a series of lectures given at the University of Washington in 1978, outlines the main concepts and techniques which have gradually evolved in the study of whale populations, and reviews their application to the problem of managing these resources. There is a description of the principal characteristics of whales, including their social structure, food, distribution, reproduction and mortality rates. Also included is a brief history of the industry and its regulation by the International Whaling Commission.

357 **Arctic chase; a history of whaling in Canada's North.**
Daniel Francis. Florida: Breakwater Books, 1984. 124p. map. bibliog.
This history of the hunting of the bowhead whale (*Balaena mysticetus*) in the eastern and western Arctic is based on seamen's diaries and ships' logbooks. In addition to describing a typical whaling season the author also considers the effects of exploitation of the whale on native people and the final decline of the industry.

358 **Whale manual '78.**
Friends of the Earth. London: The Author, 1978. 153p. bibliog.
Friends of the Earth here call for a moratorium on all commercial whaling for a minimum of ten years to prevent the extinction of currently over-exploited species. The manual summarizes all aspects of whaling including the life-cycles of whale species, the efforts of governments and the International Whaling Commission to conserve stocks, a history of legislation, the economics of whaling, assessment of whale populations, methods of killing whales and alternatives to whale products.

359 **Arctic whaling. Proceedings of the international symposium . . . February 1983.**
Edited by H. K. s'Jacob, K. Snoeijing, R. Vaughan. Groningen, Netherlands: University of Groningen, Arctic Centre, 1984. 181p. maps. bibliog. (Works of the Arctic Centre, 8).
Papers presented to the conference ranged over a broad spectrum of related topics, including 'Whale biogeography and the history of the Arctic Basin'; 'Arctic climate: past, present and future'; 'On the present state and the future fate of the arctic sea ice cover'; 'On the biology of whales'; 'History of native whaling in the Arctic and Subarctic'; 'Historical survey of the European whaling industry' and other themes.

360 **Whales, whaling and whale research; a selected bibliography.**
Compiled by L. R. Magnolia. Cold Spring Harbor, New York: Whaling Museum, 1977. 91p. (Publication no. WM-1).
Lists 1,000 English-language references on whales, whaling techniques, research and substitutes for whale-derived products.

361 **Report of the International Whaling Commission.**
Cambridge, England: International Whaling Commission, 1950- .
annual.

This annual report includes the various reports on the work of the Commission together with numerous scientific papers dealing with conservation, whale biology and population.

362 **International Whaling Commission Special Issue Series.**
Cambridge, England: International Whaling Commission, 1977- .
irregular.

This series contains the proceedings of various workshops and conferences devoted to specialized aspects of whale zoology and the whaling industry.

Sealing

363 **The war against the seals; a history of the North American seal fishery.**
Briton Cooper Busch. Kingston, Montreal: McGill-Queen's
University Press, 1985. 374p. maps. bibliog.

A comprehensive history of the sealing industry dealing with the New England sealers of the late 18th and 19th centuries who hunted the world for fur seals and nearly exterminated some species. The author also reviews the Newfoundland harp seal fishery in the 19th and 20th centuries. Thirdly, there is an account of the exploitation of the Alaskan or northern fur seal fishery of the Pribilof Islands.

364 **Seals and sealing in Canada; report of the Royal Commission.**
Royal Commission on seals and the sealing industry in
Canada. Ottawa: Ministry of Supply and Services, 1986. 3 vols.

The Royal Commission was set up by the Government of Canada in August 1984. Its mandate was to review all matters pertaining to seals and the sealing industry in Canada and to make recommendations for the development of policy. Volume one consists of a summary of the issues arising, a summary of findings and conclusions, and various recommendations. Volume two contains a review of seals and sealing, discusses public concern about sealing and reviews social and cultural issues, including the importance of sealing to native peoples in the North, together with a review of sealing issues in Norway and Greenland. Volume three deals with biological issues – methods of killing seals, the status of stocks and the impact of seals on fisheries. A concluding section deals with management issues.

365 **The Bering Sea fur seal dispute 1885-1911: a monograph on the maritime history of Alaska.**
G. O. Williams. Eugene, Oregon: Alaska Maritime Publications, 85p.
map. bibliog.

This book deals in detail with the conflict between the American and Canadian pelagic sealers and the vessels of the US Revenue Marine Service, working in conjunction with the ships of the US and British naval squadrons in the North Pacific during the years 1886-94, and again in 1907-08, against Japanese sealing vessels. Eventual control of sealing was brought about by the Pacific Fur Seal Convention of 1911. The Bering Sea fur seal dispute, of which these activities were a part, involved questions of the rights of maritime nations under international law and the 'freedom of the seas'.

Fishing

366 **Fisheries of the North Pacific: history, species, gear and processes.**
Robert J. Browning.   Anchorage, Alaska: Alaska Northwest Publishing, 1974. 408p. map.
An account of the major United States and Canadian fisheries of the northeastern Pacific Ocean stretching from the Mexican border in the south to the Bering Sea and Aleutians in the north and providing a valuable account of Alaska fisheries in particular. There is a brief review of the literature on p. 345-46.

367 **Atlas of the living resources of the seas.**
Food and Agriculture Organization.   Rome: Food and Agriculture Organization of the United Nations, 1982. [72]p. maps.
The atlas comprises three series of maps. There are ten maps illustrating the geographical distribution and present state of exploitation of the living resources of the world's oceans; seven maps giving characteristic examples of fish migration; and forty-five regional maps presenting the geographical and vertical distribution, as well as the abundance, of the main stocks in each ocean region, including arctic waters. An introductory section deals with the details of presentation. An index of fish names is appended.

368 **The fisheries resources of the ocean.**
Edited by J. A. Gulland.   West Byfleet, England: Fishing News, 1971. 255p. map. bibliog.
A useful review of the total fish resources of the world's ocean compiled from statistical information held by the United Nations Food and Agriculture Organization and intended primarily for the fishing industry and for nutritionists. Summaries of fish resources are all synthesized in sixty-two coloured maps. Sections relevant to arctic regions will be found under Northwest Atlantic, Northeast Atlantic, Northwest Pacific and Northeast Pacific.

369 **Marine fisheries.**
S. J. Holt, C. Vanderbilt.   *Ocean Yearbook*, no. 2 (1980), p. 9-56.
An overview of world fisheries catches concentrating on the nutritional use of living resources. This is an update of Holt's paper in *Ocean Yearbook* (no. 1 (1978), p. 38-83), covering the years 1938-1975.

370 **Fish and fisheries of northern Canada and Alaska.**
Compiled by Robin Minion.   Edmonton, Alberta: University of
Alberta, Boreal Institute for Northern Studies, 1985. 81p. (BINS
Bibliographic Series, no. 18).

A listing of publications compiled from the Boreal Institute's computerized library data
base, arranged by authors with geographic and author indexes. Material covered
includes monographs, theses, government documents, atlases, microforms and
periodicals.

371 **Lovely she goes!**
William Mitford.   London: Michael Joseph, 1969. 192p. map.

A first-hand account, by a trawlerman, of the voyage of a Grimsby trawler to the arctic
fishing grounds.

372 **Yearbook of Fishery Statistics.**
Food and Agriculture Organization.   Rome: Food and Agriculture
Organization of the United Nations, 1953- . annual.

Annually-updated statistics covering all aspects of world fisheries catches and
production, including Arctic waters.

Domesticated Animals

Reindeer

373 **Reindeer husbandry in Finland.**
Reijo K. Helle. *Geographical Journal*, vol. 145, part 2 (July 1979),
p. 254-64. map. bibliog.
A review of reindeer herding and husbandry in Finland and the various grazing
associations, and its coexistence with occupations like farming and forestry, to which
reindeer herding is losing out. Despite this trend the number of reindeer appears to be
larger than before, though now at a maximum.

374 **Hunters, pastoralists and ranchers. Reindeer economics and their
transformations.**
Tim Ingold. Cambridge, England: Cambridge University Press, 1980.
325p. bibliog.
A discussion, based on ethnographic material from North America and Eurasia, of the
ecological aspects of the relation between men and reindeer herds under hunting and
pastoralism, the nature and process of animal domestication, the social relations of
hunting and pastoral production, and the emergence of capitalist ranching. In an
epilogue the author takes up the problems of band organization, leadership and
ideology in hunting and pastoral and ranching societies.

375 **Caribou and reindeer in Canada and Alaska.**
Compiled by Robin Minion. Edmonton, Alberta: University of
Alberta, Boreal Institute for Northern Studies, 1984. 65p. (BINS
Bibliographic Series, no. 3).
A bibliography of 160 references, many with short contents notes, relating to all
aspects of *Rangifer* species with author, geographic and title indexes.

376 **Reindeer husbandry in North America: developments in reindeer husbandry as a native industry – Alaska and northern Canada.**
Wendlyn A. C. Nixon. Cambridge, England: Scott Polar Research Institute, 1982. 83p. maps. bibliog. (Scott Polar Research Institute, University of Cambridge, unpublished M.Phil. thesis).

Chapter one discusses the introduction of reindeer (*Rangifer tarandus*) to North America and the development of reindeer husbandry in northern Canada and Alaska. Chapter two presents a chronological review of the developments in reindeer husbandry in North America in the 1970s. In Chapter three these developments are examined in the context of changes in government policies regarding ownership and management. Chapter four discusses social and economic factors which have influenced the development of reindeer husbandry, and chapter five considers the ecological aspects of herd management – the range assessments and herding methods.

377 **Eskimos, reindeer and land.**
Richard O. Stern, Edward L. Arobio, Larry L. Naylor, Wayne C. Thomas. Fairbanks, Alaska: University of Alaska, School of Agriculture and Land Resources Management, Agricultural Experiment Station, 1980. 205p. maps. bibliog. (Bulletin 59).

Constitutes the report of a research project whose purpose was to gather data on the past and present reindeer-herding practices of northwestern Alaska, in addition to collecting information on herding and land uses, the future potential of the industry and its impact on the economy and people of the area.

378 **A selected annotated bibliography of sources on reindeer herding in Alaska.**
Compiled by Richard Olav Stern. Fairbanks, Alaska: University of Alaska Institute of Arctic Biology, 1977. 167p. (Occasional Papers on Northern Life, no. 2).

An annotated bibliography of English-language literature dealing with the socio-economic and historical aspects of reindeer herding in Alaska. Some non-annotated material is included together with two appendixes, one listing repositories holding relevant unpublished or archival material, and a second listing bibliographies and research tools used in the preparation of this work.

379 **Rangifer.**
Harstad, Norway: Nordic Council for Reindeer Research, 1981- . irregular.

Described by the publisher as 'the world's only scientific journal dealing with topics about reindeer/caribou and reindeer husbandry exclusively'. Articles are in English with Norwegian summaries. Occasional special issues are published to include reindeer conference proceedings.

Musk-oxen

380 **The history of musk-ox domestication.**
Paul F. Wilkinson. *Polar Record*, vol. 17, no. 106 (Jan. 1974),
p. 13-22. bibliog.
The realization that the musk-ox (*Ovibos moschatus*) could be domesticated can be
traced at least to the 17th century. This article traces the evolution of the domesticated
musk-ox from the first practical advocacy of the explorer Vilhjalmur Stefansson in the
1920s to the thriving industry in Alaska and northern Canada of the 1960s.

Dogs

381 **The complete Siberian husky.**
Lorna B. Demidoff, Michael Jennings. New York: Howell Book
House, 1978. 287p. bibliog.
A very full account of the history of this dog, covering its introduction to Alaska as a
sledge dog, its origins, breeding, racing, care and maintenance.

382 **The Samoyed.**
Edited by G. W. Grounds. London: Samoyed Association, 1971.
4th ed. 280p.
Used by the Samoyed peoples of arctic Siberia as reindeer-herding dogs, the Samoyed
is today a domesticated thoroughbred. This book, as well as being a guide for breeders
and owners, is a useful history of the breed.

383 **Racing Alaskan sled dogs.**
Compiled by Bill Vaudrin. Anchorage, Alaska: Alaska Northwest
Publishing, 1976. 131p.
Offers short contributions by experts on raising and racing sled dogs, together with
racing records from 1946 to 1976, and a glossary of terms.

Transport

General

384 **Arctic and Antarctic; a prospect of the polar regions.**
Colin Bertram.   Cambridge: W. Heffer, 1958. 2nd ed. 123p.

This short book contains much that is still relevant to polar transport and survival
today. Chapter four contains practical information on the husky dog and the hauling of
sledges. Chapter five reviews polar transport at the time of writing, which the author
describes as 'muscular', 'environmental' and 'mechanical'. A seasoned polar explorer,
Colin Bertram was a former director of the Scott Polar Research Institute, Cambridge,
England.

385 **IPTC 86. International polar transportation conference, Vancouver,
Canada, May 4-8, 1986. Proceedings.**
Edited by Aileen Cassidy.   Vancouver: D. F. Dickins Associates,
1986. 2 vols. bibliog.

This was the first international polar transportation conference held in conjunction
with EXPO 86, involving 200 representatives from thirteen nations presenting forty-
five invited papers. The emphasis of the conference was on recent technological
developments in polar transportation design and operating experiences with aircraft,
vessels and surface transport in polar regions.

386 **Arctic transportation.**
Compiled by Robin Minion.   Edmonton, Alberta: University of
Alberta, Boreal Institute for Northern Studies, 1984. 138p. (BINS
Bibliographic Studies, no. 11).

A bibliography of 362 references, mostly relating to northern Canada and with brief
contents notes, classified under the following headings: air, ferry, general, inland,
waterways, railroad, road and sea. Author and title indexes are included.

387 **Arctic and middle north transportation.**
Edited by Beverly F. Sater. Washington, DC: Arctic Institute of
North America, 1969. 204p. maps.

The papers presented here were read at a symposium in Montreal, 5-7 March, 1969. Its
aim was for experts from industry, universities and government to exchange experience
and opinions on the transportation problems that affect the development of northern
resources.

Primitive transport

388 **Sledges and wheeled vehicles; ethnological studies from the view-point of
Sweden.**
Gösta Berg. Stockholm: C. E. Fritzes Bokförlags Aktiebolag, 1935.
189p. bibliog.

This somewhat rare and specialized monograph contains much information on the
origins and development of sledges and wheeled vehicles in northern Scandinavia and
among the Lapps.

389 **Canoes and kayaks of western America.**
Bill Durham. Seattle: Copper Canoe, 1960. 104p. bibliog.

A detailed description, with illustrations, of the principal types of aboriginal craft used
in western America, including Eskimo and Aleut kayaks and umiaks, and canoes of
the northern interior and the northwest coast.

390 **Skinboats of Greenland.**
H. C. Petersen. Roskilde, Denmark: Viking Museum, 1986. 215p.
(Ships and Boats of the North, vol. 1).

The author discusses the construction and use of the kayak and umiak in Greenland
with reference to written sources and the study of old specimens in the museum. He
draws most strongly on his experience as a native Greenlander. He himself learned to
build these boats in order to understand fully the problems and techniques involved.
The main contribution of this book lies in its meticulous documentation of construction
techniques and materials.

Travel over snow and ice

391 **Travel over snow.**
K. M. Adam.   In: *Handbook of snow; principles, processes, management and use.* Edited by D. M. Gray, D. H. Male.   Toronto: Pergamon, 1981. p. 521-61. bibliog.

Gives a brief outline of over-snow vehicles in North America. The characteristics of each type of winter road are described along with the techniques for their construction. Finally, mention is made of the environmental impact of over-snow vehicles and snow roads.

392 **The air cushion vehicle: a possible answer to some arctic transport problems.**
Howard S. Fowler.   *Polar Record*, vol. 18, no. 114 (Sept. 1976), p. 251-58. bibliog.

A review of air cushion vehicles (ACVs) suitable for use in arctic terrain, considering problems peculiar to their operation and arctic roles for ACVs. The author concludes that there is a variety of roles that these vehicles can play in arctic operations which neither aircraft nor surface transport can perform.

393 **Snow travel and transport; the story of snowmobility in pictures.**
Walter Lorch.   Macclesfield, England: Gawsworth, 1977. 159p. map. bibliog.

A concise history of transportation on snow and ice including coverage of snowshoes and skis, dog, horse, reindeer, railways, motor power, aircraft and snowmobiles.

394 **Complete guide to snowmobiling.**
June Maxam.   Toronto: G. R. Welch, 1970. 126p.

A handbook to this popular tracked snow vehicle which includes its history, riding and safety characteristics, maintenance and other topics.

Ships, shipping, submarines and sea routes

395 **Track of the *Bear*.**
William Bixby.   New York: David McKay, 1965. 309p.

A history of this famous polar vessel which was built in Dundee, Scotland, as a sealer, subsequently serving with the US Revenue Marine Service in Alaskan waters. In the 1930s she was acquired by Richard Evelyn Byrd, the American polar explorer. After a career in World War II *Bear* became a museum. She sank in 1963.

396   *SS Windward* – whaler and arctic exploration ship.
      Alex R. Buchan.   *Polar Record*, vol. 24, no. 151 (July 1988),
      p. 213-22. map. bibliog.
A history of this famous ship, built for the whaling trade in 1860, which subsequently
took part in Frederick G. Jackson's 'Harmsworth' expedition to Novaya Zemlya (1894-
97) and Robert E. Peary's expedition to Greenland, 1897-1903.

397   **Shipping routes, ice cover and year-round navigation in the Canadian
      Arctic.**
      Balaram B. Dey.   *Polar Record*, vol. 20, no. 129 (Sept. 1981),
      p. 549-59. map. bibliog.
A major consideration in arctic hydrocarbon development is the need for safe marine
transportation to southern markets. The author firstly considers a basic methodology
which needs to be followed to ensure that shipping routes are available by regular
synoptic ice observations. An analysis of year-round shipping routes in the Canadian
Arctic follows, divided into two parts. The first is a discussion of ice conditions, in
particular during the period of polar darkness. The second makes an examination of
the type of arctic icebreaking tanker required for year-round navigation.

398   **Modern icebreakers.**
      John D. Harbron.   *Scientific American*, vol. 249, no. 6 (Dec. 1983),
      p. 53-59.
A brief review of the basic characteristics of icebreakers, the various specialized types,
techniques of icebreaking, and descriptions of some modern Canadian, Soviet and
other icebreakers.

399   **A comparative study of the Northern Sea Route and the Northwest
      Passage: with special reference to the future development of marine
      transportation along the latter route.**
      Howard Hume.   Cambridge, England: Scott Polar Research Institute,
      1984. 107p. maps. bibliog. (Unpublished thesis for the M.Phil. in Polar
      Studies, Scott Polar Research Institute, University of Cambridge).
A study of the recent historic development of the Soviet Northeast Passage (Northern
Sea Route) and the Canadian Northwest Passage, considering their economic realities,
the scientific and technical support available, sovereignty issues, strategic and
environmental problems, administration and government policy towards future
development. The author's main objective is to examine advances made by the Soviets
to see what lessons can be learnt by Canadians in the future development of arctic
marine transport along the Northwest Passage.

400   **Polar operations.**
      Edwin A. MacDonald.   Annapolis, Maryland: United States Naval
      Institute, 1969. 239p. bibliog.
Based on the author's great practical experience commanding US Navy vessels in polar
waters, this book presents useful information on the polar environment, polar
icebreakers, convoying in ice, iceworking vessels, polar navigation, seamanship,
wintering-over and safety, and survival. A revised and updated edition is due for
publication.

401 The arctic submarine: its evolution and scientific and commerical potential.

Alfred S. McLaren.   Paris: Centre National de la Recherche Scientifique, Center for Arctic Studies, 1983. 46p. bibliog.

A paper presented to the 8th International Colloquy of the Center for Arctic Studies, Paris, 7-11 November, 1983, which serves as a useful summary of the history of the arctic submarine from its origins in the mid-17th century covering its gradual development over three centuries, culminating in the development of the world's first true arctic submarine USS *Nautilus* (SSN-571). The paper concludes with a discussion of the many voyages of exploration by nuclear submarines of the USA, Great Britain and the Soviet Union which followed.

402 Maritime services to support polar resource development.

Maritime Transportation Research Board, Committee on Maritime Services to support Polar Resource Development.   Washington, DC: National Academy Press, 1981. 78p. bibliog.

This report addresses the maritime requirements and potential for servicing resource development in polar areas, and reviews the nature of marine environments, current marine systems (such as icebreakers, tugs, barges, ports), auxiliary support services (communications, navigation), and the need for these services.

403 Icebreakers and icebreaking. Citations from the NTIS data base . . . 1964-1977.

National Technical Information Service.   Springfield, Virginia: US Department of Commerce, National Technical Information Service, 1977. 203p.

The design and performance of icebreakers, icebreaking, ice navigation, and ice distribution are all reviewed in these government-sponsored research reports. This updated bibliography contains 203 abstracts.

404 Ice seamanship.

G. Q. Parnell.   London: Nautical Institute, 1986. 87p. maps. bibliog. (Nautical Institute Monograph).

This monograph is divided into two parts. Part one, 'Ice', describes different types of floating ice, the formation of ice and its changing appearance to help identification. Internationally-accepted ice terminology is explained and illustrated. Part two, 'Ice seamanship', lists seven basic safety rules, with accompanying illustrations.

405 Arctic offshore engineering, ships and marine technology: a bibliography.

P. William Penney, Richard O. Carter, Andrew W. Laws.   Newcastle upon Tyne, England: University of Newcastle upon Tyne, Department of Naval Architecture and Shipbuilding, 1985. 71p.

This bibliography relates to offshore activities in ice-infested water. Of its fourteen sections, six relate to aspects of ships and ship design for arctic conditions.

Transport. Ships, shipping, submarines and sea routes

406 **Atomic submarines.**
Norman Polmar.   Princeton, New Jersey: D. van Nostrand, 1963.
286p. maps.

The first atomic submarine was authorized by President Truman of the United States in August 1950. On August 3, 1958, she crossed the North Pole and then carried on to Iceland. Polmar's book tells the story of this and subsequent atomic submarines.

Engineering Technology

407 Geotechnical engineering for cold regions.
Edited by Orlando B. Andersland, Duwayne M. Anderson. New
York: McGraw-Hill, 1978. 566p. bibliog.

A textbook designed for civil engineering student courses with relevant specialist chapters including the geotechnical aspects of cold regions, physical and thermal properties of frozen ground, mechanical properties of frozen ground, foundations for cold regions and ice pressures and bearing capacity.

408 River and lake ice engineering.
Edited by George D. Ashton. Littleton, Colorado: Water Resources
Publications, 1986. 485p. bibliog.

An introductory source book on the general principles of engineering as they are applied to river and lake ice problems. Contributions are arranged under the following headings: (1) Introduction; (2) Ice physics; (3) Ice mechanics; (4) Thermal régime of lakes and rivers; (5) Hydraulics; (6) Ice modelling; (7) Ice control; (8) Remote sensing; and (9) Icebreakers.

**409 Civil engineering in the Arctic offshore. Proceedings of the conference
Arctic '85. Co-sponsored by the Waterway, Port, Coastal and Ocean
Division and the Technical Council on Cold Regions Engineering of the
American Society of Civil Engineers.**
Edited by F. Lawrence Bennett, Jerry L. Machemehl. New York:
American Society of Civil Engineers, 1985. 1,259p. bibliog.

Proceedings of an interdisciplinary conference which was concerned with the current state of practice and theory in the civil engineering aspects of offshore development in the Arctic. The majority of the 123 papers presented are of a technical nature, covering such topics as artificial islands, protection of the environment, properties of frozen soils and university training of specialist engineers.

410 **Ice destruction – methods and technology.**
V. V. Bogorodsky, V. P. Gavrilo, O. A. Nedeshivin. Translated from
the Russian by M. B. Rosenberg. Dordrecht, Netherlands: D. Reidel,
1987. 214p. bibliog.
Originally published under the title *Raztushenie l'da – metodi, technicheskie, sredstva*
(Moscow: Gidrometeoizdat, 1983), this textbook deals with various methods of
icebreaking – mechanical, thermal, chemical and electrophysical.

411 **Design for ice forces; a state of the practice prepared by the Technical
Council on Cold Regions Engineering of the American Society of Civil
Engineers.**
Edited by Stan R. Caldwell, Randy D. Crissman. New York:
American Society of Civil Engineers, 1983. 218p.
Part one consists of six contributions dealing with the design of offshore and coastal
structures including man-made islands, port and coastal structures, offshore pipelines
for ice environments and ships for ice environments. Part two deals with inland
waterway structures, such as river and lake processes relevant to ice loads, bridges,
navigational structures and methods of ice control.

412 **Arctic technology and policy. Proceedings of the second annual MIT sea
grant college program lecture and seminar and the third annual Robert
Bruce Wallace lecture.**
Edited by Ira Dyer, Chryssostomos Chryssostomidis. Washington,
DC: Hemisphere Publishing, [1983]. 281p. maps. bibliog.
A collection of papers dealing with various aspects of Arctic Ocean sea ice science and
technology, including policy and legal aspects.

413 **Arctic ocean engineering for the 21st century.**
Edited by B. C. Gerwick, Jr. Washington, DC: Marine Technology
Society, 1985. 234p.
This volume constitutes the proceedings of the Spilhaus Symposium, October 1984, the
first in a series of symposia addressing future developments in ocean engineering,
addressed by eminent scientists and experts. Papers published here cover such topics as
geophysical and environmental issues, arctic transportation, United States Arctic
policy, and strategic and offshore developments of the Arctic Basin.

414 **IAHR symposium on ice 1986, Iowa City, August 18-22. Proceedings
vols. I and II. Organized by the Institute of Hydraulic Research.**
Institute of Hydraulic Research. Iowa City, Iowa: University of Iowa,
College of Engineering, Institute of Hydraulic Research, [1986]. 2 vols.
bibliog.
A conference sponsored by the International Association for Hydraulic Research,
Committee on ice problems, and the US National Science Foundation, whose broad
theme is engineering for ice-covered waters. It encompasses hydraulics of ice-covered
flows and ice properties, as well as ice loads, encountered by structures and vessels.

Much of the symposium is devoted to ice formation processes and means of mitigating or ameliorating engineering problems often associated with them, such as ice jams and frazil ice.

415 Permafrost engineering design and construction.
Edited by G. H. Johnston [for] Associate Committee on Geotechnical Research, National Research Council of Canada.   Toronto: John Wiley, 1981. 540p. bibliog.

An outline of the major factors influencing the design and construction of engineering works in areas of permanently frozen ground, with suggestions as to the principles and methods that can be applied. The book is divided into two parts. Chapters one to four are intended to acquaint the reader with the main factors, such as climate, terrain features and permafrost conditions affecting engineering operations in the North, and to describe the properties and behaviour of frozen ground. Chapters five to ten deal with methods for site and route investigations, the excavation and placement of earth materials and the design and construction of engineering works in permafrost. The final chapter emphasizes the need to monitor performance, to keep detailed records and to carry out regular maintenance work.

416 Thermal geotechnics.
Alfred R. Jumikis.   New Brunswick, New Jersey: Rutgers University Press, 1977. 375p. bibliog.

This book is a theoretical treatment for practical application to the various thermal geotechnical problems that occur in soil, foundation, highway and earthwork engineering. In addition to full discussion of the fundamental theories on the freezing and thawing of soils, the author, an expert in this field, presents detailed accounts of his own experimental methods and instrumentation.

417 Ground freezing.
Edited by Seiiti Kinosita, Masami Fukuda.   Rotterdam, Netherlands; Boston, Massachusetts: A. A. Balkema, 1985. 373p. bibliog. (Proceedings of the Fourth International Symposium on Ground Freezing, Sapporo, 5-7 August 1985).

Arificial freezing of ground has been applied to increasing numbers of geotechnical construction projects in the last few decades in order to stabilize earth materials and to control ground water seepage. Many significant advances have been made in ground freezing technology. This symposium presents papers in the fields of thermal properties and processes in earth materials, frost action, mechanical properties and processes in earth materials, and engineering design and case histories.

418 Frozen ground engineering.
Arvind Phukan.   Englewood Cliffs, New Jersey: Prentice-Hall, 1985. 336p. bibliog. (Prentice-Hall International Series in Civil Engineering and Engineering Mechanics).

This textbook is based on a series of lectures given at the University of Alaska. The author's purpose is to present the 'state of the art' in frozen ground engineering in a way that is suitable for instruction at university graduate level, and for use by those interested in specializing in cold region engineering. Many engineering design and construction problems encountered in permafrost areas are described with typical solutions of foundation problems. Appendixes include a glossary of terms, conversion factors for SI units and thermal conductivity of various materials.

419 **POAC 85. The 8th international conference on port and ocean engineering under Arctic conditions, Narssarssuaq, Greenland, September 7-14, 1985. Proceedings.**
Hørsholm, Denmark: Danish Hydraulic Institute, 1985. 3 vols. bibliog.
The eighth in a series of international conferences dealing with various theoretical and practical aspects of arctic technology, this conference gave emphasis to papers dealing with coastal and offshore structures in the Arctic, and the proceedings include a large number of contributions on basic research on the properties of sea ice. Other aspects include oceanography and meteorology, and problems relating to the environment. A fourth unnumbered volume contains an index of papers.

420 **Cold regions engineering; proceedings of the fourth international conference.**
Edited by William L. Ryan. New York: American Society of Civil Engineers, 1986. 788p. maps. bibliog.
Engineers concerned with the planning, designing, constructing, operating and maintaining of facilities in cold regions must deal with all the concerns found in the more temperate areas of the world, in addition to the climatic extremes and geotechnical considerations prevalent at higher latitudes and altitudes. The papers presented here cover the areas of facilities, transportation and resources development, the latter constituting the largest category. Most of the papers in this last field relate to permafrost engineering and construction.

421 **Design of water and wastewater services for cold climate communities.**
Edited by D. W. Smith, S. E. Hrudey. Oxford: Pergamon, 1981. 184p. bibliog.
Papers presented to an international seminar in Edmonton, Alberta, 28-29 June, 1986, including studies of the impact of permafrost on the design of utilities, water distribution and sewage collection in northern North America, water treatment considerations and disposal of human waste.

422 **Proceedings. Third international speciality conference cold regions engineering. 'Northern resource development'. Vols. 1-3. April 4, 5, and 6, 1984 Edmonton, Alberta.**
Compiled and edited by Daniel W. Smith. Montreal: Canadian Society for Civil Engineering, [1984]. 3 vols. bibliog.
The objective of this conference was to focus on the civil engineering aspects of meeting the challenges of northern resource development. Many aspects of cold regions engineering are discussed, including transportation, roads, water supply, waste treatment, structures, behaviour of frozen materials, building design and ice engineering.

423 **The mechanics of frozen ground.**
N. A. Tsytovich. Edited by George K. Swinzow. New York:
McGraw-Hill; Washington, DC: Scripta, 1975. 426p. bibliog.

This volume is a translation from the Russian edition *Mekhanika merzlykh gruntov* (Moscow, Vysshaya: Shkola, 1973). The author is a foremost authority on frozen soils. The book, based upon an analysis of the results of many years of research carried out by Soviet and other investigators, sets forth the laws of frozen ground mechanics with special emphasis on the physical side of the mechanical processes that take place in freezing, frozen and thawing soils. The final section of the book discusses the application of these laws to construction on permafrost.

424 **Pipelines and permafrost; science in a cold climate.**
Peter J. Williams. Ottawa: Carleton University Press, 1986. 129p.

A readable and informative analysis of the importance of the physical environment with respect to the hazards and difficulties it presents for the construction and maintenance of northern oil and gas pipelines. The author is a leading Canadian specialist in this field.

425 **Northern Engineer.**
Fairbanks, Alaska: University of Alaska, School of Engineering,
1968- . quarterly.

A journal focusing on engineering practice and technological developments in cold regions in a broad sense, and including articles stemming from the physical, biological and behavioural sciences. It also includes correspondence and book reviews.

Building Construction

426 **Solar energy at high latitudes.**
Edited by Kerr MacGregor. Hornby, England: Ambient Press, 1986. 99p.

A description of the use of solar energy in buildings in northern and arctic environments, this article has been reprinted from the *International Journal of Ambient Energy*, (vol. 6, parts 3 and 4, 1985).

427 **Building construction in cold climates.**
Compiled by Robin Minion. Edmonton, Alberta: University of Alberta, Boreal Institute for Northern Studies, 1985. 80p. (BINS Bibliographic Series, no. 17).

A listing of publications compiled from the Boreal Institute's computerized library data base, arranged by authors with geographic and author indexes. Material covered includes monographs, theses, government documents, atlases, microforms, and periodicals.

Environment

General

428 **Ecological problems of the circumpolar area. Papers from the international symposium at Luleå, June 28-30, 1971.**
Edited by Erik Bylund, Hakon Linderholm, Olof Rune. Luleå, Sweden: Norrbottens Museum, 1974. 339p. bibliog.
The papers are arranged under the following headings: (1) The biological balance – papers dealing with biogeography and climatic change, problems of pollution and of land and forest development and conservation; (2) Circumpolar health problems emphasizing the complexity of medical problems in the Swedish north; and (3) Regional and physical planning.

429 **Land management in northern Canada and Fennoscandia.**
Julian T. Inglis. *Polar Record*, vol. 19, no. 123 (Sept. 1979), p. 543-61, maps. bibliog.
The first part of this article is concerned with recent developments in land management in the Yukon and Northwest Territories of Canada, and particularly with initiatives in land-use planning at the local, regional and national levels. The second part looks at the structures and issues which appear to characterize the land-management régimes of northern Norway, Sweden and Finland.

430 **Cold regions habitability; a selected bibliography.**
C. Burgess Ledbetter. Hanover, New Hampshire: Cold Regions Research and Engineering Laboratory, 1974. 25p.
'Habitability' is defined in various ways, for example, as 'the qualities of an environment as related to the acceptability of that environment for man'. In polar regions psychological problems can arise for various reasons, such as isolation, long hours of darkness and extremes of temperature. The bibliography analyses the problem and cites literature relating to cold regions, in particular concerning buildings, personnel problems and the environment.

431 **Arctic heritage: proceedings of a symposium.**
Edited by J. G. Nelson, R. Needham, L. Norton. Ottawa:
Association of Canadian Universities for Northern Studies (ACUNS),
1987. 653p. maps. bibliog.

An interdisciplinary symposium on ecological planning and management aspects was held at Banff, Alberta, August 1985. Over forty papers are listed under three headings. Part one, 'The natural realm in the Arctic' provides background papers on climate variation and change, marine processes, arctic landfalls, floral, faunal and limnological processes, and terrestrial and marine oases. Part two deals with 'Land use and conservation in the Arctic' and Part three covers 'National parks and protected areas in the Arctic and national perceptions and approaches to parks and reserves in Alaska, Canada, Greenland, Norway and the Soviet Arctic'.

Pollution

432 **Petroleum effects in the arctic environment.**
Edited by F. R. Engelhardt. London; New York: Elsevier Applied
Science, 1985. 281p. maps. bibliog.

This volume aims to meet the growing interest in the exploration of arctic petroleum reserves with an up-to-date and coordinated overview of the subject encompassing the entire spectrum of biological systems from microbes to man. Eight specialist contributions cover the marine ecosystem including oil spills, effects of hydrocarbons on micro-organisms, petroleum biodegradation in arctic ecosystems, effects of oil on arctic invertebrates, fish, marine birds and mammals and, finally, the effects of petroleum activities on the ecology of arctic man himself.

433 **Arctic air pollution.**
Edited by Bernard Stonehouse. Cambridge, England: Cambridge
University Press, 1986. 328p. bibliog. (Studies in Polar Research, 5).

This volume is based on papers presented to an international conference held at the Scott Polar Research Institute, Cambridge, to discuss the phenomenon of arctic haze. In addition it considered the origin and transport of pollution in the Arctic as well as the climatic, human and ecological consequences.

434 **Bibliography on the fate and effects of arctic marine oil pollution.**
Edited by Stuart C. Young. Calgary, Alberta: Arctic Science and
Technology Information System, Arctic Institute of North America,
University of Calgary, 1986. 212p. (Environmental Studies, Revolving
Funds Report, no. 026).

This bibliography contains 748 citations relating to the physical, chemical and biological dispersion, deposition, weathering and biodegradation, as well as the biological effects, of petroleum and its hydrocarbon constituents in arctic waters, including Cook Inlet and the Gulf of Alaska.

Wildlife management

435 **Environmental threats to marine mammals in the Canadian Arctic.**
Ian Stirling, Wendy Calvert. *Polar Record*, vol. 21, no. 134 (May 1983), p. 443-49. maps. bibliog.

The author reviews the environment and breeding habits of whales, seals and walruses, polar bears and arctic foxes. He then lists the largest of the resource extraction projects planned in the Canadian Arctic for 1983-86 and gives an assessment of the kind of pollution that each might generate and the danger to which wildlife might be exposed. The author concludes that there are substantial gaps in our knowledge of Arctic Ocean ecology in relation to environmental disturbance, and concludes that there is a vital need for baseline studies.

436 **Effect of the Chernobyl accident on reindeer husbandry in Sweden.**
Vincent Utsi. *Polar Record*, vol. 23, no. 147 (Sept. 1987), p. 726-28. map. bibliog.

The explosion at the nuclear reactor at Chernobyl, USSR, on 26 April 1986, was followed by fallout on Sweden and Norway two days later. A wide variety of wildlife was affected. Reindeer were especially affected because caesium is readily absorbed by lichen, the reindeer's main winter diet. The incident has had a severe effect on Lapp society. The market for reindeer meat has been badly affected by publicity and consumer resistance affects the market price.

Education

437 **Education, research, information systems and the North.**
Edited by W. Peter Adams. Ottawa: Association of Canadian
Universities for Northern Studies, 1987. 362p.

A source book for students, teachers and researchers interested in education and
research in northern Canada. The first major section is devoted to 'Education and
research' in general and contains articles on various aspects of pre-college education
and research. The second section represents the output of a workshop on higher
education and training, and the third section deals with teacher education in the North,
the first real attempt to give an overview of the diverse programmes in this area. The
fourth section contains contributions on 'Distance education' in the northern Canadian
provinces with a contribution on Alaska. The fifth section 'Information systems and the
North' provides a valuable listing of libraries, archives and information systems having
a bearing on northern studies. Finally the section headed 'The universities of Canada
and the North' constitutes a unique guide to thirty-three Canadian universities involved
in northern education and research.

438 **Native education in Canada and the United States: a bibliography.**
I. R. Brooks, A. M. Marshall. Calgary, Alberta: University of
Calgary, Indian Students University Program Services, Office of
Educational Development, 1976. 298p.

A non-annotated listing of 3,000 references arranged in sections and sub-sections. Part
four of the first section, regional reports, includes a section devoted to the Arctic.

439 **Education in the North. Selected papers of the first international conference on cross-cultural education in the circumpolar nations and related articles.**
Edited by Frank Darnell. Fairbanks, Alaska: University of Alaska and the Arctic Institute of North America, 1972. 368p. bibliog.

These twenty papers were presented by specialists from Canada, USSR, Greenland and northern Scandinavia. They attempt to identify the problems confronting educationalists in northern regions where there are majority and minority cultural groups in conflict.

440 **A selected and annotated bibliography on the sociology of Eskimo education.**
R. J. Carney, W. O. Ferguson. Edmonton, Alberta: University of Alberta, Boreal Institute for Northern Studies, 1965. 59p. (Boreal Institute Occasional Publication, no. 2).

An annotated bibliography on Eskimo education in Alaska, Canada, and Greenland numbering approximately 500 items.

Science Policy and Programmes

441 **Canada and polar science.**
W. P. Adams, P. F. Burnet, M. R. Gordon, E. F. Roots. Ottawa: Circumpolar and Scientific Affairs Directorate, 1987. 129p.

A report to the Canadian Minister of Indian Affairs and Northern Development concerning the setting up of a National Polar Institute for Canada. The institute would be first-class as regards both research and education, serving as a focus of other research institutions in Canada. The report, though stressing the importance of northern and polar research to Canada, avoids the issue by recommending other courses of action such as the establishment of an advisory Canadian Polar Research Commision, the development of a polar information system or the creation of a 'Polar House'.

442 **Arctic research and policy act of 1984.**
Washington, DC: Government Printer, 1984. [13]p. (Public Law 98-373, July 31, 1984).

This Act provides for a comprehensive national policy dealing with United States research needs and objectives to the Arctic. Its purposes are to establish an Arctic Research Commission to promote arctic research, and to recommend arctic research policy as the lead agency responsible for the implementation of such research, and to establish an Interagency Arctic Research Policy Committee to develop a national arctic research policy, and a five-year plan to implement that policy.

443 **Ten years of northern research in Canada 1974-1984. Vol. 1.**
Raymond Bergeron, Pierre Guimont. Ottawa: Department of Indian Affairs and Northern Development, 1985. 115p. maps.

A directory of research programmes in arctic Canada including details of sources of funding.

444   **The polar shelf; the saga of Canada's arctic scientists.**
Michael Foster, Carol Marino.   Toronto: NC Press, 1986. 128p. maps.

A description for the layman of the Polar Continental Shelf Project, which was created by the Government of Canada in 1958, its purpose being to strengthen Canada's sovereignty in the North. In 1960 the project mounted its first full-scale, systematic survey and research programme. This lavishly-illustrated volume celebrates the twenty-fifth anniversary of the project and reviews its various scientific projects to date.

445   **United States polar exploration.**
Edited by Herman R. Friis, Shelby G. Bale, Jr.   Athens, Ohio: Ohio University Press, 1970. 199p. (National Archives Conference on United States Polar Exploration).

This publication comprises papers presented at a conference held in Washington, DC in 1967 which marked the founding of the Center for Polar Archives in the National Archives. Relevant sections incude session one, 'Highlights of United States exploration and research in the Arctic' and session four, 'Writing and research in the Arctic'.

446   **United States arctic research plan July 1987.**
Interagency Arctic Research Policy Committee.   Washington, DC: National Science Foundation, 1987. 334p. map.

A presentation of the first five-year US Arctic Research Plan published in accordance with the Arctic Research and Policy Act of 1984. The recommendations are listed under section headings as follows: (1) Overview; (2) Atmosphere and oceans; (3) Land – its resources and environmental interactions; and (4) People. These are followed by a number of appendixes which include the 1984 Act itself, and a review of national issues and research priorities in the Arctic. A newly-published journal entitled *Arctic Research of the United States* (Washington, DC: National Science Foundation, 1987–.) will ensure that a broad audience of individuals and organizations are informed about US government-supported arctic programmes.

447   **Swedish polar research.**
Edited by Anders Karlqvist, Solgerd Björn-Rasmussen.   Stockholm: Swedish Council for Planning and Coordination of Research in co-operation with the Committee for Polar Research, Royal Swedish Academy of Sciences, 1984. 93p. (Report 84:1).

A comprehensive summary of current Swedish polar research projects, prefaced by a general introduction entitled 'Why polar research?' justifying Swedish commitment to these studies on the grounds of basic science as well as of potential application.

448   **Polar research; to the present, and the future.**
Edited by Mary A. McWhinnie.   Boulder, Colorado: Westview Press for the American Association for the Advancement of Science, 1978. 309p. (AAAS Selected Symposia Series, 7).

Offers an overview, by a number of distinguished scientists, of American research in both arctic and antarctic regions over the period 1957-77. The contributions include interdisciplinary studies on meteorology, physical oceanography, geology, and descriptions of operative biological elements and systems. Some of the papers examine the problems of biological research in marine ecosystem structures, the dynamic functions of marine mammals and ability to adapt to the harsh conditions under which they survive. Chapter two, 'Polar research: a synthesis with special reference to biology', by George A. Llano, presents an interesting contrast between the arctic and antarctic regions and summarizes biological exploration and research in the Arctic from the 19th century to the present day.

449   Towards a United States arctic research policy.
Juan G. Roederer.   *EOS. Transactions, American Geophysical Union*, vol. 64, no. 2 (Jan. 1983), p.[3]-[5], bibliog.

The article draws attention to the fact that, of all countries bordering on the Arctic, the United States is the only one without a national institute, laboratory or any other organization devoted to the sustained planning and support of arctic research. Previous attempts to implement this need are then reviewed and the difficulties surrounding the establishment of a national arctic research policy are outlined. A number of key factors which such a policy should take into account are briefly outlined and current developments in this direction are noted.

450   Polish Polar Research.
Warsaw: Polish Academy of Sciences. Committee on Polar Research. 1980- . irregular.

This publication contains accounts of the scientific work carried out by Polish expeditions to Svalbard. Book reviews are included, and many of the articles are in English.

Literature

451 **I tell of Greenland; an edited translation of the Sauðarkrokur manuscripts.**
Francis Berry.   London: Routledge & Kegan Paul, 1977. 205p. map.
The author, who has travelled widely in Greenland, has drawn on his experiences to 'edit and translate' this supposedly 11th-century autobiography of Ingolf Brandsson, which tells of his emigration from Iceland to Greenland as a child and of his experiences in that country. These include the time of Greenland's conversion to Christianity, and his participation in a Norse expedition to Vinland.

452 **Stories, essays, legends through the centuries; stories about the Russian far north.**
Compiled by Vanzetti Chukreyev.   Moscow: Raduga, 1987. 334p.
This attempts to give as full and as representative a selection as possible of the literature of the Soviet Arctic peoples from the 1930s onwards. The compiler's aim is to show the foreign reader the current state of northern literature, the way it describes the history of the north, and its approach to the problems facing northern peoples today.

453 **In the land of the musk-ox; tales of wild life in north-east Greenland.**
John Giaever.   Translated by 'Munda Whittaker and Walter Oliver.
London: Jarrolds, 1958. 191p.
A volume of reminiscences and impressions centred on Greenland wildlife, based on the author's own experiences as a hunter.

454 **Yukoners; true tales of the Yukon.**
H. Gordon-Cooper.   Vancouver: Riverrun, 1978. 127p.
Originally published in *The Whitehorse Star*, these stories are based on the author's notes kept in his days spent in the Yukon after 1947 as, variously, camp cook, bush pilot, prospector and magistrate's clerk.

Literature

455 Makpa; the story of an Eskimo-Canadian boy.
Mary Hinds. Toronto: Ryerson, 1971. 142p.

Mary Hinds spent many years in the Arctic and writes with authority. This story is about an Eskimo boy, Makpa, and his life growing up on Baffin Island.

456 The land beyond.
David Keenleyside. Toronto: Nelson, Foster & Scott; London: Robert Hale, 1975. 232p.

A novel set in the Canadian Arctic whose hero (a southerner from Montreal) finds himself drawn into the passions and conflicts of a small Eskimo community.

457 Anna's book.
George MacBeth. London: Jonathan Cape, 1983. 278p.

This novel tells the story of Nils Strindberg (nephew of the writer, August Strindberg) who was a companion of S. A. Andrée, whose ill-fated balloon trip towards the North Pole in 1907, described in *The Andrée diaries . . .* (q.v.), ended in disaster. The story is told through the words of Anna Charlier. Strindberg was her tutor and admirer and his correspondence to her records the disaster to the balloon and the growing tension that sprang up between the three aeronauts. Though a work of fiction, the novel is based on original documents.

458 Athabasca.
Alistair MacLean. London: Collins, 1980. 252p.

Two of the world's largest oilfields, one in Alaska the other in northern Alberta, Canada, are simultaneously threatened with sabotage. The oil flow down the Alaska Pipeline could be threatened. More than one million barrels a day are at risk. A team of troubleshooters are rushed in, but who are the saboteurs and what are they after?

459 Bear Island.
Alistair MacLean. London: Collins, 1971. 286p.

A vintage MacLean thriller with an arctic setting – Bear Island (Bjørnøya) a remote island in the Svalbard archipelago.

460 Tundra, arctic sled dog.
Roy Simpson Marsh. Philadelphia: Macrae Smith, 1968. 158p.

A story of gold prospecting based on the author's personal knowledge of Alaska and its Eskimo peoples.

461 The snow walker.
Farley Mowat. London: Heinemann, 1978. 222p.

One of the greatest contemporary Canadian storytellers writes here about a white man who intrudes on the life of a remote Eskimo community, and presents a vivid picture of the Arctic land and its people.

462 **Odyssey northwest; a trilogy of poems on the Northwest Passage.**
Gerald St. Maur. Edmonton, Alberta: University of Alberta, Boreal
Institute for Northern Studies, 1983. 123p. (Boreal Institute for
Northern Studies Occasional Publication, no. 18).
These narrative poems are evocative of the arctic voyages of Frobisher, Hudson and
Franklin.

463 **Arctic convoy.**
'Taffrail' (*pseud.*) (H. Taprell Dorling). London: Hodder &
Stoughton, 1956. 315p.
A story of the North Russian convoys during World War II, based on fact, and seen
through the eyes of a young officer who served on board a destroyer during, the
publisher states, 'what has been described as probably one of the worst runs of the war'

464 **Stories from the Canadian north.**
Edited by Muriel Whitaker. Edmonton, Alberta: Hurtig, 1980. 191p.
An anthology of stories from all over the Canadian north, from Ungava to the Yukon,
to the high Arctic, selected from such well-known short story writers as Jack London,
Charles G. D. Roberts, Gabrielle Roy, Farley Mowat and Rudy Wiebe.

465 **Sons of the Arctic.**
Doug Wilkinson. London: G. Bell, 1967. 172p.
The author visited the Arctic in the course of his work for the Canadian National Film
Board in 1956. Later he returned and lived for over a year with an Eskimo family on
north Baffin Island, sharing their way of life. The background and characters in this
story for young readers are, thus, authentic and the story itself based on actual
incidents.

The Arts

General

466 **Scrimshaw and scrimshanders; whales and whalemen.**
E. Norman Flyderman.   New Milford, Connecticut: The Author, 1972.
302p. bibliog.

A well-illustrated book about scrimshaw, the art of engraving on whalebone, which includes references to other allied arts including Eskimo carvings. In addition, there are background chapters dealing with the life of the whalers, the business of whaling and the various end-products.

467 **James Hamilton – arctic watercolours; an exhibition of arctic watercolours, organized by the Glenbow Museum . . . October 7, 1983-January 22, 1984.**
Constance Martin.   Calgary, Alberta: Glenbow Museum, [1984], 52p.
map. bibliog.

The illustrated catalogue of an exhibition of arctic watercolours by the American artist James Hamilton, including works by Elisha Kent Kane, for whose published journals Hamilton prepared the woodcut models. These works include *Arctic explorations; the second Grinnell expedition . . . 1856* (q.v.) and *US Grinnell expedition, in search of Sir John Franklin . . .* (q.v.). The catalogue is prefaced by an appraisal of Hamilton's work.

Native arts

468 **Eskimo art.**
Cottie Burland. London: Hamlyn, 1973. 95p. map.
An illustrated introduction to Eskimo art tracing its history from prehistoric times to
the present day. A concluding chapter relates themes in Eskimo folklore to the various
art forms.

469 **The far north; 2,000 years of American Eskimo and Indian art.**
Henry B. Collins, Frederica de Laguna, Edmund Carpenter, Peter
Stone. Bloomington, Illinois: Indiana University Press for the
National Gallery of Art, Washington, DC, 1973. 289p.
The illustrated catalogue of an exhibition of arctic art held at the National Gallery of
Art, Washington, DC in 1973, drawing on collections from many countries. In addition
to the illustrated catalogue there are essays on Eskimo and Indian art by top-ranking
experts.

470 **Lords of the stone; an anthology of Eskimo sculpture.**
Alistair Macduff, photographs by George M. Galpin. North
Vancouver, British Columbia: Whitecap, 1982. 151p. map.
The author, formerly director of the Gallery of the Arctic, Victoria, British Columbia
(1967-77) here discusses the art of the Eskimos with reference to the items of sculpture
purchased by him during this period. These are illustrated in the book with full-colour
photographs. The book begins with chapters on the cultural history of the Eskimos
(Inuit), and accounts of important artists and their materials, methods and tools, and
continues with individual chapters on Canadian arctic art based on work carried out at
individual settlements in the Canadian North. Separate chapters are devoted to the art
of Greenland Eskimos and to art at other settlements.

471 **Inuit art and artists.**
Compiled by Robin Minion. Edmonton, Alberta: University of
Alberta, Boreal Institute for Northern Studies, 1986. 79p. (BINS
Bibliographic Series, no. 26).
A listing of publications compiled from the Institute's computerized library data base,
arranged by authors with geographic and author indexes. Material covered includes
monographs, theses, government documents, microforms and periodicals.

472 **Art of the Eskimo.**
Carson I. A. Ritchie. South Brunswick; New York: A. S. Barnes;
London: Thomas Yoseloff, 1979. 175p.
A general account of the evolution of arctic art, from its origins, to the first contacts
between Eskimos and Europeans, and then to the modern period. This is followed by
basic concepts of Eskimo art – religion, folklore, costume, dwellings and hunting. The
final section of the book consists of imaginary sketches of Eskimo activities during the
'classic period'.

473 **Ivory Carving**
Carson I. A. Ritchie.   London: Arthur Barker, 1969. 136p.
A practical guide to the art of engraving on ivory with a section on scrimshaw engraving and simple tests for ivory among others.

474 **Sculpture of the Eskimo.**
George Swinton.   Toronto: McClelland & Stewart, 1987. 255p. bibliog.
This is a paperback reprint of the 1972 edition. The text outlines the ecological and cultural environment of Eskimo art and its development, and appraises contemporary sculpture since the 1950s and its place in the world of art. The second half of the book is a catalogue of the work of major Eskimo artists (many in the author's personal collection). It contains over 600 carvings and is profusely illustrated.

Folklore

475 **Myths and legends.**
Compiled by Robin Minion.   Edmonton, Alberta: University of Alberta, Boreal Institute for Northern Studies, 1984. 79p. (BINS Bibliographic Series, no. 5).
A listing of publications compiled from the Boreal Institute's computerized library data base, arranged by authors with geographic and author indexes. Material covered includes theses, government documents, atlases, microforms and periodicals.

Music

476 **Songs of the dream people; chants and images from the Indians and Eskimos of North America.**
Edited and illustrated by James Houston.   New York: Atheneum, 1972. 85p. maps. bibliog.
A selection of songs compiled by a leading Canadian anthropologist, grouped regionally and illustrated with drawings of artefacts, art objects and weapons.

477 **Music of the Americas; an illustrated music ethnology of the Eskimo and American Indian peoples.**
Willard Rhodes, Samuel Marti, Vicente T. Mendoza, Eva Lips, Rolf Krushe.   London: Curzon, 1973. 207p. maps. bibliog.
The introduction cites this as 'the firt definitive treatment of the many and varied cultural aspects of the general development of Eskimo and Indian music'. The

emphasis is placed on the special features of original significance in the life of peoples who have survived 'virtually unchanged for thousands of years'. The illustrations cover a wide range of subjects including prehistoric instruments and scenes of rituals and ceremonies in which music plays an important role.

Photography and films

478 **Expedition photography.**
John Douglas. *Geographical Journal*, vol. 145, pt. 2 (July 1979), p. 282-97.

The article is in four main sections. The first is a discussion of the photographer, his selection and pre-expedition tasks; the second deals with the choice of equipment; the third considers environmental conditions including cold environments and the fourth section discusses the scale of an expedition's photographs.

479 **Photography on expeditions; recommended techniques for different surroundings.**
D. H. O. John.   London; New York: Focal, 1965. 176p. bibliog.

A survey of the photographic requirements for unusual surroundings based on a symposium arranged by the Royal Photographic Society, London, in 1961. Section two 'Photography under cold conditions' provides detailed information on mountaineering photography and photography on polar expeditions.

480 **Films on Indians and Inuit of North America 1965-1978.**
Stephen J. Rothwell, Alex Redcrow.   Ottawa: Department of Indian and Northern Affairs, Public Communications and Parliamentary Relations Branch, Indian and Inuit Affairs Program, 1978. 264p.

A listing by title of English- and French-language films with full descriptive notes on contents, running time, colour, distributor and so on. The list is prefaced by a topic guide to the main catalogue.

Expedition Planning and Survival

481 **Exploration medicine; being a practical guide for those going on expeditions.**
Edited by O. G. Edholm, A. L. Bacharach.   Bristol: John Wright, 1965. 410p.

Medical hints to explorers based on contributions to a symposium on the subject organized by the Royal Geographical Society, London. These points of medical advice are primarily intended for the non-specialist and cover problems encountered in polar regions and cold regions generally.

482 **Man – hot and cold.**
Otto G. Edholm.   London: Edward Arnold, 1978. 60p. bibliog.

An introduction to the subject of the ways by which man can survive in all regions of the world, including the tropics and the polar regions. At the time of writing Dr Edholm was one of Britain's leading experts in the field of cold-climate physiology.

483 **Winter skills.**
Rob Hunter.   London: Constable, 1982. 246p. bibliog.

A handbook for the winter traveller with chapters on clothing, equipment, hardware, winter living, travel on ski and snowshoe, shelter, first-aid and special hazards. Appendixes include kit lists, stockists, tour operators and national tourist boards.

484 **Polar expeditions.**
Edited by Geoff Renner.   London: Royal Geographical Society. Expedition Advisory Centre, 1984. 183p. bibliog.

Twenty-five contributions from specialists introducing the potential polar expeditioner to a wide range of topics, some of immediate practical concern, such as radio, medicine, dentistry, equipment and safety, clothing, food and cooking and photography. Other subjects covered are technical or scientific and include satellite photography, glaciology, surveying and meteorology.

485 **Not by bread alone.**
Vilhjalmur Stefansson. New York: Macmillan, 1946. 339p.
In this classic account of polar nutrition the author argues from his personal experience of living among the Eskimo hunters that pure meat, raw or cooked, is the best for arctic survival and for antiscorbutic value.

486 **Expedition planners' handbook and directory 1988/89.**
Edited by Nigel Winser, Shane Winser, Louise Henson. London:
Royal Geographical Society, Expedition Advisory Centre, [1988], 319p.
Advice to expedition planners by numerous specialists covering such subjects as planning, organization, choice of projects, scientific fieldwork, logistics, managing an expedition, photography, radio, catering, post-expedition responsibilities, and expedition directories.

Sports and Recreation

487 **Ski touring; an introductory guide.**
William E. Osgood, Leslie J. Hurley.   Rutland, Vermont: Charles E. Tuttle, 1972. 148p. bibliog.

Topics covered in this book include: preparation, maps and compasses, automobile maintenance; skis, boots, bindings, waxing, clothing and snowshoes; skiing techniques; safety on snow; and camping, igloos, tents, heating and food. Appended is a wind-chill factor table.

488 **The snowshoe book.**
William Osgood, Leslie Hurley.   Brattleboro, Vermont; Lexington, Massachusetts: Stephen Greene, 1983. 3rd ed. 149p. bibliog.

A comprehensive coverage of the history and technique of snowshoeing, including hints on selecting the correct type, construction and maintenance, travel technique, safety, winter camping, snowshoes and sport and how to make snowshoes.

Libraries, Museums, Archives and Academic Institutions

489 **To the farthest ends of the earth; the history of the Royal Geographical Society 1830-1980.**
Ian Cameron. London; Sydney: Macdonald, 1980. 288p. map. bibliog.
A comprehensive and well-illustrated history of the Royal Geographical Society which has been involved in very many polar expeditions and whose library and archives constitute one of the world's primary sources for polar history. There are two chapters in this volume specifically concerned with arctic exploration: Chapter two, 'The search for a Northwest Passage', and Chapter five, 'The conquest of the North Pole'. Appendixes list past presidents and secretaries of the Society, medallists and the principal expeditions aided by the Society.

490 **The Boreal Institute for Northern Studies. An information centre for the North.**
G. A. Cooke. *Library Association of Alberta Bulletin*, vol. 5, no. 2 (April 1974), p. 66-69. Reprinted, *Boreal Institute for Northern Studies Contribution*, no. 23.
Presents an account of this important collection of published and other material in the Boreal Institute for Northern Studies, University of Alberta, Edmonton, Alberta, Canada, established in 1960. It is especially strong in material on the western Canadian Arctic.

491 **Proceedings of the eleventh Northern Libraries Colloquy, Luleå, Sweden, June 9-12, [1986].**
Edited by Terje Höiseth, Ann-Christine Haupt. Luleå, Sweden, CENTEK, [1986], 210p.
The Northern Libraries Colloquy is a conference of librarians and information specialists held every two years, concerned with information and documentation concerning polar regions, more especially the Arctic. This volume constitutes a selection of papers presented to the 1986 colloquy. Not all the papers are strictly

concerned with libraries and information, but the majority focus on research, source materials, information services, archives, computer databases and information networks, and other matters of interest to northern librarians and researchers. The *Proceedings of the twelfth Northern Libraries Colloquy*, ed. by Ann M. Brennan and Martin Andrews have recently been published [Boulder, Colorado: World Data Center for Glaciology and the Institute of Arctic and Alpine Research, 1988. 331p. (Glaciological Data Report, GD–22)].

492 **Library of the U.S. Army Cold Regions Research and Engineering Laboratory, Hanover, N.H.**
Nancy C. Liston. In: *Education, research, informations systems and the North.* Edited by W. Peter Adams. Ottawa: Association of Canadian Universities for Northern Studies, 1987, p. 210.

A short account of this library which was formed in 1952 to support research on physics and mechanics of cold regions materials, and on engineering in cold regions. This article outlines the history of the library, its policy, special services and publications. For information concerning the published bibliography see *Bibliography on cold regions science and technology* (q.v.).

493 **Polar and cold regions library resources: a directory.**
Compiled and edited by Robin Minion, Geraldine A. Cooke. Edmonton, Alberta: Northern Libraries Colloquy, University of Alberta, Boreal Institute for Northern Studies, 1985. 2nd ed. 383p.

A directory of libraries and manuscript archives relating to the polar regions, representing twenty-two countries and 162 libraries, archives and collections. The descriptions are based on questionnaires detailing the history of each institution, a description of the polar collection, size, acquisitions policy, classification used, publications available and other information.

494 **Northern studies assessment project: a report.**
Margot Macnaughton, Marie Muren. Ottawa: National Library of Canada, 1985. 20p.

An assessment of the National Library of Canada's northern studies collection, comparing it with the holdings of the Scott Polar Research Institute at the University of Cambridge, England, and the Arctic Institute of North America at the University of Calgary, Alberta.

495 **Alaskan arctic information resources.**
Barbara Sokolov. In: *Education, research, information systems and the North.* Edited by W. Peter Adams. Ottawa: Association of Canadian Universities for Northern Studies, 1987, p. 214-15.

A general review of libraries and other information resources in Alaska with special emphasis on the Arctic Environmental Information and Data Center (AEIDC), University of Alaska, located in Fairbanks. This is a centre concerned with the transfer and referral of environmental information and with applied research. It is not a conventional repository library.

496 **The International Glaciological Society; fifty years of progress.**
Peter Wood.   Cambridge, England: International Glaciological
Society, 1986. 128p. bibliog.

A history of the formative years of the society from its origins in 1935, as the
Association for the Study of Snow and Ice, through its change in 1945 to the British
Glaciological Society, and finally its evolution to international status. A brief
description of the society's official organ *Journal of Glaciology* has been published.

497 **The Center for Northern Studies.**
Oran R. Young.   *Polar Record*, vol. 21, no. 132, (Sept. 1982),
p. 299-300.

The centre, founded in 1971, is located at Wolcott, Vermont. It is an independent,
non-profit-making organization devoted to research and education in all aspects of the
circumpolar north. The centre is the only organization in the USA currently offering
an integrated programme of studies covering the socio-economic, political and legal
issues arising in the region, together with the physical and biological environments of
the Arctic and Subarctic.

498 **Norsk Polarinstitutt Årbok.**
Oslo: Norsk Polarinstitutt, 1960- . annual.

The annual report of the Norwegian Polar Institute in Oslo, published in English and
containing brief articles relevant to the institute's work.

499 **Northern Libraries Bulletin.**
Juneau, Alaska: Alaska Division of State Libraries, 1971- . irregular.

A news bulletin published on behalf of the Northern Libraries Colloquy which
provides brief information on northern libraries' activities, developments and
cooperation. New publications and bibliographies are listed.

Bibliographies

500 **Databases from the Boreal Institute for Northern Studies Library.**
G. A. Cooke. In: *Education, research, information systems and the North.* Edited by W. Peter Adams. Ottawa: Association of Canadian Universities for Northern Studies, 1987, p. 217-18.
An account of the library databases of this multidisciplinary library with emphasis on the western Canadian Arctic. It is the only general northern collection in Canada.

501 **National Library of Canada services and resources in support of northern research and northern libraries.**
Mary Joan Dunn. In: *Education, research, information systems and the North.* Edited by W. Peter Adams. Ottawa: Association of Canadian Universities for Northern Studies, 1987, p. 205-06.
A brief overview of the National Library of Canada's services and collections, highlighting northern research and northern libraries, but focusing specifically on the National Library's DOBIS data base, an on-line catalogue covering all Canadiana.

502 **SPRILIB: a new look for the Scott Polar Research Institute library.**
Valerie Galpin. *Polar Record,* vol. 23, no. 146 (May 1987), p. 601-02.
A description of the newly-established database of the Scott Polar Research Institute, set up with assistance from the Cambridge University Computer Service. The software package BIBCAT enables searches to be made by author, title, subject, library classification number (Universal Decimal Classification), or any combination of these. To date (1988) the database contains 27,000 bibligraphic records and progress is being made on the conversion of the existing card catalogues.

503 **The Arctic Science and Technology Information System (ASTIS).**
Ross Goodwin. In: *Education, research, information systems and the North.* Edited by W. Peter Adams. Ottawa: Association of Canadian Universities for Northern Studies, 1987, p. 216.

An account of this multidisciplinary arctic bibliography database which is centred on the Arctic Institute of North America, University of Calgary, Alberta. Its main geographic emphasis is on arctic and Canadian arctic waters, with some relevant material on Alaska, Greenland, Scandinavia and the Soviet Arctic. The database includes full abstracts and subject and geographic indexing.

504 **Arctic bibliography.**
Edited by Marie Tremaine. Washington, DC: Department of Defense; Montreal: Arctic Institute of North America, 1953-75. 16 vols. maps.

The most ambitious attempt yet to produce a definitive bibliography of the Arctic with full abstracts covering all subjects likely to increase man's understanding of the Arctic and its native populations. The publications listed (over 108,000) are written in some forty languages. The main areas of interest include northern Canada and Labrador, Greenland, Svalbard (Spitsbergen), northern Scandinavia, the USSR and Kamchatka, the arctic seas and straits and the North Polar Basin. Later volumes include material on Canada's 'Middle North' and the corresponding parts of Eurasia. The earlier volumes (especially the first three) are of particular interest to historians on account of their detailed historical coverage. Volume eight contains a separate listing compiled by Andrew Taylor entitled *British parliamentary papers on exploration in the Canadian north* (items 45212-45275) (q.v.). Each volume is accompanied by detailed subject and geographical indexes. The series ceased with volume sixteen as a result of lack of funding.

505 **ASTIS Current Awareness Bulletin.**
Calgary, Alberta: University of Calgary, Arctic Institute of North America, 1978. six-times-yearly.

A bimonthly update of publications added to the Arctic Science and Technology Information Systems multidisciplinary arctic data base. Each issue contains about 300 abstracts, and geographic and author indexes are appended. An annual cumulation is published on microfiche as *ASTIS bibliography* which includes the entire contents of the data base together with detailed subject, geographic, author, title and serial indexes. The online database is available through QL Systems Ltd.

506 **Recent Polar and Glaciological Literature.**
Cambridge, England: Scott Polar Research Institute, 1973- . quarterly.

This bibliography covers both arctic and antarctic publications, including books, monographs and journal articles, indexed in the library of the Scott Polar Research Institute, and supplemented by contributions from World Data C 'Glaciology' and from the International Glaciological Society. It is a selective listing of the current literature of the polar regions aiming for a comprehensive coverage of all relevant subjects. References are grouped in broad subject categories, and are accompanied by brief indicative notes. Each issue contains an author index.

The Arctic Regions

Svalbard (Spitsbergen and its Neighbouring Islands)

Geography

507 Spitsbergen; an account of exploration, hunting, the mineral riches and future potentialities of an arctic achipelago.
R. N. Rudmose Brown. London: Seeley, Service, 1920. 306p. maps.
Despite its date this book remains a useful source for information on the area. The author, who knew the islands well, attempts to trace the history, exploration and economic development of the country and draws attention to the potential of its economic resources.

508 Svalbard; Norway in the Arctic Ocean.
Tim Greve. Oslo: Grøndahl, 1975. 85p. map.
A useful short introduction to the islands, offering sections on geography, climate, flora and fauna, history, the Spitsbergen Treaty, administration, economic activities, environmental protection, the Svalbard community, communications, exploration and research, and place-names.

509 The year-long day: one man's Arctic.
A. E. Maxwell, Ivar Ruud. London: Gollancz, 1977. 240p. map.
Describes twelve months in the life of Norwegian trapper Ivar Ruud, living alone in latitude 77°N in a hunter's cabin in Hornsund, southwest Spitsbergen. This was his fourth winter in the Arctic. The book is a translation of Ruud's diaries and reminiscences. Chapters are entitled 'Afternoon', 'Evening', 'Night', 'Dawn', and 'Morning', each one being a description of the hunter's activities in each season, giving detailed accounts of the habits of seals, geese, foxes and bears.

510 **The place-names of Svalbard.**
Norges Svalbard-og Ishavs-undersøkelser. Oslo: Jacob Dybwad, 1942.
539p. map. bibliog. (Skrifter om Svalbard og Ishavet, no. 80).
An historical gazetteer of Svalbard place-names, prefaced by an account of the origin
of the place-names and their development. A supplement to this volume dealing with
new names 1935-55, compiled by Anders K. Orvin, has also been published
(Universitetsforlaget, Oslo, 1958 [Norsk Polarinstitutt Skrifter no. 112]).

511 **Stratigraphy of Spitsbergen.**
Edited by V. N. Sokolov. Translated by E. T. Francis, G. Klener.
Boston Spa, England: British Library, Lending Division, 1977. 2nd ed.
298p. maps. bibliog.
Collected papers on the geology and stratigraphy of Svalbard which are based on
materials from Soviet investigations started in 1962.

History and expeditions

512 **The first crossing of Spitsbergen.**
Sir William Martin Conway, with contributions by J. W. Gregory,
A. Trevor-Battye, E. J. Garwood. London: J. M. Dent, 1907. 371p.
maps.
The author, a seasoned mountaineer, spent the summers of 1896 and 1897 exploring
the interior of Spitsbergen. This volume is an account of the first season's voyage to the
island and various trips made there including an overland crossing from Advent Bay to
Bell Sound, northward to Sassen Bay and from there to Agardh Bay. In all, thirteen
mountains were climbed and a survey of 600 square miles of central Spitsbergen was
made.

513 **America in Spitsbergen, the romance of an arctic coal-mine. With an
introduction relating the history and describing the land and the fauna
and flora of Spitsbergen.**
Nathan Haskell Dole. Boston, Massachusetts: Marshal Jones, 1922.
2 vols.
A full and detailed history of Longyearbyen, the coal-mine on the island of Spitsbergen
founded by an American John Munro Longyear, together with chapters on such topics
as the geography and fauna and flora.

514 **Young men in the Arctic; the Oxford University Arctic Expedition to
Spitsbergen 1933.**
A. R. Glen. London: Faber & Faber, 1935. 329p. map.
An account, by its leader, of an Oxford University expedition whose aim was to
explore by sledge parties the northern New Friesland peninsula region of Spitsbergen.
Appendixes by various members of the expedition constitute a preliminary account of
the scientific work accomplished.

515   **Svalbard: Svalbard's historie 1596-1965.**
Adolf Hoel.   Oslo: Sverre Kildahls Boktrykkeri, 1966. 3 vols. maps.
bibliog.

This constitutes the definitive history of Svalbard's mineral industry, and is based on
unpublished material in various scientific and commerical organizations. Unfortunately, no English translation has been attempted yet.

516   **Spitsbergen; the story of the 1962 Swiss-Spitsbergen expedition.**
Hugo Nünlist.   Translated from the German by Oliver Coburn.
London: Nicholas Kaye, 1966. 191p. map.

First published as *Spitzbergen* (Zürich: Orell Fussli Verlag, 1963), this is an account of
a Swiss mountaineering expedition to North West Spitsbergen where many new peaks
were conquered and much valuable mapping accomplished.

517   **Journey into silence.**
Jack Denton Scott.   New York: Reader's Digest, 1976. 200p. maps.

The author's description of a boat journey from Longyearbyen in Spitsbergen which
circumnavigated North East Land (Nordauslandet). Observations on the country,
scientists, explorers and wildlife are made.

Politics and international law

518   **Svalbard in the changing Arctic.**
Trygve Mathisen.   Oslo: Glydendal Norsk Forlag, 1954. 112p. map.
bibliog.

A discussion of the part played by Svalbard in international politics since 1925.
Chapters cover the following topics: (1) government; (2) mining and exploration in the
inter-war period; (3) Svalbard during World War II; (4) negotiations about a revision
of the Svalbard Treaty; (5) post-war reconstruction; and (6) the changing economic
and strategic pattern of the Arctic.

519   **Politics in high latitudes; the Svalbard archipelago.**
Willy Østreng.   Translated by R. I. Christophersen. London:
C. Hurst, 1975. maps. bibliog.

Originally published under the title *Det politiske Svalbard* (Oslo: Gyldendahl, 1975),
this book outlines the geographical, historical and economic background to this group
of islands. The framework of the discussion consists of the principles of the Svalbard
Treaty of 1920, the text of which is appended, and how these principles have been
observed by the nations active in Svalbard since 1925. Also appended is the Mining
Code of 1925 and the Svalbard Act enacted by the Norwegian Parliament in 1925.

520 **The Spitsbergen (Svalbard) question: United States foreign policy, 1907-1935.**
Elen C. Singh. Oslo: Universitetsforlaget, 1980. 244p. bibliog.
Combining information from the papers of the former Arctic Coal Company, the United States Department of State, the Royal Norwegian Ministry of Foreign Affairs and various published sources, the author accounts for the development of United States foreign policy regarding Spitsbergen. Essentially, this monograph is an account of attempts to find an answer to the international political question: 'how should a resource-rich arctic archipelago, legally considered terra nullius, be administered?'

Bibliographies

521 **Svalbardliterature; a bibliography.**
Tor Sveum, Per Kyrre Reymert, Marit Anne Hauan. Tromsø, Norway: Universitetsbiblioteket i Tromsø, Tromsø Museum, 1987. 54p.
A bibliography of 304 titles, without annotations and with an author index, covering the following subjects: newspapers, journals, yearbooks, general works; travels and expeditions (chronological); history and politics; hunting; and fiction.

Jan Mayen

522 **Historical remains on Jan Mayen.**
   Susan Barr. *Norsk Polarinstitutt Meddelser* no. 108 (1985), 67p. map.
   bibliog.
A short history of the island of Jan Mayen followed by a descriptive list of historic
sites. The text is in English and Norwegian.

Greenland

General

523 **Greenland.**
Michael Banks.   Newton Abbot, England: David & Charles, 1975.
208p. maps. bibliog.
The author, a well-known explorer and climber, here describes the country's history,
geography and wildlife. The final chapters are devoted to the mapping and exploration
of Greenland and its ice sheet.

524 **Staunings Alps – Greenland. Scoresby Land and Nathorsts Land.**
Donald J. Bennet.   Reading, England: Gaston's Alpine Books & West
Col, 1972. 120p. maps. bibliog.
An account of this large peninsular region of west Greenland, compiled as background
reading for mountaineers. There are short chapters dealing with the general
geography, mountains climbed, a chronological history of mountaineering expeditions,
flora and fauna, and information for expedition planning, together with a specimen
food and equipment list.

525 **City under the ice; the story of Camp Century.**
Charles Michael Daugherty.   New York: Macmillan, 1963. 156p.
maps. bibliog.
In 1960 the United States Army Polar Research and Development Center established a
scientific laboratory on the Greenland ice sheet constructed in trenches excavated in
the ice. It was the first community in the world to be completely supplied with light,
heat and power by a nuclear reactor. This book tells the story of this pioneering
achievement and the impressions of the author based on his first-hand experience of
this unusual isolated community.

526 **Greenland past and present.**
Edited by Knud Hertling, Erik Hesselbjerg, Svend Klitgaard, Ebbe
Munck, Olaf Petersen. Copenhagen: Edvard Henriksen, [1970]. 370p.

A lavishly-illustrated account of Greenland, with expert contributions on every
conceivable aspect of the country, including history, exploration, geography, climate
and weather, fauna and flora, geology, mining, law, administration, education, the
church, economic problems and contemporary life.

527 **Arctic riviera; a book about the beauty of northeast Greenland.**
Ernst Hofer. Berne, Switzerland: Kümmerly & Frey, 1957. 125p.

The author, a professional photographer, based this account on four expeditions to the
region. A narrative of his experiences, it is more especially a camera's-eye-study of the
flora, fauna and scenery of one of Greenland's most spectacular and least accessible
regions.

528 **Greenland: a country in transition.**
Tom Høyem. *Polar Record*, vol. 24, no. 148 (Jan. 1988), p. 9-14.

Offers an account of the events leading to Greenland's independence, present Danish
arctic policy, Greenland's home rule, resource exploitation, technology and research,
the need for a Danish arctic research centre, and other related topics.

529 **Danish Greenland, its people and products.**
Henrik Rink. London: C. Hurst, 1974. 468p. map.

Hinrik (or Henrik) Johannes Rink, natural scientist and humanitarian, arrived in
Greenland from Denmark in 1848 to prospect for mineral deposits. He was
unsuccessful in this venture, but continued his geological investigations in north
Greenland until 1851, making the first survey of the coal deposits there as well as the
first geological map. Later Rink joined the Danish administration and showed a keen
interest in the welfare of the native Greenlanders. It was as royal inspector of south
Greenland in 1858-68 that he wrote this comprehensive survey of the country and its
people. This volume is a reprint of the first English edition (London: Henry S. King,
1877).

530 **Greenland's future development: a historical and political perspective.**
Jørgen Taagholt. *Polar Record*, vol. 21, no. 130 (Jan. 1982), p. 23-32.
map. bibliog.

Throughout their history Greenlanders have struggled, not against invaders but against
a harsh environment. Their close association with the environment is reflected in a
well-developed descriptive language. However, Greenlanders have a less-developed
capacity for abstract thought and, as a result, they find discussion of national problems,
such as security, far removed from the daily debate. In this article Greenland's
development is traced and her strategic position in the North Atlantic is discussed in
terms of national interests and international cooperation.

531 **Meddelser om Grønland.**
Copenhagen: Kommissionen for videnskabelige undersøgelser i
Grønland, 1879- . irregular.

A learned journal, with many English language contributions, devoted to various
aspects of Greenland. Since 1979 it has been split into three separate series: *Man and
Society*, *Bioscience* and *Geoscience*.

Geography

532 **Geology of Greenland.**
Edited by Arthur Escher, W. Stuart Watt. Copenhagen: Geological
Survey of Greenland, 1976. 603p. maps. bibliog.

This is the first comprehensive book on the geology of Greenland. It is an up-to-date
survey of Greenland geology covering most aspects of the subject. Twenty chapters
deal with the main subdivisions of Greenland geology, written by experts.

533 **The Greenland ice cap.**
Børge Fristrup. Copenhagen: Rhodos, 1966. 312p. map. bibliog.

The Greenland ice cap (more correctly ice sheet), covering some eighty per cent of the
land mass, is the largest glaciated region outside Antarctica. This well-illustrated book,
based on first-hand experience, contains a general account of the ice sheet, the history
of its exploration and details of scientific investigations up to the early 1960s. The book
concludes with chapters discussing the climate, thickness, age, movement and early
formation of the ice sheet.

Flora and fauna

534 **The flora of Greenland.**
Tyge W. Böcher, Kjeld Holmen. English translation by T. T.
Elkington, M. C. Lewis. Copenhagen: P. Haas & Son, 1968. 312p.
map.

A standard reference book which discusses 500 species of vascular plants (flowering
plants and ferns). The determination of species is facilitated by numerous keys and
black-and-white illustrations. For each species a morphological description, and
chromosome number and the distribution of the species in Greenland are given, and
there is a glossary of botanical terms.

535 **Grønlands blomster./Flowers of Greenland.**
Jon Feilberg, Bent Fredskild, Sune Holt.   Copenhagen: Forlaget
Regnbuen, 1984. [98]p. map.

A simplified pocket guide to the most common plants of Greenland with colour
photographs of 170 species and a brief description of each. The guide is compiled by
staff of the Greenland Botanical Survey. Habitat and distribution details are given with
reference to the nearest town.

536 **Polar animals.**
Alwin Pedersen.   Translated from the French by Gwynne Vevers.
London: George G. Harrap, 1962. 188p. map.

A description of the wildlife of northeast Greenland, based on a six-year series of field
trips. Animals described include the musk-ox, arctic wolf, arctic fox, polar bear,
lemming and ermine, walrus, seal, ptarmigan and common sea birds and upland birds.

Prehistory and archaeology

537 **Voyage to Greenland; a personal initiation into anthropology.**
Frederica de Laguna.   New York: W. W. Norton, 1977. 285p. map.

An account of a leading anthropologist's voyage to Greenland and sojourn there
through the summer of 1929. She accompanied the Danish archaeologist and arctic
explorer, Therkel Mathiasson, in the making of the first archaeological survey ever
undertaken there. The expedition took the two scientists to Upernivik on the west
coast of Greenland. In her journal and correspondence home the author tells of the
primitive life of the Eskimos at that time and of the archaeological work achieved.

538 **Land under the pole star; a voyage to the Norse settlements of Greenland
and the saga of the people that vanished.**
Helge Ingstad.   Translated from the Norwegian by Naomi Walford.
London: Jonathan Cape, 1966. 381p. maps. bibliog.

First published as *Landet under leidarstjernen* (Oslo: Gyldendal Norsk Forlag (1959)
this book relates the early history of Greenland and its colonization by the Vikings – a
colony which subsequently vanished. In 1953 Helge Ingstad, a former governor of
Spitsbergen, sailed to Greenland to study the remains of the Norse settlements. The
conclusion that he drew from his discoveries led to five more expeditions between 1960
and 1964, summarized here in an appendix.

539 **The last kings of Thule; with the polar Eskimos as they face their
destiny.**
Jean Malaurie.   Translated from the French by Adrienne Faulke.
London: Jonathan Cape, 1982. 489p. maps. bibliog.

Originally published in a slightly different form as *Les derniers rois de Thule* (Paris:
Plon, 1976). The author of this well-illustrated edition, a professor of anthropology at
the University of Paris, spent fourteen months among the Thule Eskimos of northeast

Greenland in 1950-51. There he carried out scientific research, and also learned the Eskimo language, which gave him a keen insight into their way of life. The book, a classic of its kind, is devoted to the social anthropology of these peoples. The final chapters are devoted to an account of a 1,000-miles-long sledging journey northeast to Inglefield Land, Kane Basin, and then over the sea ice to Ellesmere Island in northern Canada.

History

General

540　**The history of Greenland: including an account of the mission carried on by the United Bretheren in that country . . . with a continuation to the present time; illustrative notes; and an appendix, containing a sketch of the Bretheren in Labrador.**
David Crantz.　London: Longman, Hurst, Rees, Orme & Brown, 1820. 2 vols. in 1.
An abridged and revised edition of the English translation of the German edition of 1767, with some added material. In addition to a full account of the history of Greenland, its geography and Eskimo inhabitants, there is much about the origins of the Moravian mission which dates from 1733.

541　**Greenland then and now.**
Erik Erngaard.　Copenhagen: Lademann, 1972. 240p.
A popular, lavishly-illustrated account of Greenland's past history and of modern Greenland society.

542　**The spread of printing – western hemisphere – Greenland.**
Knud Oldendow.　Edited by Colin Clair. Amsterdam: Vangendt, 1969. 72p. map.
Presents a history of printing in Greenland from the establishment of the first press in 1857 at Godthaab by Hinrik Rink.

543　**The history of Greenland.**
Finn Gad.　London: Christopher Hurst (vols. I-II), 1972-73; Copenhagen: Nyt Nordisk Forlag/Arnold Busck (vol. III), 1982. 3 vols. maps. bibliog.
This is a translation from the Danish edition *Grønlands historie*. Periods covered are: Vol. I Earliest times to 1700; Vol. II 1700-1782; and Vol. III 1782-1808. This is a detailed and definitive history of the country, though, as yet, it is incomplete.

544 **Greenland: being extracts from a journal kept in that country in the years 1770 to 1778 . . .**
Hans Egede Saabye. Introduction by G. Fries. London: Boosey & Sons, 1818. 293p. map.

First published in Danish in 1816 this journal, by the grandson of the Danish missionary to Greenland, Hans Egede, contains extracts concerning the customs of the Eskimos and reactions to the changes brought about by the introduction of Christianity; witchcraft and religion; and notes on climate, education, domestic life and so on. The introduction by G. Fries contains descriptions of west Greenland Eskimos, Lutheran missions and centres of population.

Voyages and expeditions

545 **Journal of a voyage to the northern whale-fishery including researches and discoveries on the eastern coast of west Greenland made in the summer of 1822 in the ship Baffin of Liverpool.**
William Scoresby, Junior. Edinburgh: Archibald Constable; London: Hurst Robinson, 1823. 472p. maps. Reprinted, Whitby, England: Caedmon of Whitby, 1980.

Between 1803 and 1822 William Scoresby Junior and his father, William Scoresby Senior, made some twenty voyages to Spitsbergen waters and Greenland in pursuit of whales and seals, and also in an attempt to promote geographical knowledge in the Arctic. This account records the most notable of these voyages, in which the younger Scoresby surveyed and charted the icebound east coast of Greenland and made detailed notes on plants, animals and rock specimens, as well as compiling meteorological tables and observations on magnetism. The narrative constitutes a companion volume to Scoresby's *An account of the arctic regions* (q.v.).

546 **Northward over the 'great ice'.**
Robert E. Peary. London: Methuen, 1898. 2 vols. maps.

An account of the author's two expeditions to Greenland, made in 1886 and in 1891-92. The first involved a manhauled sledge trip east of Disko Bay to about 100 miles from the edge of the inland ice sheet. The second expedition delineated the northern extension of the ice sheet and discovered ice-free land masses on the northern coast. Extensive reports on the Eskimos are included in the narrative.

547 **The first crossing of Greenland.**
Fridtjof Nansen. London: Longmans, Green, 1890. 2 vols. maps.

This edition is a translation of the Norwegian *Paa ski over Grønland* (Kristiania: Aschehoug, 1890), comprising the official narrative of Nansen's expedition with Otto Sverdrup and four companions to east Greenland to cross the ice sheet, in 1888-89. The book contains a survey of previous attempts to explore the region, a detailed account of the crossing from Umivik to Godthaab on skis, the wintering at Godthaab and observations on Eskimo life as well as a summary of the scientific work accomplished.

548 **Lost in the Arctic; being the story of the 'Alabama' expedition, 1909-1912.**
Ejnar Mikkelsen. London: William Heinemann, 1913. 400p.

An account by the leader of a Danish expedition on the *Alabama* to the east coast of Greenland in 1909-12 to search for Mylius-Ericksen and Høeg Hagen, and their records, lost on an earlier expedition in 1907. Only a few notes were found. Following the wreck of the *Alabama*, Mikkelsen's party had to await rescue in 1912. Extensive journeys were made along the coast, including one on the ice sheet, and there is much information on, for example, natural history and the weather.

549 **Greenland journey; the story of Wegener's German expedition to Greenland in 1930-31 as told by members of the expedition and leader's diary.**
Edited by Else Wegener, Fritz Loewe. London; Glasgow: Blackie, 1939. 295p. maps.

Alfred Lothar Wegener, leader of this expedition, was the first to propose a scientifically acceptable theory of 'continental drift'. The object of this expedition in 1930 was to set up a scientific station on the Greenland ice sheet, named 'Eismitte', from which experiments for measuring the thickness of the ice, and other scientific observations, could be made. It was on this expedition that Dr Wegener met his tragic death.

550 **Northern lights; the official account of the British Arctic Air-route expedition 1930-31.**
F. Spencer Chapman. London: Chatto & Windus, 1932. 304p. map.

The general objective of this expedition, under the leadership of H. G. (Gino) Watkins, was to study the possibilities of a short air route from Britain to Canada across Greenland. The immediate aim was to investigate the least well-known region from the east coast over the central ice sheet, with a base headquarters established at Angmagssalik. From here a weather station was to be established on the ice sheet, ground and air surveying carried out, and a general scientific programme pursued. Chapter ten is written by August Courtauld and is an account of five months spent in total isolation in the under-snow 'Ice Cap' station on the Greenland ice sheet.

551 **Watkin's last expedition.**
F. Spencer Chapman. London: Chatto & Windus, 1934. 291p.

An account of H. G. (Gino) Watkin's second and last expedition (1932-33) to survey the hinterland of east Greenland north of Angmagssalik. Less than a month after the establishment of the base camp Watkins disappeared; only his upturned kayak bore witness to the tragedy that overtook him. The three remaining members of the expedition continued their survey work and scientific research in the face of difficult ice conditions.

552 **North ice; the British North Greenland Expedition.**
C. J. W. Simpson. London: Hodder & Stoughton, 1957. 384p. maps.

The leader's account of a scientific expedition in 1952-54 to Dronning Louise Land in north Greenland, to carry out geophysical, glaciological and meteorological work. The expedition had the backing of the Royal Society of London with logistic support of the Navy, Army and Air Force.

553 **Mischief in Greenland.**
H. W. Tilman. London: Hollis & Carter, 1964. 192p. map.
An account of two voyages from Lymington, England, to southwest Greenland, in
1961 and 1962, with mountaineering as the purpose.

554 **Vikings, Scots and Scraelings.**
Myrtle Simpson. London: Victor Gollancz, 1977. 189p. maps.
An account of a canoe and camping trip along the southwest coast of Greenland to
investigate the fate of the former Viking settlers.

Peoples

555 **Eskimo diary.**
Thomas Frederiksen. Translated into English by Jack Jensen, Val
Clery. London: Pelham, 1981. 148p. maps.
The author, a Greenland hunter and fisherman, was born in 1939. From his early youth
he kept a diary, which is reproduced in this book and illustrated with the author's own
watercolours. The diary extracts are accompanied by English translations. They give a
vivid impression of the life and customs of a simple Eskimo fishing community.

556 **The snow people.**
Marie Herbert. London: Barrie & Jenkins, 1973. 229p. map.
An account of a sixteen-month sojourn (1971-72) among the Thule Eskimos of north
west Greenland by the author and her husband, the explorer Wally Herbert. Here
Marie Herbert recounts what it was like to live among these still-primitive people, to
take part in their hunting expeditions and to live off the land.

557 **Hunters of the polar north: the Eskimos.**
Wally Herbert. Amsterdam: Time Life Books, 1981. 168p. bibliog.
(Peoples of the Wild).
A personal account of the Eskimos of northwest Greenland by an experienced Arctic
traveller and explorer, in cooperation with photographer Bryan Alexander, both of
whom spent ten months in the region collecting material for this book.

558 **Eskimo life.**
Fridtjof Nansen. Translated by William Archer. London: Longmans,
Green, 1894. 2nd ed. 350p.
A translation from the Norwegian edition *Eskimoliv* (Kristiania: H. Aschehoug, 1891),
in which the author contributes his account of the origins and distribution of the
Eskimos of west Greenland as he, and travellers before him, found them. This detailed
description of their lifestyle includes appearance, dress, social life and customs,
property, food and dwellings, religion and art.

559 **The people of the polar north; a record.**
Knud Rasmussen. Compiled from the Danish original and edited by
G. Herring. London: Kegan Paul, Trench, Trübner, 1908. 358p. map.

A compilation from the author's Danish language publications, resulting from the
Danish Literary Expedition to Greenland of 1902-04, which visited three different
regions inhabited by Eskimos, more especially northwest Greenland. Subjects covered
include customs, beliefs, fables and legends.

560 **Tales and traditioins of the Eskimo.**
Henrik Rink. London: C. Hurst, 1974. 472p.

This was first published in 1875 (London, Edinburgh: William Blackwood). Rink, who
was Royal Inspector of south Greenland in 1858, became interested in the language
and religion of the western Greenland Eskimos. These tales are primary source
material in the field of anthropology and constitute a rich source of information on the
beliefs and concepts of the supernatural which dominated the lives of these people. A
preliminary chapter is devoted to a general account of the Greenland Eskimos.

Language

561 **Tunumiit oraasiat: the east Greenlandic Inuit language.**
P. Robbé, Louis-Jacques Dorais. Québec: Université Laval, 1986.
265p. (Collection Nordicana, 49).

An introduction to the language of east Greenland. The book is divided into four
sections: (1) a series of tables outlining the main forms of east Greenlandic grammar;
(2) a list of about 300 frequently used postbases with examples; (3) a thematic
dictionary of over 3,000 words; and (4) an alphabetical index of east Greenlandic
words. Translations are given in west Greenlandic (the official language of Greenland),
Danish, English and French.

562 **Dictionary of the west Greenlandic Eskimo language.**
C. W. Schultz-Lorentzen. Copenhagen: C. A. Reitzl, 1927. 303p.
Reprinted from *Meddelselser om Grønland*, vol. 69.

The English edition of a dictionary compiled for practical use among Danes and
Greenlanders limiting itself to the translation of words without explanations. The
spelling is not phonetic and a guide to the phonetic value of the written language is
added.

Politics and the legal system

563 **Greenland: political structure of self-government.**
Jens Dahl. *Arctic Anthropology*, vol. 39, no. 3 (1986), p. 223-31.
map.

A discussion of Greenland home rule introduced in 1979.

564 **Home rule in Greenland.**
Isi Foighel. Copenhagen: Commission for Scientific Research in
Greenland, 1980. 21p. (Meddelelser om Grønland. Man and society, 1).
Home Rule was established in Greenland within the Unity of the Danish Realm by an
Act of 29 November, 1978. The Act on Home Rule is discussed here with special
reference to the historical and political background, the Act itself being appended.

565 **The Greenland criminal code.**
South Hackensack, New Jersey: Fred B. Rothman; London: Sweet &
Maxwell, 1970. 47p. (American Series of Foreign Penal Codes).
Translated at the Center for Studies in Criminal Justice, University of Chicago Law
School, here with an introduction by Verner Goldschmidt. The Greenland criminal
code is unique in its creation of a system of sanctions which are inspired not by the
gravity of the offence, but by a desire to rehabilitate the offender and to perfect
society.

The arts

566 **Classification of traditional Greenland music.**
Michael Hauser, H. C. Petersen. Copenhagen: Commission for
Scientific Research, 1985. 50p. bibliog. (Meddelelser om Grønland.
Man and society, 7).
Covers the usage and performance of Greenlandic music, divided into eleven different
categories. Ten of these groups deal with traditional Greenlandic music and one group
concerns acquired Euro-American music. An elaborate bibliography is appended.

567 **The art of Greenland; sculpture, crafts, paintings.**
Bodil Kaalund. Translated by Kenneth Tindall. Berkeley, California:
University of California Press, 1979. 224p. map. bibliog.
A translation of *Grønlands kunst* (Copenhagen: Politkens forlag, 1979), this is a
comprehensive, fully-illustrated work about Greenland art.

Museums

568 **Greenland's museum laws: an introduction to Greenland's museums
under Home Rome.**
Arctic Anthropology, vol. 23, nos. 1-2 (1986), p. 239-46. maps.
Jurisdiction concerning Greenland's museums was transferred to Home Rule
authorities on 1 January 1986. This paper discusses the work carried out by the
Greenland National Museum. An appendix contains the main portions of the relevant
laws.

Bibliographies

569 **Groenlandica. Catalogue of the Groenlandica-collection in the National Library of Greenland.**
Edited by Benny Høyer. Nuuk, Greenland: Nunatta Atuagaateqarfia, 1986. 585p.

On 9 February, 1968, the National Library of Greenland was destroyed by fire; since then the collection has been rebuilt. The catalogue is divided into four parts: (1) books in Greenlandic; (2) books on Greenland and the Arctic; (3) an alphabetical index; and (4) a classified index. Bibliographic entries include brief descriptive notes.

Arctic Canada

General

570 **Science, history and Hudson Bay.**
   Edited by C. S. Beals.   Ottawa: Department of Energy, Mines and
   Resources, 1968. 2 vols. maps. bibliog.
A comprehensive review of the Hudson Bay region with contributions by various
specialist writers. The following subject areas are covered: prehistory; history; people;
geography; climate; water and ice; marine life; flora and fauna of land areas; geology;
geophysical studies; upper atmosphere research; transport and communications;
defence forces operations; economic possibilities; and theories of origin.

571 **Arctic Canada from the air.**
   Moira Dunbar, Keith Greenaway.   Ottawa: Queen's Printer for
   Defence Research Board, 1956. 541p. maps. bibliog.
Originally intended as an aid to air navigation in the Canadian Arctic, this compilation
still serves as a valuable summary of the history and physiography of the Canadian
Arctic islands. The description of each geographical area is preceded by a brief history
of its exploration, followed by sections on topography, drainage, coastline, and
population. Accompanying each chapter is a map and the relevant air photographs.
The book concludes with a list of Canadian arctic expeditions.

572 **The living Arctic.**
   Fritz Müller.   Toronto: Methuen, 1981. 233p. bibliog.
The late Professor Müller, who taught glaciology at McGill University, spent twenty-
one years leading a research expedition to Axel Heiberg Island in the Canadian Arctic.
This well-illustrated account of the Arctic today is written for the layman and is based
on three independent but inter-connected sources – the author's own scientific research
and experience, the specialized literature for sections dealing with biology, exploration, history and native peoples, and, finally, reports of various expedition members.

Arctic Canada. General

573 **Canada's North.**
R. A. J. Phillips. Toronto: Macmillan of Canada, 1967. 306p. maps.
An historical and geographical introduction to the Yukon and Northwest Territories by a former Federal Government administrator. The book makes a pertinent comparison with the advanced development in the Soviet North.

574 **The unbelievable land.**
Edited by L. Norman Smith. Ottawa: Queen's Printer for the Department of Northern Affairs and National Resources and the Northern Service of the Canadian Broadcasting Corporation, [1964]. 140p.
A series of twenty-nine essays descriptive of the Canadian North. Originally broadcast on the Canadian Broadcasting Corporation's Northern Service by persons eminent in their respective fields, they cover such topics as landscape and wildlife, snow, ice and permafrost, the ocean, aurora, native peoples and scientific research.

575 **Canada Year Book.**
Ottawa: Minister of Supply and Services, 1905- . annual.
A useful source of information on the Canadian North, especially when up-to-date statistical information is required. Appendixes include sections on government organizations, bibliography and commissions of enquiry.

576 **Canada's North; the Reference Manual.**
Canada. Department of Indian and Northern Affairs. Ottawa: Supply & Services Canada, 1985- . irregular.
A looseleaf manual providing general information about northern Canada, Yukon and the Northwest Territories, compiled by the Department of Indian and Northern Affairs, Ottawa. Headings include: (1) Introduction; (2) Physical environment; (3) People; (4) History; (5) Native organizations and land claims north of 60°N.; (6) Government; (7) Renewable resources; (8) Non-renewable resources; (9) Northern hydrocarbon transportation proposals; (10) Transportation; (11) Communications; (12) Socio-economic infra-structure; (13) Tourism and recreation; and (14) Locations of government offices in the North.

577 **News North.**
Yellowknife, Northwest Territories: Northern News Services, 1981- . weekly.
A newspaper covering the Canadian Arctic, and more especially the Yellowknife district, Northwest Territories. A useful source of information on, for example, business, mining operations and social problems.

578 **Northern Perspectives.**
Ottawa: Canadian Arctic Resources Committee, 1973- . two-monthly.
A periodical containing brief popular articles dealing with aspects of Canadian Arctic development and Canadian relationships with the circumpolar world.

579 **Whitehorse, Yukon Star.**
Whitehorse, Yukon Territory: Whitehorse Star. 1907- . daily.
An old-established daily newspaper covering the Canadian Yukon and Northwest Territories, with editorial comment on political development in the region.

Geography

General

580 **The physiography of arctic Canada with special reference to the area south of Parry Channel.**
J. Brian Bird.   Baltimore, Maryland: Johns Hopkins University Press, 1967. 336p. maps. bibliog.
A textbook reviewing the physiography of the southern half of the Canadian Arctic (excluding Labrador-Ungava and the Queen Elizabeth Islands). It incorporates the author's own fieldwork in the late 1940s. In addition to chapters dealing with the formation and structure of the landscape there are 'background' chapters covering geology, climate, glaciers, permafrost and soils and vegetation.

581 **The climate of the Canadian arctic islands and adjacent waters.**
J. B. Maxwell.   Ottawa: Environment Canada, Atmospheric Environment Service, 1980. 2 vols. maps. bibliog. (Climatological Studies, no. 30).
A comprehensive handbook of all aspects of climate in Canada's arctic islands. The object of the publication is to draw together all climatic information available relevant to all types of transportation, energy, communications, engineering design and construction, the defence industry, and to hydrological, environmental and ecological problems. The emphasis is on probability estimates of extremes, as well as on deviations of critical weather types, particular attention being paid to wind chill factor, inversions and sea ice.

582 **Canadian nordicity; it's your North, too.**
Louis-Edmond Hamelin.   Translated by William Barr. Montreal: Harvest House, 1979. 373p. maps. bibliog.
In this book Professor Hamelin is concerned to convert southern Canadians to the idea that the Canadian 'North', being the Northwest Territories, the Yukon Territory, northern Quebec, the northern parts of seven provinces, and the adjacent areas, constitutes an entity, or 'nordicity', which poses special problems. The book revolves in particular around the Northwest Territories and northern Quebec, looking at their relationships with Federal Government, populations, economic development and underdevelopment, and big business activities and their effect on local people.

583 **Canadian inland seas.**
Edited by I. P. Martini. Amsterdam: Elsevier, 1986. 494p. maps. bibliog.
A comprehensive review, by a number of expert contributors, of Hudson Bay, James Bay and Foxe Basin, with chapters on geological history, stratigraphy, economic geology, glaciation, climate, ice cover, shipping patterns, islands, seafloor morphology and sediments, oceanography, sea ice and icebergs, and marine ecology, including birds and mammals.

584 **Canadian Geographer.**
Montreal: Canadian Association of Geographers, 1951- . quarterly.
A long-established professional journal, with articles in French and English, dealing with all aspect of Canada's geography, and with much relevant to the Canadian Arctic.

585 **Canadian Geographic.**
Ottawa: Royal Canadian Geographical Society, 1930- . two-monthly.
A popular magazine devoted to every aspect of geography – historical, human, physical and economic – with occasional articles concerned with the Canadian Arctic.

Towns and communities

586 **Settlements of northern Canada: a gazetteer and index.**
Compiled by Roy Jackson Fletcher. Edmonton, Alberta: University of Alberta, Boreal Institute for Northern Studies, 1975. [n.p.]. maps. bibliog. (Occasional Publication, no. 11).
A gazetteer of the Yukon Territory, the Northwest Territories, Labrador, Ungava-Quebec and Newfoundland. The listing attempts to provide a comprehensive record of past and present settlements with their latitudes and longitudes and a key to their locations on the maps appended. Each place-name is also identified by its particular functions and facilities, such as gold mine, summer fishing or whaling station.

587 **Communities and towns of the Northwest Territories.**
Compiled by Robin Minion. Edmonton, Alberta: University of Alberta, Boreal Institute for Northern Studies, 1985. 100p. (BINS Bibliographic Series, no. 23).
A listing of publications compiled from the Boreal Institute's computerized library database, arranged by authors with geographic and author indexes. Material covered includes monographs, theses, government documents, atlases, microforms and periodicals.

Flora and fauna

588 **Truelove Lowland, Devon Island, Canada: a high Arctic ecosystem.**
Edited by L. C. Bliss. Edmonton, Alberta: University of Alberta
Press, 1977. 714p. maps. bibliog.
A series of research studies on the ecology of a sixteen-square-miles corner of the
northeastern coast of Devon Island (lat. 75°33'N) in the Canadian Arctic archipelago,
forming the most northern component of the International Biological Programme.
Papers cover the various vegetation communities as well as the invertebrate and
vertebrate consumers.

589 **Flora in the Yukon and NWT.**
Compiled by Robin Minion. Edmonton, Alberta: University of
Alberta, Boreal Institute for Northern Studies, 1984. 95p. (BINS
Bibliographic Series, no. 10).
A bibliography of 238 items, many with brief indicative contents notes, dealing with
the flora of arctic Canada. Author, geographic and title indexes are appended.

590 **High Arctic; an expedition to the unspoiled north.**
George Miksch Sutton. New York: Paul S. Eriksson, 1976. 119p.
A personal record of a distinguished ornithologist's visit to Bathurst Island, Canadian
Arctic, in 1962, to study the behaviour, life history and distribution of arctic
shorebirds. The book also contains information on arctic mammals such as arctic hares,
lemmings, wolves, foxes, walruses, caribou and musk-oxen.

Prehistory and archaeology

591 **Thule pioneers.**
Edited by E. Bielawski, Carolynn Kobelka, Robert R.
Janes. Whitehorse, Northwest Territories: Prince of Wales Northern
Heritage Centre, [n.d.] 110p. maps. (Occasional Paper, no. 2).
A description of the Thule culture in arctic Canada with details of an archaeological
dig on Banks Island, Northwest Territories.

592 **Canadian arctic prehistory.**
Robert McGhee. Toronto: Van Nostrand Reinhold, 1978. 128p.
maps. (Canadian Prehistory Series).
A popular introduction to migration routes of the ancestral Eskimo peoples and the
archaeological evidence for the Dorset and Thule cultures of arctic North America and
Greenland.

593 **Archaeology in northern Canada.**
Compiled by Robin Minion. Edmonton, Alberta: University of
Alberta, Boreal Institute for Northern Studies, 1985. 63p. (BINS
Bibliographic Series, no. 20).

A listing of publications compiled from the Boreal Institute's computerized library
database arranged by authors with geographic and author indexes. Material covered
includes monographs, theses, government documents, atlases, microforms and
periodicals.

594 **Canadian Journal of Archaeology.**
Victoria, British Columbia: University of Victoria, Department of
Anthropology, 1977- . twice-yearly.

An academic journal with frequent articles and book reviews relating to the
archaeology of northern Canada.

595 **National Museum of Man Mercury Series.**
Ottawa: National Museums of Canada, National Museum of Man,
[1972]- . irregular.

The object of this series is to permit the rapid dissemination of information pertaining
to those disciplines for which the National Museum is responsible. Especially relevant
to this bibliography are the sub-series Archaeological Survey of Canada papers and the
Canadian Ethnology Service papers both of which are frequently devoted to arctic or
subarctic topics.

History

General

596 **Maintain the right; the early history of the North West Mounted Police
1873-1900.**
Ronald Atkin. London: Macmillan, 1973. 400p. maps. bibliog.

An account which attempts to present 'the unvarnished story' of the North West
Mounted Police (now the Royal Canadian Mounted Police), compiled from the
reports, diaries and memoirs of the men themselves.

597 **The British search for a North-west Passage: maps of exploration (1818-1823).**
Michael Trevor Bravo. Cambridge, England: Darwin College, 1987. 45p. maps. (Thesis submitted to the Faculty of Philosophy for the M.Phil. degree in the Department of History and Philosophy of Science, University of Cambridge).

A discussion of the underlying philosophy behind British naval exploration for a Northwest Passage, with special reference to Sir John Barrow's captains, William Edward Parry and John Ross.

598 **Canada's colonies: a history of the Yukon and Northwest Territories.**
Kenneth Coates. Toronto: James Lorimer, 1985. 251p.

A history of the Yukon and Northwest Territories including material on the fur trade, gold mining, whaling, oil exploration and recent resource projects.

599 **The exploration of northern Canada 500 to 1920; a chronology.**
Alan Cooke, Clive Holland. Toronto: Arctic History, 1978. 573p. maps. bibliog.

A chronological list of expeditions to northern Canada, the region being interpreted in the broadest sense, including geographical discoveries, the collection of scientific information and many lesser journeys resulting in some kind of publication. All known Northwest Passage expeditions are listed. Each entry gives details of an expedition including its date, nature, national, commercial or other association, leader, captain and, frequently, other senior members, and ship. At the beginning of each entry is a statement of the expedition's points of departure and return and the dates of its duration, if known, followed by an account of what the expedition attempted and achieved. Accompanying these details is a bibliography, a list of the members of expeditions mentioned, maps and an index. This is an indispensable research tool, but one which was, unfortunately, published in a limited edition. A preliminary publication appeared in the journal *Polar Record* (vol. 15, 1970-71; vol. 16, 1972-73).

600 **Discovery of the North: the exploration of Canada's Arctic.**
Daniel Francis. Edmonton, Alberta: Hurtig, 1986. 224p. maps.

An account of Arctic exploratory expeditions covering the period from the 16th century to the early 20th century.

601 **Fur trade and exploration, opening the far northwest 1821-1852.**
T. J. Karamanski. Vancouver: University of British Columbia Press, 1983. 330p. maps. bibliog.

A readable yet scholarly account of the Hudson's Bay Company's exploration in northern British Columbia and the Yukon, based on the Hudson's Bay Company archives in Winnipeg. The focus is on the explorers, such as John M. McLeod and Robert Campbell, who laboured mainly on the notoriously difficult Liard River. The book benefits from the fact that the author is himself an expert canoeist who understands the idiosyncracies of navigating northern rivers.

602 **Nineteenth century expeditions in the Arctic and Canada.**
Compiled by Robin Minion. Edmonton, Alberta: University of
Alberta, Boreal Institute for Northern Studies, 1984. 102p. (BINS
Bibliographic Series, no. 4).

A bibliography of 255 references, many with brief contents, notes, indexed under
authors, geographic names, titles, expedition leaders and ships.

603 **Tundra; selections from the great accounts of Arctic land voyages.**
Farley Mowat. Toronto: McClelland & Stewart, 1973. 415p. maps.
bibliog. (The Top of the World, vol. III).

Presents selections from the journals of the following explorers of Arctic Canada:
Samuel Hearne (1769-72); Alexander Mackenzie (1789); John Franklin (1819-22);
George Back (1833-35); Frank Russell (1892); Royal North West Mounted Police
(1916-18); Vilhjalmur Stefansson (1916); John Hornby and Edgar Christian (1926-27);
and Thierry Mallet (1925-29).

604 **Company of adventurers.**
Peter C. Newman. Markham, Ontario: Viking, Penguin Canada,
1985. 2 vols. maps. bibliog.

A history, based on the archives in Winnipeg, of the Hudson's Bay Company whose
agents were largely responsible for opening up the North American Arctic in the 17th,
18th and 19th centuries. The second volume carries the cover title *Caesars of the
wilderness.*

605 **Narratives of voyages towards the north-west in search of a passage to
Cathay and India 1496 to 1631.**
Thomas Randall. London: Hakluyt Society, 1849. 259p. maps.

Documented accounts of the following voyages in search of a Northwest Passage:
Sebastian Cabot (1496); Sir Martin Frobisher's three voyages (1576, 1577, 1578 and a
fourth projected in 1581); John Davis's three voyages (1585, 1586 and 1587); George
Waymouth (1602); John Knight (1606); Henry Hudson (1610); Sir Thomas Button
(1612); James Hall (1612); Captain Gibbons (1614); Robert Bylot and William Baffin
(1615); Captain Hawkridge (1619); Captain Luke Foxe (1631); and Captain James
(1631).

606 **The fur trade and the Northwest to 1857.**
E. E. Rich. Toronto: McClelland & Stewart, 1967. 336p. maps.
bibliog.

This history, written by a leading authority on the fur trade, traces the penetration of
present-day Canada by the early fur traders, both French and British. It deals with the
rivalry between the various competing companies and traces the incidental exploration
of northern Canada by such pathfinders as Samuel Hearne, David Thompson, Simon
Fraser and Alexander Mackenzie.

607 **The North-West Passage.**
George Malcolm Thomson. London: Secker & Warburg, 1975. 288p.
map. bibliog.
A popular history of the search for the Northwest Passage from the days of John Cabot
and Martin Frobisher to the first east-west traverse of the passage by the Norwegian
explorer Roald Amundsen in *Gjøa*, in 1903-05.

608 **The Navy, the Company and Richard King; British exploration in the
Canadian Arctic, 1829-1860.**
Hugh N. Wallace. Montreal: McGill-Queen's University Press, 1980.
232p. maps. bibliog.
A history of the first half-century of the exploration of northern Canada by the Royal
Navy and by the Hudson's Bay Company, analysing the organizational difference
between the large-scale sea expeditions and the lightweight land expeditions, as
exemplified by the journeys of Richard King, surgeon with the Arctic explorer George
Back.

609 **The North West Company.**
Marjorie Wilkins Campbell. Vancouver; Toronto: Douglas &
McIntyre, 1983. 295p. map. bibliog.
Offers a history of this fur trading company, founded in Montreal in 1779. Its activities
came to span the entire North American continent to the boundaries of the Arctic.
Associated with the company were such famous names in arctic history as Pond,
Frobisher, Mackenzie, Thompson and Fraser. In 1821 the company merged with the
Hudson's Bay Company, formerly its bitter rival.

610 **The subarctic Indians and the fur trade, 1680-1860.**
J. C. Yerbury. Vancouver: University of British Columbia Press,
1986. 189p. maps.
An account of the changes to the Athapaskan-speaking peoples of the Canadian
subarctic following European contact.

611 **A century of Canada's arctic islands 1880-1980.**
Edited by Morris Zaslow. Ottawa: Royal Society of Canada, 1981.
358p. maps. bibliog.
Presents the proceedings of a symposium marking the transfer of Canada's arctic
islands from British sovereignty in 1880. The papers read are interdisciplinary in scope
covering history, politics, scientific exploration, economic development and peoples,
with concluding contributions on 'Northern Canada today', 'Canada and the
circumpolar world', and 'The Arctic and Canadian culture'.

612 **The opening of the Canadian North 1870-1914.**
Morris Zaslow. Toronto; Montreal: McClelland & Stewart, 1971.
339p. maps. bibliog. (Canadian Centenary Series).
A pioneer study of Canada's northward expansion in the years after confederation. At
first fur-traders, missionaries and gold-seekers were in the forefront with provincial and

federal governments concerned for authority and economic development. Later the Geological Survey, the North-West Mounted Police and the Departments of the Interior, Indian Affairs and Marine and Fisheries, gained new importance.

613 **Beaver.**
Winnipeg; Manitoba: Hudson's Bay Company. 1922- . quarterly.
An illustrated magazine devoted to all aspect of Canada's history, with much about the exploration of the Arctic and Subarctic and their native peoples. Many of the articles are based on the Hudson's Bay Company's extensive archives in Winnipeg.

614 **Canadian Historical Review.**
Toronto: University of Toronto Press, 1919- . quarterly.
A journal of high academic rating with occasional articles and book reviews relating to the history of Canada's North.

Voyages and expeditions

615 **The three voyages of Martin Frobisher in search of a passage to Cathaia and India by the North-west A.D. 1576-8. Reprinted from the first edition of Hakluyt's voyages with selections from manuscript documents in the British Museum and State Paper Office.**
Edited by Richard Collinson.   New York: Burt Franklin, [n.d.]. 374p. maps. (Reprint of Hakluyt Society, First Series, no. 38, 1867).
An annotated edition of George Beste's narrative, *A true discourse of the late voyages of discoverie for the finding of a passage to Cathaya, by the north-west, under the conduct of Martin Frobisher general.* (London: 1578). This is the first account of all the three voyages of Frobisher in 1576, 1577 and 1578 by George Beste who sailed with him. It includes a descriptive catalogue of the relics of these expeditions discovered by Charles F. Hall while voyaging in search of Sir John Franklin in 1860-62. Hall himself wrote of these expeditions in *Life with the Esquimaux* . . . (q.v.).

616 **Tokens of possession; the northern voyages of Martin Frobisher.**
W. A. Kenyon.   Toronto: Royal Ontario Museum, 1974. 164p. maps.
A heavily edited version, for the non-specialist, of the three voyages of Martin Frobisher, 1576, 1577 and 1578, following the text of George Beste's narrative, *A true discourse of the late voyages of discoverie, for the finding of a passage to Cathaya . . .* (London: 1578). In 1974 Dr Kenyon led an archaeological expedition to Frobisher Bay, Northwest Territories, to see what traces were still to be found of Frobisher's expeditions. An account of this constitutes the concluding chapter of the book. An analysis of the rocks taken from Frobisher's workings is analysed in an appendix.

617 **North west to Hudson Bay; the life and times of Jens Munk.**
Thorkild Hansen.   Translated by James McFarlane, John Lynch. London: Collins, 1970. 348p. maps.
An abridged translation of the life of the Danish arctic explorer Jens Eriksen Munk culminating in his voyages to Hudson Bay in 1619-20 with the ships *Unicorn* and

Lamprey, at the' behest of King Christian of Denmark. After encountering much ice, Munk finally reached what is today Port Churchill, on the west shore of Hudson Bay, where he decided to winter. The expedition suffered terribly from malnutrition and scurvy. By the time the snow had melted only Munk and three others remained alive. Eventually they managed to summon up sufficient strength to sail the *Lamprey* home to Denmark.

618   **A journey from Prince of Wales's fort in Hudson's Bay to the northern ocean undertaken by order of the Hudson's Bay Company, for the discovery of copper mines, a North West Passage, &c in the years 1769, 1770, 1771, & 1772.**
Samuel Hearne.   London: A. Strahan & T. Cadell, 1795. 458p. maps.
Reprinted, Amsterdam: N. Israël; New York: Da Capo, 1968.

Hearne, an employee of the Hudson's Bay Company, explored the northern parts of Canada over a period of thirty-two months between 1769-72. He discovered the Coppermine River and became the first European to reach the Arctic Ocean overland at Coronation Gulf, and the first to see and cross Great Slave Lake. The book, published three years before Hearne's death, marks him as a significant early naturalist.

619   **Exploring the northwest territory; Sir Alexander Mackenzie's journal of a voyage by bark canoe from Lake Athabasca to the Pacific Ocean in the summer of 1789.**
Alexander Mackenzie.   Edited by T. H. McDonald. Norman,
Okahoma: University of Oklahoma Press, 1966. 133p. maps. bibliog.

Mackenzie, a young director of the North West Fur Company was the first white man to navigate the Mackenzie River, in the Northwest Territories of Canada, from Lake Athabaska to the Arctic Ocean in June-September 1789. This account of his journey has been edited from a transcript of Mackenzie's original manuscript in the British Museum, thought to be more accurate than the published account attributed to Mackenzie, *Voyages from Montreal . . . to the frozen and Pacific oceans; in the years 1789 and 1793* (London: T. Cadell, 1801). The editor travelled the same route as Mackenzie himself, by canoe in 1965, and has illustrated the text with comparative photographs.

620   **A voyage of discovery, made under the orders of the Admiralty, in His Majesty's ships Isabella and Alexander, for the purpose of exploring Baffin's Bay, and inquiring into the probability of a North-West Passage . . .**
John Ross.   London: John Murray, 1819. 252p. maps.

Ross entered Lancaster Sound to the north of Baffin Island on 30 August 1818 but refused to sail westward believing the passage to be barred by a range of mountains. William Edward Parry, accompanying Ross in command of *Alexander*, believed these mountains to be a mirage, a belief in which he was justified by a subsequent voyage about which he published a narrative (q.v.). On returning to England Ross became involved in a controversy with the Admiralty over his decision leading to a life-long quarrel between himself and the Second Secretary of Admiralty, John Barrow.

621 **Journal of a voyage for the discovery of a North-West Passage from the Atlantic to the Pacific; performed in the years 1819-20, in His Majesty's ships Hecla and Griper, under the orders of William Edward Parry, RN, FRS . . . With an appendix, containing the scientific and other observations.**
William Edward Parry. London: John Murray, 1821. 310p. [& 179]p.
On this voyage Parry was to disprove John Ross's theory that Lancaster Sound was an inlet (put forward by Ross in his narrative of his voyage [q.v.]) by sailing through the Sound and Barrow Strait as far west as Melville Islands, where the ships wintered. The expedition also discovered Prince Regent Inlet, Banks Island, and surveyed the south shore of Barrow Strait. Parry's narrative is accompanied by nine scientific appendixes (separately paged) including remarks on the health of the crew. A supplement to the second edition of this narrative, containing *An account of the subjects of natural history*, was subsequently published (London: John Murray, 1824, p. clxxix-cccx, 6 plates).

622 **Narrative of a journey to the shores of the polar sea in the years 1819, 20, 21, and 22. With an appendix on various subjects relating to science and natural history.**
John Franklin. Rutland, Vermont: Charles E. Tuttle, 1970. 768p. maps.
This is reprint of the original edition (London: John Murray, 1823). It is the author's journal account of an expedition overland in northwestern Canada, exploring the upper reaches of the Coppermine River, wintering at Fort Enterprise (between Great Slave and Great Bear Lakes), descending the Coppermine and exploring the coast of Coronation Gulf eastward for 500 miles, and finally returning over the Barren Grounds to Fort Enterprise. On the return journey extreme hardship prevailed leading to starvation, murder, and even cannibalism. The illustrations by Lieutenants George Back and Robert Hood are of unusual interest and ability. Hood's illustrations are also featured in his book *To the Arctic by canoe . . .* (q.v.).

623 **To the Arctic by canoe; the journal and paintings of Robert Hood midshipman with Franklin.**
Robert Hood. Edited by C. Stuart Houston. Montreal; London: Arctic Institute of North America, McGill-Queen's University Press, 1974. 217p. maps. bibliog.
A less formal and more lively account of John Franklin's first overland expedition to the Arctic Ocean in 1819-22 than Franklin's own *Narrative of a journey . . .* (q.v.). This edited field diary, illustrated with twenty-four reproductions of Hood's own watercolour sketches of landscape and wildlife (especially birds), is prefaced by an introductory résumé of Hood's work. This is followed by a narrative of the progress of the expedition up to 15 September 1820, just over a year before the author's tragic death. There are two chapters presenting Hood's observations on ethnology (Cree Indians) and natural sciences (buffalo, climate, aurora borealis and magnetic phenomena). The final chapters provide details of Hood's painting, his death and the men of the expedition.

624 **Arctic ordeal; the journal of John Richardson surgeon-naturalist with Franklin 1820-1822.**
John Richardson. Edited by C. Stuart Houston. Kingston, Montreal: McGill-Queen's University Press; Gloucester, England: Alan Sutton, 1984. 349p. maps. bibliog.
A journal of the first Franklin overland expedition, subject of other works by Franklin and Hood (q.v.), by the medical officer and naturalist. In addition to an account of the descent of the Coppermine River to the Arctic Ocean there is an eye-witness account of the gruelling return across the Barren Lands in which only nine of the twenty men survived. Precise, and rich in detail, this is an invaluable historical and scientific record of the expedition. As well as a commentary on the journal there are four appendixes devoted to Richardson's natural history observations, and two notes on his contributions to lichenology and geology, by experts.

625 **Journal of a second voyage for the discovery of a North-West Passage from the Atlantic to the Pacific; performed in the years 1821-22-23 in His Majesty's ships Hecla and Fury under the orders of Captain William Edward Parry . . .**
William Edward Parry. London: John Murray, 1824. 572p. maps.
The narrative of an attempt to find a Northwest Passage by way of Hudson Bay. Parry's expedition, having wintered at Winter Island, to the south of Melville Peninsula, sailed northward to Fury and Hecla Strait, spending a second winter at Igloolik. The deteriorating health of his crew forced Parry to return to England in October 1823. Parry's journal gives a detailed account of the voyage and explorations along the coast of NE Melville Peninsula and the west coast of Baffin Island, with details of ice conditions, wintering the ships, and relations with the Eskimos. The plates include engravings of sketches by Captain G. F. Lyon of HMS *Hecla* who also published his private journal of the voyage (q.v.). A vocabulary of Eskimo words is appended.

626 **The private journal of Captain G. F. Lyon of H.M.S. Hecla during the recent voyage of discovery under Captain Parry.**
George Francis Lyon. London: John Murray, 1825. 468p. map.
A record by the captain of HMS *Hecla* during William Edward Parry's expedition to the Canadian Arctic in 1821-23 described by Parry himself in *Journal of a third voyage for the discovery of a North-West Passage . . .* (q.v.). Lyon's journal includes a detailed account of the Eskimos of southern Baffin Island and Melville Peninsula, ice conditions and natural history.

627 **Journal of a third voyage for the discovery of a North-West Passage from the Atlantic to the Pacific; performed in the years 1824-25, in His Majesty's Ships Hecla and Fury, under the orders of Captain William Parry . . .**
William Edward Parry. London: John Murray, 1826. 151p. maps.
Presents the narrative of Captain Parry's third expedition to the Canadian Arctic, this time to continue the exploration of Prince Regent Inlet, discovered in 1819-20. Bad ice conditions compelled the expedition to winter on the west coast of Baffin Island. Later, the coast of Somerset Island was explored but eventually *Fury* had to be abandoned at

latitude 72°42'N while *Hecla* sailed home to England. Parry's journal contains a day-to-day narrative of events and includes seventeen observational appendixes plus three chapters on zoology, botany and geology.

628 **Narrative of a second expedition to the shores of the polar sea in the years 1825, 1826 and 1827 . . . including an account of the progress of a detachment to the eastward by John Richardson.**
John Franklin. Edmonton, Alberta: M. G. Hurtig, 1971. 320 [& 157]p. maps.
This is a reprint of the original edition (London: John Murrary, 1828). In June 1826 Franklin, accompanied by the naturalist Dr John Richardson, sailed from winter-quarters at Fort Franklin on Great Bear Lake, Northwest Territories of Canada, down the Mackenzie River to its delta on the Arctic Ocean. From here Richardson and Ernest Kendall explored eastward to the Coppermine River (900 miles) and thence back to Fort Franklin. Franklin's party turned westward to link up with a support expedition under Captain F. W. Beechey RN, in command of HMS *Blossom*, but the latter was prevented by heavy ice conditions from making a contact. Franklin explored the arctic coast to Return Point (Alaska), about longitude 147°W (374 miles). These journeys, plus *Blossom*'s cruise, added notably to the known shoreline of North America. This volume contains Franklin's and Richardson's narratives plus a separately-paged appendix containing scientific observations.

629 **To the Pacific and Arctic with Beechey; the journal of Lieutenant George Peard of H.M.S. 'Blossom' 1825-1828.**
George Peard. Edited by Barry M. Gough. Cambridge, England: Cambridge University Press for the Hakluyt Society, 1973. 272p. maps. bibliog. (Hakluyt Society, Second Series, no. 143).
A journal account of the voyage of HMS *Blossom* under the command of Captain Frederick William Beechey, RN, 1825-28, by the ship's first lieutenant. The object of the expedition was to relieve the expeditions of Franklin and Parry in Bering Strait. Beechey sailed around Cape Horn and eventually reached Kotzebue Sound, Alaska in July 1826. He continued north to Icy Cape from where he sent his ship's mate, Thomas Elson, along the coast to Point Barrow in the hope of meeting up with Franklin, but without result. Beechey returned to Bering Strait in 1827 but again failed to meet up with expeditions from the east.

630 **Narrative of a second voyage in search of a North-West Passage and of a residence in the Arctic regions during the years 1829, 1830, 1831, 1832, 1833 . . . including the reports of James Clark Ross . . . and the discovery of the North Magnetic Pole.**
John Ross. London: A. W. Webster, 1835. 740p. maps.
Ignored by the Admiralty since the debacle of 1818-19, described by Ross in *A voyage of discovery* . . . (q.v.), Captain Ross led his own expedition to the Canadian Arctic in 1829 with the *Victory*, the first steam-propelled vessel used for polar exploration. Accompanying him was his nephew, Commander James Clark Ross. The expedition traversed Lancaster Sound and Prince Regent Inlet and discovered the Boothia Peninsula (named for Felix Booth, Lord Mayor of London and financial backer of the expedition). *Victory* remained ice-bound for three winters, but overland sledge trips led to the discovery of the North Magnetic Pole by James Clark Ross on the western

coast of Boothia. Subsequently *Victory* was abandoned and Captain Ross decided to return north in boats and sledges. He was forced to spend a fourth winter on Somerset Island, but the following spring reached Lancaster Sound where the expedition was rescued by the whaler *Isabella* and returned safely to London. The narrative contains a wealth of scientific and ethonological information. The volume contains plates engraved from Ross's original sketches now held by the Scott Polar Research Institute in Cambridge, England. In 1835 an *Appendix to the narrative* was published (A. W. Webster, London, [443]p.) containing additional ethnological information with sections on natural history, the surgeon's report and gazetteer, and additional plates.

631 **Narrative of the Arctic land expedition to the mouth of the Great Fish River and along the shores of the Arctic Ocean in the years 1833, 1834 and 1835.**
George Back. London: John Murray, 1836. 663p. map.

An overland expedition to the Northwest Territories of Canada to search for Captain John Ross's expedition, detailed in *Narrative of a second voyage of discovery* (q.v.), now officially overdue. Back's party travelled by canoe to Great Slave Lake and finally down Great Fish River (now Back River) to the shores of the Arctic Ocean. By then, unbeknown to Back, Ross's expedition had been rescued. Back's narrative contains much information on landscape, flora and fauna and the physical anthropology of the Netsilik Eskimos. A reprint of this volume has been published (Edmonton, Alberta: M. G. Hurtig, 1970).

632 **Frozen in time; the fate of the Franklin expedition.**
Owen Beattie, John Geiger. London: Bloomsbury, 1987. 180p. maps. bibliog.

An investigation of tissue samples taken from three Eskimo skeletons and a Franklin expedition crewman on King William Island, Northwest Territories, suggested lead poisoning from canned food as a source of death. In 1984 the perfectly preserved bodies of Able Seaman John Hartnell and Royal Marine William Braine of HMS *Erebus* and Petty Officer John Torrington of HMS *Terror* were found in the permafrost of Beechey Island. An autopsy revealed high levels of lead in these bodies also. The authors claim, not entirely convincingly, that lead poisoning played an important role in the declining health of the members of Franklin's expedition.

633 **Sir John Franklin's last arctic expedition; a chapter in the history of the Royal Navy.**
Richard J. Cyriax. London: Methuen, 1939. 222p. maps. bibliog.

A well-researched and scholarly history of a British naval expedition under the leadership of Sir John Franklin, commanding HMS *Erebus* and *Terror*, whose object was to sail from the Atlantic to the Pacific through a Northwest Passage. The expedition left London on 19 May 1845 never to return. A series of official and unofficial search expeditions followed over a period of more than ten years culminating in the expedition of Sir Francis McClintock, 1857-59, described in his book *The voyage of the 'Fox' in the arctic seas; a narrative of the discovery of the fate of Sir John Franklin and his companions* (q.v.), and the finding of the evidence pointing to the fate of Franklin and his men.

634 **The Franklin era in Canadian Arctic history.**
Edited by Patricia D. Sutherland. Ottawa: National Museums of
Canada, 1985. 220p. (Mercury Series. Archaeological Survey of
Canada, paper no. 131).

This volume comprises a series of sixteen papers presented at a multidisciplinary
symposium held at the National Museum of Man, Ottawa, Canada, entitled 'The
Franklin era in Canadian Arctic history, 1845-1859'. The papers submitted examine a
wide range of topics including the art and literature of the period, climatic conditions
at the time of Franklin's last voyage, the contribution of private expeditions and of
whalers to the search for Franklin, the effectiveness of man-hauled sledging traditions
of the British Royal Navy, the impact of nineteenth-century European exploration on
native culture, and recent archaeological and osteological investigations of the Franklin
expedition sites and Franklin search expeditions sites.

635 **The land that devours ships; the search for the Breadalbane.**
Joe MacInnis. Montreal: CBC Enterprises, 1985. 191p. bibliog.

An account of the locating of the remains of the supply ship HMS *Breadalbane*, sunk
in 100 metres of water south of Beechey Island, Northwest Territories of Canada, by a
diving crew led by Dr Joe MacInnis in 1980-83. *Breadalbane* was sent to relieve Sir
Edward Belcher's fleet searching for Sir John Franklin. She was nipped in the ice and
sunk on 21 August 1853.

636 **The discovery of the North-West Passage by H.M.S. *Investigator*, Capt.
R. M'Clure 1850, 1851, 1852, 1853, 1854.**
Edited by Commander Sherard Osborn, from the logs and journals of
Capt. Robert Le M. M'Clure. London: Longman, Brown, Green,
Longmans, & Roberts, 1856. 405p. map.

An account of a British naval expedition which set sail in 1850 to search for Sir John
Franklin's lost expedition in the Canadian Arctic following the western approaches to
the Arctic Ocean via Bering Strait. M'Clure's ship *Investigator* succeeded in reaching
Banks Island, wintering to the south of it in Prince of Wales Strait, but heavy ice
prevented him from sailing on into Melville Sound. A second winter was spent off
Banks Island during which the ship was abandoned. A second search vessel, *Resolute*,
rescued M'Clure's men, but was itself later frozen in the ice and abandoned.
Eventually, the crews of both ships were rescued and returned to England on board
North Star in 1854, this time by the eastern approaches. In this indirect way the
Northwest Passage was finally traversed from west to east for the first time in history.

637 **The U.S. Grinnell expedition, in search of Sir John Franklin; a personal
narrative.**
Elisha Kent Kane. London: Sampson Low, 1854. 552p. map.

A narrative, by the surgeon, of the first Grinnell expedition commanded by Lieutenant
E. J. De Haven on the *Advance* and *Rescue* to the Lancaster Sound, Wellington
Channel region of the Canadian Arctic in 1850-51, giving details of Eskimos, natural
history, hunting and ice conditions. Much of the voyage was spent drifting in the pack
ice and no signs of Franklin's expedition were reported.

638 **Arctic explorations; the second Grinnell expedition in search of Sir John Franklin, 1953, '54, '55.**
Elisha Kent Kane.   Philadelphia: Childs & Peterson, 1856. 2 vols. maps.

An expedition in search of Franklin sponsored by Henry Grinnell, George Peabody and various scientific institutions in the United States. This narrative, based on selected passages from Kane's journal, gives an account of the organization of the expedition voyage of the ship *Advance* to Smith Sound, the wintering at Rensselaer Harbour, NW Greenland, and several sledge expeditions, one of which explored Kane Basin. *Advance* was abandoned in 1855 and Kane's party returned in small boats to Upernarvik, Greenland. Various scientific reports are summarized in the eighteen appendixes.

639 **The open polar sea; a narrative of a voyage of discovery towards the North Pole in the schooner 'United States'.**
Isaac Israel Hayes.   London: Sampson Low, Son & Marston, 1867. 454p. maps.

Hayes, who had served on Henry Grinnell's second expedition under Elisha Kent Kane in 1853-55, described in a narrative by Kent Kane (q.v.), in 1860 led another expedition, again financed by Grinnell, in the hope of achieving the North Pole via the open polar sea, which many believed to exist north of latitude 85°N. Visits were made to west Greenland and Ellesmere Island, but the ship met very heavy ice at Smith Sound and here the expedition wintered; they were joined by the local Eskimos. In 1861 Hayes made sledge trips in northern Ellesmere Island hoping to find an open polar sea, but eventually had to return home to Boston, further exploration being frustrated by the outbreak of the Civil War. Numerous scientific reports were, however, completed.

640 **The voyage of the 'Fox' in the arctic seas; a narrative of the discovery of the fate of Sir John Franklin and his companions.**
Francis Leopold M'Clintock.   London: John Murray, 1860. 406p. maps.

A narrative of the final expedition (1857-59) financed by Sir John Franklin's widow, Lady Jane Franklin, to search for traces of her husband's expedition. Led by Captain M'Clintock in command of the yacht *Fox*, the expedition voyaged through Lancaster Sound and Prince Regent Inlet to Bellot Strait, overwintering in Port Kennedy. From here sledge journeys were made along the west coast of Boothia, Prince of Wales Island and King William Island, leading to the discovery of many relics and two records of Franklin's expedition. Observations were also made on geology, meteorology and biology.

641 **Weird and tragic shores: the story of Charles Francis Hall, explorer.**
Chauncey C. Loomis.   London: Macmillan, 1971. 379p. maps. bibliog.

The story of Charles Francis Hall, a Cincinnati business man, who, at the age of thirty-eight, abandoned his career to explore the Arctic in search of evidence relating to the fate of Sir John Franklin's expedition. In all, he commanded three expeditions between 1860-71, learned to live among the Eskimos, and eventually died in the Arctic in mysterious circumstances, possibly of arsenic poisoning, according to an autopsy attended by the author of this book in 1968.

642 **Life with the Esquimaux; a narrative of arctic experience in search of survivors of Sir John Franklin's expedition.**
Charles Francis Hall. Introduction by G. Swinton. Edmonton, Alberta: M. G. Hurtig, 1970. 547p. map.

A reprint of the first edition (London: Sampson Low, 1865) with a new introduction by Professor George Swinton. The narrative was, in fact, written by W. Parker Snow making use of Hall's journals. It covers the voyage of the whaling barque *George Henry* to west Greenland and thence to the Frobisher Bay region of Baffin Island in 1860-62, where much surveying and mapping was achieved. Throughout the book details are given of Eskimo life, a subject in which Hall was especially interested, with notes on sledging, food, the effects of cold and so on. The actual object of the expedition was to shed light on the fate of Franklin's expedition. The American edition of this work was published under the title *Arctic researches and life among the Esquimaux* (Harper, 1865).

643 **Narrative of the second arctic expedition made by Charles F. Hall: his voyage to Repulse Bay, sledge journeys to the Straits of Fury and Hecla and to King William Land and residence among the Eskimos during the years 1864-69.**
J. E. Nourse. Washington, DC: Government Printing Office, 1879. 644p. maps.

This expedition, like Hall's expedition of 1860-62, was undertaken to search for records of the Franklin expedition and according to the introduction to this volume, 'to promote and benefit the cause of geography, navigation, history and science'. From winterquarters in Wager Inlet and Repulse Bay, Hall explored the shores north and west from Melville Peninsula to King William Island, 1864-69. The narrative was edited after Hall's death, from his journals and associated material, by Professor Nourse, on behalf of the United States Naval Observatory.

644 **Narrative of the North Polar expedition. U.S. Ship Polaris, Captain Charles Francis Hall commanding.**
Edited by C. H. Davis. Washington, DC: Government Printing Office, 1876. 696p. maps.

The official narrative, compiled from the journals of the men and officers, of the *Polaris* expedition (1871-73) to seek the North Pole, explore the regions north of Smith Sound and to make scientific investigations. The expedition wintered at Thank God Harbour on the northwest coast of Greenland having achieved a record northern latitude of 82°11′N. On 8 November 1871 Hall died in mysterious circumstances, possibly as a result of arsenic poisoning, the question of which is discussed in Chauncey C. Loomis' book, *Weird and tragic shores* . . . (q.v.). *Polaris* was subsequently beset in the ice and abandoned, the crew being rescued by a whaler. A second party, carried away from the ship on an ice floe, was likewise rescued by a sealer.

645 **Three years of arctic service; an account of the Lady Franklin Bay expedition of 1881-84 and the attainment of the farthest north.**
Adolphus W. Greely. London: Richard Bentley, 1886. 2 vols. maps.

The official narrative, based on Greely's journals, of a United States expedition based at Fort Conger, Lady Franklin Bay, on the east coast of Ellesmere Island, Northwest

Territories, Canada (lat. 81°45′N) in support of the First International Polar Year, 1882-83. The expedition explored the north coast of Greenland, and the interior and coast of Grinnell Land (northern Ellesmere Island). As relief ships failed to reach them, members of the expedition set to march from Hall Basin; all but seven died of starvation before being rescued at Cape Sabine, Smith Sound, by the whaler *Thetis*. Scientific data are discussed in the ten appendixes.

646 **The boundary hunters: surveying the 141st meridian and the Alaskan Panhandle.**
Lewis Green.   Vancouver, London: University of British Columbia Press, 1982. 214p.

Describes 'the most arduous and protracted survey operation that has ever been undertaken'. The need for an agreed demarcation between Canada and Alaska became urgent after the discovery of gold in the Yukon River area between 1893-96. Fieldwork started in 1904 but was not completed until sixteen years later, since surveying could only take place in the summer months. Reports of the fieldwork are enlivened by extracts from the reports of the surveyors themselves.

647 **Hunters of the Great North.**
Vilhjalmur Stefansson.   London: George G. Harrap, 1923. 288p. map.

A popular account of Stefansson's first expedition to the Mackenzie River delta region of northern Canada and northern Alaska in 1906-07, compiled from his diaries sixteen years after the event. There are chapters on hunting caribou, seals and polar bear and details of how to build a snow house or igloo. It was during his first experience of an arctic winter that Stefansson learned how to live with the Eskimos and this made him realize that competence in their skills would allow him to accomplish an ambitious programme of arctic exploration and research of information on Eskimo life and customs, their modes of thought, and the physical geography of the region. The results of the expedition include reports on topography, geology and flora and fauna.

648 **My life with the Eskimo.**
Vilhjalmur Stefansson. Appendix by Rudolph M. Anderson.   New York: Macmillan, 1943. 538p. maps.

The full narrative of Stefansson's second expedition to the Mackenzie River delta region of northern Canada with Rudolph M. Anderson as assistant, 1908-12. It was Stefansson's first published book (New York: Macmillan, 1913). The main object of the expedition was to locate and study the so-called 'Blond Eskimos' reported by the whaling captain Klinkenberg and believed to live on Victoria Island, Northwest Territories. It was not until April 1910 that Stefansson was able to make the trip to Victoria Island and the account of his meeting with these very primitive Copper Eskimos, as they are better known, makes fascinating reading. Anderson contributed a natural history appendix to this volume.

649 **My life among the Eskimos; Baffinland journeys in the year 1909 to 1911.**
Bernhard Hantzsch. Translated from German and edited by Leslie H. Neatby. Saskatoon, Saskatchewan: University of Saskatchewan, 1977. 386p. map. bibliog. (Mawdsley Memoir, 3).

The edited journals of Bernhard Hantzsch (1875-1911), son of a Dresden schoolmaster and an experienced ornithologist, describe his remarkable journey from Cumberland Sound across Baffin Island to Foxe Basin and up the coast to Piling Bay, April 1910-May 1911. The object of the expedition, on which Hantzsch was accompanied by an Eskimo family, was to learn the language of the Eskimos and to study their way of life.

650 **The friendly Arctic; the story of five years in polar regions.**
Vilhjalmur Stefansson. New York: Macmillan, 1943. new ed. 812p. maps.

A revised version of the original edition of 1921, containing an additional preface and a new chapter, 'The friendly Arctic twenty-one years after'. This is an account of the Canadian Arctic Expedition of 1913-18 organized by the Canadian government and led by Stefansson. Its purpose was to explore the little-known area of the western Canadian Arctic. The expedition was divided into two parts: a Northern Division, under Stefansson, to carry out geographical discovery in the Beaufort Sea, and a Southern Division under Rudolph Anderson to carry out scientific work in Coronation Gulf. Stefansson's ship *Karluk* was beset in the Beaufort Sea and eventually sank. Eight members of the ship's party were lost, the remainder reaching Wrangell Island where they were eventually rescued. In this narrative Stefansson describes his own travels eastwards along Melville Island, McClure Strait, Banks Island and a visit to Herschel Island, Victoria Island and the Copper Eskimos, and finally the subsequent wintering on Melville Island. This book – perhaps Stefansson's best-known – is an eloquent testimony to the author's belief that the Arctic is indeed friendly to those travellers who take the trouble to adapt to Eskimo lifestyles.

651 **Across arctic America; narrative of the Fifth Thule Expedition.**
Knud Rasmussen. London: G. P. Putnam's, 1927. 388p. maps.

An account of the Danish ethnographical expedition to arctic North America 1921-24, led by Knud Rasmussen; it consisted of five Danish scientists and assistants who investigated extinct and living cultures in northern Canada and Alaska for general interest and for data on the origin and migrations of Eskimos. The scientific reports were to be published in twelve projected volumes, most of which have been published (Copenhagen: Gyldendalske boghandel, 1927-45).

652 **The land that God gave Cain; an account of H. G. Watkins's expedition to Labrador, 1928-1929.**
J. M. Scott. London: Chatto & Windus, 1933. 282p. maps.

A personal account of an expedition to map the complex system of falls whose existence had been reported in the region of the Hamilton River. It was hoped to find lakes suitable as bases for an air survey of the largely unmapped interior. Journeying was by canoe and by dog sledge and involved an exploration of the rivers and lakes between Hamilton River and the Eskimo settlement of Hopedale.

653 **Northwest Passage.**
William D. Smith. New York: American Heritage, 1970. 204p. map.
A newspaperman's account of the voyage of the supertanker SS *Manhattan* in 1969 which set out to prove that a year-round commercial sea route could be opened through the ice-clogged Northwest Passage westwards to the North Slope of Alaska where large reserves of oil were about to be exploited.

Peoples

654 **Nanook of the North.**
Julian W. Bilby. London: Arrowsmith, 1925. 319p.
A classic account of the life and customs of the primitive Eskimos of Baffin Island, Northwest Territories of Canada, which centres round the daily life of Nanook the hunter, a fictitious figure based on fact. A silent film of the book, going by the same name, made and directed by Robert Flaherty, was distributed in 1922.

655 **Living Arctic; hunters of the Canadian north.**
Hugh Brody. London; Boston, Massachusetts: Faber & Faber, 1987. 254p. maps. bibliog.
Published in collaboration with the British Museum and Indigenous Survival International in connection with the 'Living Arctic' exhibition, this is an account of the native peoples of arctic and subarctic Canada – Indians and Eskimos – by a professional sociologist and anthropologist, well acquainted with the North over many years. It is an attempt to describe the culture of these peoples, 'in defiance of the stereotype', as Mr Brody puts it. Southerners regard the way of life of these peoples as primitive, their wealth from hunting as 'poverty'. These attitudes, the author asserts, deny them their natural rights. The book is brought to life with carefully chosen photographs and the quoted words of the peoples themselves.

656 **List of Canadian native periodicals held by the INAC library.**
Canada. Department of Indian and Northern Affairs. Ottawa: Indian & Northern Affairs Canada, 1985. 18p.
Offers a complete listing of Canadian native periodical titles held by the library of the Canadian Department of Indian and Northern Affairs, together with holdings for each title. The listing is updated periodically.

657 **Inuit youth; growth and change in the Canadian Arctic.**
Richard G. Condon. New Brunswick; London: Rutgers University Press, 1987. 252p. maps. bibliog.
An ethnographical description of the life of young people between the ages of nine and twenty in the small isolated Inuit (Eskimo) community of Holman Island, Northwest Territories. The book opens with an overview of the historical development and contemporary situation of the community with emphasis on the rapid social, material and political changes taking place, and the impact of these changes on the behaviour,

167

attitudes and aspirations of the new generation of Inuit. The lifestyle of a former hunting and trapping society has been radically changed by the introduction of schooling, radio and television, subsidized housing and wage employment. The author describes the day-to-day activities of Inuit youth and concludes with a description of adolescence in Holman Island and a discussion of how it compares with similar stages in other cultures.

658 **Resources for native peoples studies.**
Nora T. Corley. Ottawa: National Library of Canada, Resources Division, Collections Development Branch, 1984. 342p. maps. bibliog. (Research Collections in Canadian Libraries, 9).

A comprehensive review of Canadian libraries holding collections relating to native peoples. A total of 356 libraries of all types are listed under provinces, with brief reviews of, amongst other things, their policies and holdings. Appended are bibliographies of periodicals about native peoples published both within and without Canada, and a list of reference works useful for native peoples' studies.

659 **A history of the original peoples of northern Canada.**
Keith J. Crowe. Montreal; London: McGill-Queen's University Press for the Arctic Institute of North America, 1974. 226p. maps. bibliog.

A history of northern native peoples from their first arrival to the beginnings of their tribal groups, languages and customs. It gives an account of the changes resulting from foreign intrusion – fur-trading, whaling and missionary activity. Today, northern peoples are subjected to military, industrial and government power. A list of associations serving the needs of northern peoples is appended.

660 **The road to Nunavut; the progress of the eastern Arctic Inuit since the Second World War.**
R. Quinn Duffy. Kingston; Montreal: McGill-Queen's University Press, 1988. 308p. map. bibliog.

Previously the Eskimo (Inuit) hunters and trappers of the eastern Arctic were largely unorganised. They have now become a sedentary population tied to the economy of southern Canada and politically developed to the level of demanding self government in a region they call 'Nunavut' ('Our land'). This book is an analysis of federal government policy on the social and economic problems of the Eskimos. The author describes economic, political and social changes in the eastern Arctic and provides historical background to the current debate on Nunavut land claims and political subdivision of the Northwest Territories. Finally, the author, having outlined the Eskimos' dependence on Canadian government responsibility for social services, and the inevitable side-effects of this (delinquency and alcohol abuse, for example) describes how they have begun to assume responsibility for improving their situation, are gradually developing political maturity, as expressed through their own political organizations, and are pressurizing for regional self-determination.

661 **The Inuit; life as it was.**
Richard Harrington. Edmonton, Alberta: Hurtig, 1981. 143p.

An account of the author's travels among the Canadian Eskimos, 1947-53, at a time when they were still following their traditional life-style as primitive hunters. The book is plentifully illustrated with the author's photographs.

662 **The native peoples of Canada: an annotated bibliography of population biology, health and illness.**
Compiled, edited and annotated by C. Meiklejohn, D. A.
Rokala. Ottawa: National Museums of Canada, 1986. 564p.
(Canadian Museum of Civilization Mercury Series. Archaeological
Survey of Canada, paper no. 134).

A valuable research tool covering much interdisciplinary material scattered throughout professional publications, journals and books. This computer-based bibliography includes references to the people of North America, including Greenland, and is fully abstracted.

663 **A status report and bibliography of cultural studies in the Canadian Arctic to 1976.**
James F. V. Miller, Alexander M. Ervin. Saskatoon, Saskatchewan:
Institute for Northern Studies, 1981. 113p. (Musk-Ox Special
Publication).

A bibliography of 1,489 references, mostly in the English language, extending from 1744 to 1976 and dealing with human conditions and behaviour values in the widest anthropological sense. The bibliography is arranged in three sections: (1) A general bibliography; (2) An annotated bibliography; and (3) An index.

664 **Native rights in Canada.**
Compiled by Robin Minion. Edmonton, Alberta: University of
Alberta, Boreal Institute for Northern Studies, 1984. 102p. (BINS
Bibliographic Series, no. 1).

A bibliography of 280 references, many with brief contents' notes, covering various aspects of Canadian native peoples' rights including land claims and settlements and ownership of natural resources. Author, geographic and title indexes are appended.

665 **Aboriginal peoples and the law: Indian, Metis and Inuit rights in Canada.**
Edited by Bradford W. Morse. Ottawa: Carleton University Press,
1985. 800p. bibliog. (Carleton Library Series).

Although this volume does not encompass all relevant aspects of the law of Canadian aboriginal peoples it does attempt, through its several specialist-contributed chapters, to provide a basic resource work of reference, and includes excerpts from selected materials and original texts regarding certain of the critical issues in this field. The introductory chapter describes the general position of the indigenous population today. The following chapters deal with the influence of international law on aboriginal and treaty rights. The final themes addressed concern the details and impact of land rights and the land claims process.

666 **Inuit du Nouveau-Québec. Bibliographie (The Inuit of Nouveau Québec. Bibliography).**
Pierette Pageau. Québec: Ministère des Affaires Culturelles, Service d'Archéologie et d'Ethnologie, 1975. 175p. maps. (Dossier, 13).
A bibliography of references, arranged thematically, in English and French relating to the Eskimos of northern Quebec province, Canada. It includes some references to neighbouring Labrador.

667 **Nunaga: ten years among the Eskimos.**
Duncan Pryde. London: Eland, 1985. 286p.
An autobiographical account of the author's life among the hunters and traders of the Canadian Arctic in which he describes the customs and lifestyle of the Eskimos. As an accepted member of one of the last traditional Eskimo societies his experiences are unique.

668 **Our land; native rights in Canada.**
Donald Purich. Toronto: James Lorimer, 1986. 252p. bibliog.
A review of the history of the native peoples' rights movement in Canada and the future of native rights.

669 **Northern nomadic hunter-gatherers; a humanistic approach.**
David Riches. London: Academic, 1982. 242p. bibliog.
A fresh look at the main issues that have occupied social anthropologists in the field of nomadic hunting and gathering societies, focusing on Canadian Eskimo societies in particular. Issues discussed are: (1) Why do hunter-gatherers assemble in camps of different sizes from season to season? (2) What is the basis to the variation in patterns of social organization and leadership among these peoples? (3) What underlies the existence of territorial notions in hunter-gatherer cultures? (4) How may we best apprehend the changes in social organization and culture of nomadic hunter-gatherers under the impact of contact with European culture?

670 **Whaling and Eskimos: Hudson Bay 1860-1915.**
W. Gillies Ross. Ottawa: National Museum of Man, 1975. maps. bibliog. (Publications in Ethnology, no. 10).
Based on ships' logbooks and private journals, this scholarly monograph gives an account of the relationship built up between the hunters of the bowhead whale in Hudson Bay between 1860 and 1915 and the local Eskimo peoples. The latter became indispensable to the whalemen in a number of different ways, such as whale hunting and overland travel, while the whalemen, for their part, came to be essential to the new Eskimo way of life, for example, through imported trade goods, firearms and whaleboats.

671 **Inuit; the North in transition.**
Ulli Steltzer. Seattle: University of Washington Press, 1982. 216p. map.
A largely visual account of the Eskimos of northern Canada, based on the author's year-long travels (1980-81) from the Yukon to Labrador, taking photographs and talking to the local people.

672 **Natives and newcomers; Canada's 'heroic age' reconsidered.**
Bruce G. Trigger. Kingston: McGill-Queen's University Press, 1985.
430p.
A re-evaluation of the interactions between native and European cultures in early
Canadian history with reference to recent ethnological and archaeological findings.

673 **The changing role and significance of native peoples in Canada's
Northwest Territories.**
William C. Wonders. *Polar Record*, vol. 23, no. 147 (Sept. 1987),
p. 661-71. maps. bibliog.
A general review of the present status of the Indians and Eskimos (Inuit) of the
Northwest Territories, covering their numbers, demography and way of life. The
article concludes with a brief summary of the native peoples' future role and life-style
in the Northwest Territories and questions of comprehensive land claims, the political
division of the Territories, and the relationship between native and national goals.

Languages

674 **Uqausigusiqtaat: an analytical lexicon of modern Inuktitut in
Quebec-Labrador.**
Louis-Jacques Dorais. Québec: Les Presses de l'Université Laval,
1983. 150p. maps.
A 2,100 word Inuktitut (Eskimo) vocabulary of words adapted to accommodate Euro-
American acculturation changes. There are borrowings from foreign languages, and
traditional words are invested with novel meanings. A major part of the vocabulary of
the Eskimos in Quebec-Labrador has been altered by contact.

675 **Inuit and Indian languages, including educational concerns and
materials in these languages.**
Compiled by Robin Minion. Edmonton, Alberta: University of
Alberta, Boreal Institute for Northern Studies, 1985. 77p. (BINS
Bibliographic Series, no. 16).
A listing of publications compiled from the Boreal Institute's computerized library
database, arranged by authors with geographic and author indexes.

676 **English-Eskimo/Eskimo-English dictionary.**
F. W. Peacock. St. John's, Newfoundland: Memorial University of
Newfoundland, [1978]. 2 vols.
A dictionary of the Labrador Eskimo language, using the German alphabet employed
by the Moravian missions in their work among this people.

677 **Conversational Eskimo; a self-guide to the language of the Inuit.**
F. W. Peacock. Portugal Cove, Newfoundland: Breakwater Books, 1977. 135p.

A booklet intended to help non-native people living among the Eskimos (Inuit), especially social workers, teachers, nurses and policemen. The spelling follows that used by the Moravian Brethren on the coast of Labrador for over 200 years.

678 **English Eskimo/Eskimo-English dictionary.**
Arthur Thibert. Ottawa: Research Center of Amerindian Anthropology, 1954. 2 vols. bibliog.

Based on Father Thibert's twenty-seven years of missionary work among the Eskimos of Chesterfield Inlet, Eskimo Point, Southampton Island, Baker Lake and Churchill, Northwest Territories, and incorporating the work of numerous pioneer linguists in this field. The dictionary was compiled primarily for missionaries and social workers.

Missions

679 **The Anglican Church from the Bay to the Rockies; a history of the ecclesiastical province of Rupert's Land its diocese from 1820 to 1950.**
T. C. B. Boon. Toronto: Ryerson, 1962. 480p. maps. bibliog.

The Church of England came to this region, initially, by way of Nova Scotia, British Columbia and Ontario. Finally it reached Rupert's Land by the canoe routes of the fur traders working for the Hudson's Bay Company, between the years 1820-70. This is a history of those pioneer years and the years that followed up until the 1950s.

680 **Archibald the Arctic.**
Archibald Lang Fleming. New York: Appleton-Century-Crofts, 1956. 399p. map.

Bishop Fleming went north to Baffin Island in the Northwest Territories of Canada in July 1909, to work as a missionary, at the age of twenty-five. After subsequent ordination in Canada he returned north to become Archdeacon of the Arctic in 1926. In 1933 he was consecrated first Bishop of the Arctic. He built up an organization known as the 'Fellowship of the Arctic' with some 3,000 members worldwide. For many years, until his retirement through ill health in 1949, Bishop Fleming travelled widely through his vast diocese, covering an area of some 1,200,000 square miles using ship, sledge and airplane. He established many new schools, hospitals and missions throughout the North.

681 **Beyond traplines.**
Charles E. Hendry. Toronto: Ryerson, 1969. 102p. bibliog.

A report for the Anglican Church of Canada on the Indians, Métis and Eskimos of Canada and the forces that have shaped their present condition, especially their massive poverty and alienation. The report recommends organized public pressure and person-to-person humanitarian services.

172

682 **Missionary in Labrador and New Quebec (Lionel Scheffer, O.M.I.).**
Alexis Joveneau, Laurent Tremblay. Translated by Emmett O'Grady.
Montreal: Rayonnement, 1971. 127p. map.
A biography of Bishop Lionel Scheffer, OMI, first bishop of Labrador-Schefferville,
northern Quebec, and missionary to the Eskimos.

683 **The impact of the Grenfell Mission on southern Labrador.**
John C. Kennedy. *Polar Record*, vol. 24, no. 149 (July 1988),
p. 199-206. map.
The mission discussed here was established in northern Newfoundland and Labrador
by the British medical missionary Wilfred Grenfell, in the late 19th and early 20th
centuries. This article describes the mission's approach to health, education,
agricultural and industrial development, and its impact on the region of southeast
Labrador.

684 **And to the Eskimos.**
Gleason H. Ledyard. Chicago: Moody, 1958. 254p.
An account of the work of two American missionaries among the Caribou Eskimos of
Canada's Northwest Territories.

685 **The life and work of the Rev. E. J. Peck among the Eskimos.**
Arthur Lewis. London: Hodder & Stoughton, 1904. 350p.
Describes the work of a Church of England missionary in the eastern Canadian Arctic,
1876-1902. An appendix reproduces Peck's remarks on the Eskimo language and a
table of syllabic characters adapted for the Eskimos.

686 **Echoes from a frozen land.**
Donald B. Marsh. Edited by Winifred Marsh. Edmonton, Alberta:
Hurtig, 1987. 187p. map.
Donald Marsh first went to the Arctic in 1926 when he established a Christian mission
among the Padlimiut (or Caribou) Eskimos on the western shore of Hudson Bay.
There he remained, serving these people in many capacities for some eighteen years.
In 1950 he became Anglican Bishop of the Arctic, a diocese covering over eight million
square kilometres. After his death in 1974 his widow worked on his notes and
photographs to form the basis of this account of his life and activity among the
Eskimos.

687 **The Moravian Brethren – a historical introduction.**
T. D. Regehr. *Musk-ox*, no. 62 (summer 1980), p. 80-81.
Gives a brief history of this Protestant religious group leading to its work in Labrador
in the mid-19th century.

688 **Culture change and religious continuity among the Arviligdjuarmiut of Pelly Bay, N.W.T., 1935-1963.**
Cornelius H. W. Rennie. *Inuit Studies*, vol. 7, no. 2 (1983), p. 53-77, bibliog.
The author sets out to demonstrate that the opening of a mission post at Pelly Bay, Northwest Territories, Canada, in 1935 by the Oblate Fathers did not bring about the complete collapse of the Arviligdjuarmiut Eskimos' traditional religion. He shows that, on the contrary, it remained intact to a considerable extent and was effective in several domains of domestic and social life, at least until the early 1960s. In brief, the traditional religion continued to exist alongside the new.

689 **Arctic News.**
Toronto: Diocese of the Arctic, 1944- . twice-yearly.
A news bulletin covering events in the Canadian Diocese of the Arctic which includes the Northwest Territories and northern Quebec province. It includes short articles of local interest and much biographical information.

690 **Eskimo.**
Churchill, Manitoba: Diocese of Churchill-Hudson Bay, 1943- . twice-yearly.
A journal devoted to the Catholic mission in northern Canada, which is valuable for the information it provides on the Eskimo community and biographies of missionary priests.

Constitution and law

691 **The Northwest Territories and its future constitutional and political development: an examination of the Drury Report.**
Bernard W. Funston. *Polar Record*, vol. 21, no. 131 (May 1982), p. 117-25. bibliog.
A useful summary of the political status of the Canadian Northwest Territories and its historical background, together with a commentary on the commission set up in 1977 by order-in-council, chaired by C. M. Drury, which published its findings and recommendations in March 1980. The report does not, finally, prescribe a provincial model, or any other model, for the Northwest Territories which, it seems, must continue to look to the Federal Government for financing and for constitutional change.

692 **The north.**
Michael S. Whittington. Toronto: University of Toronto Press, 1985. 183p. map.
A collection of essays on the role of the northern territories of Canada in political, social and economic terms, written by leading scholars working in the field of northern development, and presented to a seminar on economic development organized by a

Royal Commission on the subject. Following a general review on northern studies there are sections on: development planning north of 60; requirements and prospects; political and constitutional development in the Northwest Territories and the Yukon; the issues and interests of northern political development within Canadian federalism; environmental perspectives in the 1980s; sovereignty and the Canadian north; and a southern perspective on northern economic development.

Strategic aspects

693 **Arctic imperative: is Canada losing the North?**
John Honderich. Toronto: University of Toronto Press, 1987. 258p.

The author, a journalist on the *Toronto Star*, argues the case for an integrated policy on sovereignty, security and economic development which will meet the challenge to Canada's control of the Northwest Passage from the United States government's Strategic Defense Initiative ('Star wars').

694 **Northern development, northern security.**
Nils Ørvik. Kingston: Queen's University, Centre for International Relations, 1983. 196p. (Northern Studies Series, no. 1/83).

A series of essays by the Director of the Centre for International Relations at Queen's University, Kingston, Ontario, dealing with problems relating to the economic and political development of northern Canada. Special reference is made to the environmental hazard posed by the proposed Arctic Pilot Project (APP), a scheme for the bulk transport of oil and gas through arctic waters. The book concludes with considerations of Canadian national security policy in the North, and relations with such northern neighbours as the USA, Greenland, Iceland and with NATO.

Economic resources and development

695 **Power from the North.**
Robert Bourassa. Scarborough, Ontario: Prentice-Hall, 1985. 182p. maps.

A description of the hydroelectric resources of Quebec province, tracing the history of the James Bay hydroelectric project and the future economic prospects for similar developments.

696 **Northern mineral policy.**
Canada. Department of Indian Affairs and Northern Development. Ottawa: The Author, 1986. 65p. maps.

An outline of policy decisions relating to the mining industry in the Northwest Territories and the Yukon Territory.

697 **The northern mineral sector: a framework for discussion.**
Canada. Department of Indian Affairs and Northern
Development. Ottawa: The Author, 1985. 74p. maps.

An examination of how economic concerns influence the exploitation of minerals in the
Northwest Territories and the Yukon Territory.

698 **National and regional interests in the North; third national workshop on
people, resources and the environment north of 60°; Yellowknife,
Northwest Territories 1-3 June 1983.**
Canadian Arctic Resources Committee. Ottawa: The Author, 1984.
758p. map.

The goal of this workshop was to 'explore policy alternatives for resource management
that accommodate the growing demands of northerners in a way that respects the
interests of all Canadians in the development of these resources'. Topics on which
papers are presented include: regional planning and land-use planning; conservation of
environmentally significant areas; mineral development; renewable resources management; inland water resources; and ocean management and development in the
Beaufort Sea region.

699 **Prospects for the northern Canadian native economy.**
Bruce A. Cox. *Polar Record*, vol. 22, no. 139 (Jan. 1985), p. 393-400.
bibliog.

This paper re-examines the debates over the prospects for a native hunting economy in
northern Canada and supports the arguments in favour. The author argues that given
proper institutional support a wage economy can co-exist, and this mixed economy
should persist into the next century, thereby showing that critics of the bush economy
have underestimated its contribution to the welfare of the northern natives.

700 **The Canadian North: source of wealth or vanishing heritage?**
Bruce W. Hodgins, Jamie Benedickson, Richard P. Bowles, George A.
Rawlyk. Scarsborough, Ontario: Prentice-Hall, 1977. 257p. bibliog.
(Canada Issues and Options Series).

A selection of documents culled from, for example, the press, and government
statements, providing a broad range of opinion and historical background on the issues
of northern development. Appended to each document are questions designed to
stimulate further thought and questioning. Issues covered include the need for an oil
and gas pipeline in the Mackenzie Valley and other economic considerations; social
considerations in the North; and historical roots and future prospects.

701 **Yukon wildlife; a social history.**
Robert G. McCandless. Edmonton, Alberta: University of Alberta
Press, 1985. 200p.

A history of the economic development of the Yukon Territory including details of
hunting and trapping activities and game laws.

702 **Northern development; the Canadian dilemma.**
Robert Page. Toronto: McClelland & Stewart, 1986. 360p. (Canada in Transition Series).

An examination of two landmark northern development public policy forums in Canada during the 1970s: the Commission on the Mackenzie Valley Pipeline, chaired by Mr Justice Thomas Berger, and the National Energy Board hearing on northern pipeline development. This account of these two enquiries analyses the complex problems facing all northern development schemes, more especially environmental concerns, native land claims, technological problems and the enormous capital requirements of resource exploitation in this region. The author also shows how these themes have evolved in the first half of the 1980s.

703 **Economic theory and development planning in the arctic regions; a study in plural economy.**
Joseph R. Potvin. Cambridge, England: Scott Polar Research Institute, 1986. 107p. maps. bibliog. (Thesis submitted for the M.Phil. in Polar Studies, University of Cambridge).

A discussion of the possibilities of applying economic method and strategy to the task of practical development planning in a peripheral regional economy. This thesis addresses the theory and strategy of economic development in the Northwest Territories of Canada. It is essentially an essay in methodology. There are four main sections: (1) The regional context of planning is proposed with a consideration of questions concerning capital and labour mobility. (2) The case of plural economy is examined in theory and practice. (3) The determinants and mechanisms of economic growth are dealt with. (4) The last section consists of a draft proposal for an economic model suitable for the Northwest Territories. The thesis concludes with a variety of suggestions on how to construct a long-term economic plan.

704 **The political economy of the Canadian North; an interpretation of the course of development in the northern territories of Canada to the early 1960s.**
K. J. Rea. Toronto: University of Toronto Press and University of Saskatchewan, 1968. 453p. map. bibliog.

A study of the processes of development which shaped and limited the growth of economic and political life in the Yukon and Northwest Territories between the 1890s and the early 1960s. Much emphasis is placed on the role of government policy which was one of 'developmental *laissez-faire*' until after World War II. However, in subsequent years there has been great expansion in government activity in welfare and public services. The author examines the effect of this programme and suggests the future course of action.

705 **Canadian Mining Journal.**
Don Mills, Ontario: Canadian Mining Journal, 1879- . monthly.

A journal directed at the mining industry with much of relevance to the Arctic. It contains regular reviews of mines and their output, arranged by provinces.

706 **Northern Miner.**
Toronto: Northern Miner, [1950]- . weekly.
A mineral resources newspaper covering the whole of Canada, and including current information on such topics as geological and geophysical exploration, new mineral deposits and gas pipelines.

Employment

707 **A bibliography on labour, employment and training in the Canadian north: some important issues.**
Compiled by Kenneth de la Barre, Denise Harvey. Montreal: Département de démographie, Committee on Northern Population Research, 1983. 106p. (ASTIS Occasional Publication; no. 8).
This bibliography focuses on population-related material concerned primarily with labour, employment and training issues in the Canadian North. Approximately 500 entries, in French and English, cover the period 1970-83.

708 **The training and employment of northern Canadians: an annotated bibliography.**
Edited by J. C. Finley, C. R. Goodwin. Ottawa: Environmental Studies Revolving Funds, 1986. 206p. (Environmental Studies Revolving Funds, report no. 050).
A bibliography of references concerning the training and employment of northern Canadians including those in the oil and gas industry, mining, tourism, government and communications.

Transport

709 **The White Pass and Yukon Railway 1898-1982.**
Peter B. Clibbon. Sillery, Quebec: Laurentia, 1986. 16p. (Northern Canada and Alaska Series Collection, no. 2).
A short history of the White Pass and Yukon Railway, linking Whitehorse, Yukon Territory, with the Pacific coast at Skagway, Alaska, and its significance to the economic development of the region.

710 **Transit management in the Northwest Passage; problems and prospects.**
Edited by Cynthia Lamson, David L. Vanderzwaag. Cambridge, England: Cambridge University Press, 1988. 316p. maps.
A collection of eight contributory chapters analysing various aspects of marine transportation through the Northwest Passage, from the Canadian viewpoint. The first

six chapters summarize major problem areas which must be considered in designing an integral ocean management régime. Chapter two highlights important environmental and human concerns at stake in arctic resource development. Chapter three reviews the economic difficulties in developing northern ocean industries. Chapter four surveys arctic marine technologies such as icebreaking vessels, submarine tankers, artificial islands. Chapter five sets forth Canadian arctic marine transportation capabilities and probable future needs. Chapter six provides an overview of the administrative and legislative framework for Canadian northern decision making. Chapter seven explores the evolving political development of the Northwest Territories. A final chapter examines alternative conceptual models for designing a transit management system and advocates an integrated research strategy.

Environment

711 **Canadian national parks.**
Compiled by Robin Minion. Edmonton, Alberta: University of Alberta, Boreal Institute for Northern Studies, 1985. 72p. (BINS Bibliographical Series, no. 22).

A listing of publications compiled from the Boreal Institute's computerized library database arranged by authors with geographic and author indexes. Material covered includes monographs, theses, government documents, atlases, microforms and periodicals. A listing of parks is also included.

712 **North of 50°: an atlas of far northern Ontario.**
Royal Commission on the Northern Environment, J. E. J. Fahlgren, Geoffrey Matthews. Toronto: University of Toronto Press, 1985. 119p. maps.

Provides detailed maps of the national environment, human occupation, administrative divisions and economic activities of this area.

713 **Environmental Studies Revolving Funds Reports.**
Ottawa: Department of Energy, Mines and Resources; Department of Indian Affairs and Northern Development. 1985- . irregular.

These reports are financed from special levies on the oil and gas industry and support specialized research and publication in a multitude of fields covering environmental studies in northern Canada.

Education

714 **The universities of Canada and the north – a guide.**
In: *Education, research, information systems and the north.*
Edited by W. Peter Adams. Ottawa: Association of Canadian
Universities for Northern Studies, 1987, p. 239-362.
Thirty-five profiles submitted to the Association of Canadian Universities for Northern
Studies providing information specifically designed to be of use to northern residents
and stressing not only northern studies but also aspects of these institutions of
particular interest to people living in the North.

Literature

715 **Isumaksaqsiurvik: the first Canadian collection of Inuit literature.**
Jennifer Cram. *Polar Record*, vol. 23, no. 143 (May 1986), p. 203-04.
Gives an account of the Hochelaga Research Institute, Montreal, Canada, and its
collection of Inuit (Eskimo) language literature, catalogued with an IBM word-
processor with a programme able to transliterate roman orthography to Eskimo
syllabics and vice versa. The collection spans Inuit publications from the 18th century
to the present and includes biblical translations, diaries, government publications,
novels, poems, articles and songs. All Inuit groups of Canada are represented in the
collection as are those of Alaska, Greenland and the Soviet Union.

716 **Canadian Inuit literature: the development of a tradition.**
Robin McGrath. Ottawa: National Museums of Canada, 1984. 230p.
bibliog. (Mercury Series. Canadian Ethnology Service, paper no. 94).
In Canada there is now a considerable body of Inuit literature available in both
Inuktitut, the native Eskimo language, and English. This monograph examines the
development of this literature. A brief history of European contact as it affected
literacy, a consideration of the movement from the oral to the written tradition, and a
description of early Inuktitut publications, lead to a discussion of the poetry and prose
of both oral and written traditions. Appendixes include an illustrated account of
Inuktitut writing systems, a listing of 100 relevant periodicals by and about the Inuit
(Eskimos) and a primary bibliography of 750 books, articles, stories and poems by
native authors.

Bibliographies

717 **Bibliography of the Quebec-Labrador peninsula.**
Compiled by Alan Cooke, Fabien Caron. Boston, Massachusetts:
G. K. Hall, 1968. 2 vols. (Centre d'Études Nordiques, Université
Laval, Québec).
A comprehensive bibliography of this region of northern Canada, including books and journal articles.

718 **Bibliography of Canadian bibliographies.**
Compiled by Douglas Lochhead. Toronto: University of Toronto
Press in association with the Bibliographical Society of Canada, 1972.
2nd ed. 312p.
This alphabetical listing of over 2,300 titles has a name and subject index. Relevant subject headings include 'Arctic'; 'Eskimos'; 'Indians'; 'Labrador'; 'Northwest Passage'; and 'Yukon'.

719 **Yukon Bibliography.**
Edited by Geraldine A. Cooke. Edmonton, Alberta: Boreal Institute
for Northern Studies, 1973- . irregular.
A bibliography covering the literature of the Yukon Territory of Canada. The first volume, published in 1973, was an update for 1963-1970 and formed a companion volume to James R. Lotz's *Yukon bibliography* (Ottawa: Department of Northern Affairs and National Resources, 1964. 155p). It has been updated at intervals subsequently, the most recent being for 1983 (published 1986). The listings, which are on a computer database, include books, government reports, theses, periodical articles and certain unpublished material.

Alaska

General

720 **Alaska: the complete travel book.**
Norma Spring.   London: Collier-Macmillan, 1970. 248p.
An introduction for the intending visitor based on the author's extensive travel in the state. Chapters cover general information on the country, including, for example, its people, towns and cities, weather and clothing, with a chapter on the Arctic.

721 **Here is Alaska.**
Evelyn Stefansson.   New York: Charles Scribner's Sons, 1973. 3rd ed. 178p. map.
A short popular introduction to the state, based largely on the author's travels, with an account of its development since the 1950s and the discoveries of vast oil and gas reserves in the far north.

722 **Alaska.**
Anchorage, Alaska: Alaska Publishing Properties, 1940- . monthly.
A popular magazine covering all aspects of life in Alaska with emphasis on the history of the state and the 'great outdoors'.

Geography

723 **Glacier Bay, icy wilderness.**
Alaska Geographic, vol. 15, no. 1 (1988), 103p. map. bibliog.
A popular, profusely-illustrated, account of Glacier Bay National Park and Preserve, which encloses Glacier Bay itself and is bounded by the Gulf of Alaska on its seaward edge. Individual sections cover minerals, ice ages and glaciers, exploration, marine environment and wildlife, transportation and tourist information.

724 **Mt. McKinley; the pioneer climbs.**
Terris Moore. College, Alaska: University of Alaska Press, 1967. 202p. maps. bibliog.
Offers a history of Alaska's highest mountain with a documentary account of the pioneer climbs to 1932, together with a glossary of mountaineering terms and a note on Dr Frederick Cook's claim to have conquered the peak in 1906.

725 **Dictionary of Alaska place names.**
David J. Orth. Washington, DC: US Government Printing Office, 1967. 1,084p. maps. bibliog. (Geological Survey Professional Paper, 567).
This is an alphabetical list of the geographic names that are now applied, and have been applied, to places and features of the Alaskan landscape. Each entry provides the application and location of a place-name together with the history and the meaning of the name. Also given is a number reference to the US Geological Survey's 1:250,000 scale quadrangle map on which the name is shown.

726 **Notes on the islands of the Unalaska District.**
Ivan Veniaminov. Edited by Richard A. Pierce, Richard A. Fairbanks. Kingston, Ontario: Limestone, 1984. 511p. maps. (Alaska History, 27).
A reprint of the original 1840 edition, containing geographical descriptions of the Aleutian Islands and details of flora, fauna and native peoples.

727 **Alaska Geographic.**
Anchorage, Alaska: Alaska Geographic Society, 1975- . quarterly.
This journal is issued on subscription to the Alaska Geographic Society. Each number, published in album-style format with lavish colour illustrations and maps, is devoted to some special aspect of Alaskan geography, such as a national park, natural history, native peoples or information for travellers.

Flora and fauna

728 A guide to the birds of Alaska.
Robert H. Armstrong.   Anchorage, Alaska: Alaska Northwest
Publishing, 1981. 309p. map. bibliog.

This book was designed to aid the identification of the 386 species of birds in Alaska
(as at 25 June 1979). The book relies on colour photographs or paintings as a means of
identification, along with the status and distribution of each bird.

729 Wild Alaska.
Dale Brown.   New York: Time Life, 1976. 184p. maps. bibliog. (The
American Wilderness).

A well-informed, splendidly-illustrated travelogue on Alaska, based on the author's
extensive travels from the southeastern 'Panhandle' to the northern Brooks Range.
The text is especially informative on the natural history of the region.

730 Flora of Alaska and neighbouring territories. A manual of the vascular plants.
Eric Hultén.   Stanford, California: Stanford University Press, 1968.
1,008p. maps. bibliog.

A monumental work by a pre-eminent authority on arctic flora, and a comprehensive
botanic manual for this region based on more than forty years of study. The book
describes and illustrates some 1,974 taxa belonging to 1,559 species which occur in
Alaska, the Yukon, District of Mackenzie and the eastern extremity of Siberia. For
1,735 of these, detailed descriptions, nomenclature, plant drawings and range maps are
provided. An introduction describes the background natural history of the area.

731 A naturalist in Alaska.
Adolph Murie.   New York: Devin-Adair, 1961. 302p.

Presents an account of the larger mammals of Alaska – grizzly bear, wolf, lynx,
wolverine, Dall sheep, caribou and arctic fox – and their interrelationships. The author
is a field biologist serving with the US National Park Service.

732 The mosses of arctic Alaska.
William Campbell Steere.   Vaduz, Liechtenstein: J. Cramer, 1978.
508p. map. bibliog.

This definitive work is based on the author's extensive field work as the first bryologist
to set foot in Alaska. The volume consists of a description of the arctic environment,
followed by an account of the physiographic provinces. Six floristic elements are then
considered and summarized. An account of the commonness and abundance of arctic
Alaskan mosses is followed by a gazetteer of collecting localities.

733 **Anderson's flora of Alaska and adjacent parts of Canada.**
Stanley L. Welsh.   Provo, Utah: Brigham Young University Press,
1974. 724p.

This volume of flora owes its inspiration to the late Dr J. P. Anderson. It covers all of
Alaska, the Yukon and adjacent British Columbia. It attempts to bring together
current information on the indigenous and common cultivated plants of Alaska and the
Yukon. The presentation differs from traditional floras in that the treatment is in
alphabetical order by families, genera and species with only the major categories being
in phylogenetic order.

734 **A flora of the Alaskan Arctic slope.**
Ira L. Wiggins, John Hunter Thomas.   Toronto: University of Toronto
Press, 1962. 425p. maps. bibliog. (Arctic Institute of North America
Special Publication, no. 4).

This book provides a full coverage of the classification of the flowering plants, ferns
and fern-allies growing naturally on the northern slopes of the Brooks Range and the
tundra between that range and the Arctic Ocean within the State of Alaska. The book
is chiefly intended to provide assistance for biologists active in the region.

Prehistory and archaeology

735 **Nunamiut ethnoarchaeology.**
Lewis R. Binford.   New York: Academic, 1978. 509p. maps. bibliog.

A simultaneous description of the subsistence practices of the Nunamiut Eskimo of
Anaktuvuk Pass, Brooks Range, north Alaska, in both behavioural and archaeological
terms. The focus is on hunting and the attendant techniques of procurement, storage
and consumption of food. The book claims to be a unique description of a group of big
game hunters designed to elucidate the archaeological remains generated during the
course of their annual round of activities.

736 **The archaeology of Cape Nome, Alaska.**
John R. Bockstoce.   Philadelphia: University of Pennsylvania, 1979.
132p. maps. bibliog. (University Museum Monograph, 38).

This is an account of the author's archaeological excavations at Cape Nome, Seward
Peninsula, Alaska. The first part of the monograph deals with previous archaeological
work in the Bering Strait region and Cape Nome. The relevant aspects of the Cape
Nome area are discussed and then the excavations and the archaeological findings are
described in detail. With this as background, the cultural changes that took place near
Bering Strait, based on the evidence from Cape Nome, are explained and the author's
theories presented. Finally, a brief assessment of the present state of archaeological
knowledge of the Bering Strait region is made.

737 **Koniag prehistory; archaeological investigations at late prehistoric sites on Kodiak Island, Alaska.**
Donald Woodforde Clark. Stuttgart: Verlag W. Kohlhammer, 1974.
271p. maps. bibliog. (Tübinger Monographien zur Urgeschichte, Bd. 1).

Kodiak Island lies southeast of the Alaskan Peninsula along the western side of the Gulf of Alaska. This report describes part of the archaeological work undertaken by the University of Wisconsin Department of Anthropology and Zoology on the native culture at, and shortly preceding, the time of historical contact. An introductory chapter contains a succinct historical and geographical summary of the region including remarks on the native inhabitants and the archaeology of the island.

738 **Koniag-Pacific Eskimo bibliography.**
Donald W. Clark. Ottawa: National Museums of Canada, 1975. 97p.
map. (National Museum of Man Mercury Series. Archaeological Survey of Canada Paper, no. 35).

Presents approximately 500 published and manuscript sources, of which two-fifths relate to anthropological and ethnohistorical topics. The Pacific Eskimos here include the Koniag of Kodiak Island, Alaska, and the adjacent mainland; the Chugach of Prince William Sound; and the Eskimos of the intervening Kenai Peninsula–outer Cook Inlet area. The bibliography further focuses on the Koniag, their Kodiak Island habitat, and the history of the Kodiak Island region.

739 **The archaeology of Cook Inlet, Alaska.**
Frederica de Laguna. Anchorage, Alaska: Alaska Historical Society, 1975. 2nd ed. 264p. maps. bibliog.

The objective of the author's research was to determine the antiquity of the presence of Tanaina Athabascan Indians in Cook Inlet, southwest Alaska, and to investigate the possibility that they had been preceded on these shores by early Eskimo cultures. The basic achievement of this monograph has been the definition and preliminary periodization of a long-lived Eskimo cultural tradition in the area. This report is supplemented by a concluding chapter by Bruno Oetteking on 'Skeletal material from Cook Inlet and Prince William Sound'.

740 **The Eskimos and Aleuts.**
Don E. Dumond. London: Thames & Hudson, 1977. 180p. maps.
bibliog.

The author regards the region between Bering Strait on the north and the Aleutian Islands and Alaska Peninsula on the south, where the majority of the Eskimos and their cousins the Aleuts live, as the key to the prehistory of these peoples. This region, which displays a surprisingly homogeneous culture has, the author feels, been neglected by prehistorians and the aim of this book is to redress the balance. By marshalling the latest evidence, the author attempts to answer such questions as: when did the ancestral Eskimo-Aleuts arrive in the New World? How were they able to colonize these inhospitable regions? What accounts for the mixture of cultural diversity and homogeneity among their descendants?

741 **The archaeology of Cape Denbigh.**
J. L. Giddings. Providence, Rhode Island: Brown University Press, 1964. 331p. maps. bibliog.

A detailed analysis of the author's archaeological excavations on the Alaskan coast of the Bering Sea, 1948-52, concerned with the origins and identity of the Eskimos. The book reports in detail, for the first time, on the remains of three prehistoric cultures, commenting on the kind of natural resources in the regions available for each culture and their exploitation in the light of these artefactual remains. The monograph is illustrated with seventy-three plates and numerous line drawings.

742 **The anthropology of Kodiak Island.**
Aleš Hrdlička. Philadelphia: Wister Institute of Anatomy and Biology, 1944. 486p. maps. bibliog.

This monograph presents the author's final seven-and-a-half season's work on the physical anthropology and archaeology of Kodiak Island and the neighbouring mainland, and their natives, the Koniag and pre-Koniag populations.

History

General

743 **The battle for Alaska statehood.**
Ernest Gruening. College, Alaska: University of Alaska Press; Seattle; London: University of Washington Press, 1967. 122p.

This history of Alaska, by a leading Alaskan politician and governor of the former Territory of Alaska, traces in outline the fight to achieve statehood for Alaska. This was finally obtained in 1958, when the Territory became the 49th State of the USA.

744 **The State of Alaska.**
Ernest Gruening. New York: Random House, 1954. 606p. maps. bibliog.

Represents a standard history of the former Territory of Alaska, by a one-time governor, politican and journalist. The history traces the early Russian period in outline, but concentrates mainly on the American period, commencing with a chapter entitled 'The era of total neglect' (1867-1884), and concluding with 'The era of growing awareness' (1933-1954) covering the New Deal and the war years. Final chapters discuss land rights, native claims, economics, transportation and 'Self-government: the quest for statehood' – not, of course, achieved until after the publication of the book.

745 **The Americanization of Alaska, 1867-1897.**
Ted C. Hinckley. Palo Alto, California: Pacific Books, 1967. 285p.
map. bibliog.

This is a review of the background of the sale of Alaska by Russia to the United States.
The author goes on to show how, despite parallels with the pioneer occupation of the
trans-Mississippi West, the settlement of Alaska was different. After 1867 this
settlement was borne northward by sea rather than wagon train and was motivated
more by speculation in mining than by settled farming. Until the government and the
pioneers came to appreciate Alaska's uniqueness her growth was impeded. By the end
of the third decade of settlement southeastern Alaska was beginning to display a
semblance of law and order.

746 **An interpretative history of Alaskan statehood.**
Claus-M. Naske. Anchorage, Alaska: Alaska Northwest Publishing,
1973. 192p. bibliog.

A re-examination of Ernest Gruening's theme, published in *The battle for Alaska
statehood* (q.v.). The author covers the early history of the region, to its incorporation
as a Territory in 1912, and then traces the attempts to achieve statehood which only
entered its 'populist' stage after World War II when the Federal Government suddenly
realized Alaska's strategic importance. Eventually, statehood was achieved in 1958,
but this was due chiefly to pressure from Alaskans themselves.

747 **Discovery in Russian and Siberian waters.**
L. H. Neatby. Athens, Ohio: Ohio University Press, 1973. 226p.
bibliog.

A history of exploration in the Russian Arctic, covering 400 years. In the 16th century
most voyages to this region were made by the English and Dutch in an attempt to open
up trade with Muskovy and find a Northeast Passage to China. In the 18th century the
Russian Imperial Government sent Bering to Alaska and Kamchatka and instigated
the exploration of northern Siberia. Later, Cook and Wrangell surveyed in Bering
Strait. From 1870 onwards adventurers of all nations penetrated into the Russian
Arctic culminating in Nansen's drift in *Fram*. Dr Neatby's history concludes
with chapters covering Andrée's balloon flight, the voyage of the Duke of Abruzzi
(1899-1900), Anthony Fiala's 'Ziegler' expedition to Franz Josef Land (1903-04), and
the North Polar flights of Nobile and Amundsen in the 1920s.

748 **The Alaska boundary dispute: a critical reappraisal.**
Norman Penlington. Toronto: McGraw-Hill, Ryerson, 1972. 141p.
maps. bibliog. (The Frontenac Library).

An investigation into Canada's reaction to the Alaska boundary problem in which
Great Britain, Canada and the USA were involved and the solution of which was
decided in 1903. The author challenges the generally accepted view that Canada did
not deserve the 'humiliation' of the boundary settlement and sets out, using maps and
other evidence, to show that the Canadians were responsible for their own
predicament.

749 **Archives of the Russian Orthodox Church in Alaska.**
Antoinette Shalkop. In: *Arctica 1978: 7th Northern libraries colloquy 19-23 September 1978.* Edited by Sylvie Devers. Paris: Editions du Centre National de la Récherche Scientifique, 1982, p. 287-91. bibliog.
A brief review of the history of Russian church documents left behind in Alaska after the sale to the USA in 1867, and of microfilming achieved by the Alaskan State Library in Juneau.

750 **Alaska and its history.**
Edited by Morgan B. Sherwood. Seattle; London: University of Washington Press, 1967. 475p. maps. bibliog.
An anthology of scholarly articles covering the history of Alaska, selected from various journals and books, all by experts in various fields. The chronological selection is representative only and attempts to cover as many important topics as possible.

Voyages and expeditions

751 **Where the sea breaks its back; the epic story of a pioneer naturalist and the discovery of Alaska.**
Corey Ford. London: Victor Gollancz, 1967. 206p. bibliog.
The author, himself a naturalist, accompanied the Alaska Game Commission's cruiser *Brown Bear* on a cruise of the Aleutian Islands in 1941. This account of the great German naturalist, Wihelm Georg Steller, who accompanied Vitus Bering's second voyage in 1741-42, is retold, inspired by the author's own experiences in this region. The source used is principally F. A. Golder's edition of Bering's voyages (q.v.).

752 **A history of the Russian-American Company.**
P. A. Tikhmenev. Translated and edited by Richard A. Pierce and Alton S. Donnelly. Seattle; London: University of Washington Press, 1978. 522p. maps.
The Russian-American Company was chartered by the Russian government in 1799 to conduct monopoly trading in the Aleutians and Alaska, and played a major role in the affairs of the North Pacific during the following half century. The original Russian text of this classic work was written at company behest, a few years before the sale of Alaska to the USA and the liquidation of the company.

753 **Russian round-the-world voyages, 1803-1849, with a summary of later voyages to 1867.**
N. A. Ivashintsov. Translated by Glynn R. Barrett. Edited by Richard A. Pierce. Kingston, Ontario: Limestone, 1980. 156p.
(Material for the Study of Alaska History, no. 14).
This book, the Russian original of which was published in St. Petersburg in 1848 and 1849, was written by a distinguished hydrographer and naval historian for the guidance of Russian naval officers. During the early 19th century there were many Russian voyages made between European Russia and points in the Pacific, usually involving

Russian-America (now Alaska). These voyages were often of scientific importance and, as a major factor in the development and maintenance of the Russian colonies, form an essential part of the history of the European colonization of North America.

754 **Exploration of Alaska 1865-1900.**
Morgan B. Sherwood. New Haven, Connecticut; London: Yale University Press, 1965. 207p. maps. bibliog. (Yale Western Americana Series, 7).
A history of United States government explorations in Alaska in the second half of the 19th century, beginning with the Russian American Telegraph Expedition, of 1865, and ending with the Harriman Alaska Expedition of 1899.

755 **Compilation of narratives of explorations in Alaska.**
US Senate. Committee on Military Affairs. Washington, DC: Government Printing Office, 1900. 856p. maps.
This compilation is, basically, a report to the United States Senate on the extent to which what was then the Territory of Alaska had been explored by the US Army, with the long-term view of opening up the country and developing its resources. The report embraces in narrative form an account of fifteen expeditions between 1869 and 1899, all controlled by the Army, and constitutes a remarkable historical documentary record of Alaska's history.

756 **Looking far north; the Harriman expedition to Alaska 1899.**
William H. Goetzmann, Kay Sloan. Princeton, New Jersey: Princeton University Press, 1982. 244p. bibliog.
An account of the wealthy publisher Edward H. Harriman's expedition to Alaska on the ship *George W. Elder* in 1899. The expedition, which boasted all the trappings of a luxury cruise, produced important scientific results, Harriman subsidizing some thirteen volumes of reports contributed by the twenty-five scientists on the ship's complement. The results themselves are summarized in a concluding chapter.

Alaska purchase

757 **The annexation of Russian America to the United States.**
Victor J. Farrar. New York: Russell & Russell, 1966. 142p. bibliog.
An account of the purchase of Alaska from Russia by the United States using Russian archive material in the archives of the US Department of State. A concluding chapter 'Why did the United States purchase Alaska?' concludes that the question is still unanswered.

758 **The Alaska purchase and Russian-American relations.**
Ronald J. Jensen. Seattle; London: University of Washington Press, 1975. 185p. map. bibliog.
A comprehensive study of Russian-American relations during the period of the Alaska Purchase in the 1860s, providing an explanation of the agreement and its role in the

history of the two countries. The author re-examines the course of the negotiations in the context of Russian-American commercial expansion and, using public records, provides a candid view of the personalities of the chief negotiators themselves.

Gold rush

759 **Life on the Yukon 1865-1867.**
George R. Adams.   Edited by Richard A. Pierce. Kingston, Ontario: Limestone, 1982. 219p. maps. bibliog. (Alaska History, no. 22. Western Union Telegraph Expedition, 1).
An autobiographical sketch and account of the author's adventures as a member of the Western Union Telegraph Expedition to the Yukon in 1865-67. The sketch, written over half a century after the 'account' complements the details lacking in the latter. The expedition itself was part of an ambitious project to link North America with Siberia, via Bering Strait, with an overland telegraphy. However, the completion of an Atlantic telegraph brought an end to this particular project resulting in considerable financial loss, to some extent compensated for by the valuable scientific work accomplished, and the drawing of the attention of the United States to the economic potential of Alaska.

760 **Klondike, the last great gold rush 1896-1899.**
Pierre Berton.   Toronto: McClelland & Stewart, 1972. 2nd ed. 472p. maps. bibliog.
The story of the Klondike gold rush forms what the author describes as a 'gaudy interlude between the two epic tales of post-Confederation western development – the building of the railway and the mass settlement of the plains'. This is a highly-readable account of an extraordinary episode in the history of the American Northwest with emphasis on the heroes and villians involved.

761 **Sourdough sagas: the journals, memoirs, tales and recollections of the earliest Alaskan gold miners, 1883-1923.**
Edited by Herbert L. Heller.   Cleveland, New York: World Publishing, 1967. 273p. map.
A selection of contemporary accounts by the gold seekers and adventurers who made their way north to Alaska in the days of the gold rush.

Peoples

762 **Raven's journey; the world of Alaska's native people.**
J. Barsness.   Philadelphia: University of Pennsylvania, University Museum, 1986. 208p. maps. bibliog.
This volume is based on a cultural exhibition held at the University of Pennsylvania Museum. Lavishly-illustrated, its aim is to examine the physical, social and spiritual

adaptation of the late 19th, early 20th century Alaskan Eskimo, along with the Athabaskan and Tlingit Indians. The lifestyle of these people is also examined by placing ethnographic objects in the cultural contexts in which they were made and used.

763 **Eskimo kinsmen; changing family relationships in northwest Alaska.**
Ernest S. Burch, Jr. St. Paul, Minnesota: West Publishing, 1975.
352p. maps. bibliog.

A study of kinship and social change among the Eskimo in the area of Alaska west and north of the Yukon drainage, encompassing an area of some 150,000 square miles, and including the entire domain of the Inupik-speaking Eskimos. The research is based on field work spanning the years 1960-70 and claims to reconstruct the kinship system as it existed in 1850.

764 **The central Yupik Eskimos.**
Inuit Studies, vol. 8, Supplementary Issue (1984), 218p. map. bibliog.

Brings together ten papers representing current research on ethnological and linguistic research aspects of the Yupik Eskimos of southwestern Alaska. Includes an introductory chapter by Ernest S. Burch, Jr., who defines the term 'Yupik' and outlines the nature of ethnographical research on these people since the early 19th century.

765 **Eskimo medicine man.**
Otto George. [Portland, Oregon]: Oregon Historical Society, 1979.
109p. map.

This is a record of the author's life as a 'travelling physician' in the remote areas of Alaska during the 1930s. The book deals with the Eskimos of the Bering Sea, along the Arctic Ocean, the areas of the Kuskokwin rivershed and the lower Yukon.

766 **An Eskimo village in the modern world.**
Charles Campbell Hughes, Jane M. Hughes. Ithaca, New York:
Cornell University Press, 1960. 419p. maps. bibliog.

A study of the Yupik-speaking Eskimo community of Gambell, St. Lawrence Island, in the Aleutian chain, carried out in 1954. It was a follow-up of an earlier study in 1940, since when many changes had taken place. This scholarly study in anthropology covers the history, population statistics, morbidity and mortality, diet, occupations, housing and institutions of these people. A glossary of Eskimo terms is appended.

767 **Eskimos of northwestern Alaska; a biological perspective.**
Edited by Paul L. Jamison, Stephen L. Zegura, Frederick A.
Milan. Stroudsburg, Pennsylvania: Dowden, Hutchinson & Ross,
1978. 319p. bibliog. (US/IBP Synthesis Series, vol. 8).

Offers twenty-two contributions by specialist authors, relating to biological variation in the Eskimos of northwest Alaska. The articles are interdisciplinary and include demography, morphology, biochemistry, biomedical parameters, nutrition, physiology, genetics and behaviour. The investigations reported took place as part of the Human Adaptability component of the International Biological Program (IBP).

768   **Aleuts in transition; a comparison of two villages.**
Dorothy M. Jones.   Seattle; London: University of Washington Press
for the Institute of Social, Economic and Government Research,
University of Alaska, 1976. 125p. bibliog.
A study of the Aleut people, considering their adjustment to contact with the western
world. The author's research centred on two villages on the Alaska Peninsula, Iliaka
and New Harbor, the latter a remote fishing village and the former, on the island of
Bright Bay, displaying 'jolting contrasts' between the old style of life and the new
western model. The study is prefaced by an outline of Aleut history.

769   **Alaska native culture and history. Papers presented at the second
international symposium National Museum of Ethnology, Osaka, August
1978.**
Edited by Yoshinobu Kotani, William B. Workman.   Osaka, Japan:
National Museum of Ethnology, 1980. 321p. maps. bibliog. (Senri
Ethnological Studies, no. 4).
A collection of papers in the fields of Alaskan ethnology and anthropology including a
review of Alaskan studies by Japanese anthropologists.

770   **Ethnohistory in southwestern Alaska and the southern Yukon; method
and content.**
Edited by Margaret Lantis.   Lexington: University Press of Kentucky,
1970. 311p. maps. bibliog. (Studies in Anthropology, 7).
Five contributions by well-known anthropologists relating to the Aleuts, the Indians
and the Eskimos of southwestern Alaska (especially those of the interior) and the
Indians living on the boundary of the Yukon Territory and British Columbia. In the
first part the authors seek to reconstruct the early contacts between these peoples and
western civilization, from the points of view of archaeology, archival history and folk
history. The second part studies the effect of conquest on the non-material culture of
the Aleuts.

771   **Aleuts, survivors of the Bering land bridge.**
William S. Laughlin.   New York: Holt, Rinehart & Winston, 1980.
151p. map. bibliog. (Case Studies in Cultural Anthropology).
This book is based on the author's many visits to, and field work on, Umnak Island in
the Aleutian chain. Physically, linguistically, culturally and geographically the Aleuts
are a highly distinct people. These characteristics are considered in separate chapters
dealing with environment, hunting, village life, whaling, language, the Russian
influence, and modern life in an ancient village.

772   **Lost heritage of Alaska; the adventure and art of the Alaskan coastal
Indians.**
Polly Miller, Leon Gordon Miller.   New York: Bonanza, 1967. 289p.
map. bibliog.
This plentifully-illustrated volume describes the arts and history of Alaska's Tlingit and
Haida Indians. The authors have made use of quotations from contemporary explorers'

narratives to evoke the European reaction to the native artefacts at a period when Indian artistic culture was most flourishing. With the advent of Alaska's acquisition by the USA this flourishing culture was to become a lost heritage.

773 **Ethnohistory in the Arctic; the Bering Strait Eskimo.**
Dorothy Jean Ray. Edited by R. A. Pierce. Kingston, Ontario: Limestone, 1983. 274p. maps. bibliog.

A collection of articles complementing Dorothy Ray's earlier works in this field including pieces on the first Russian contacts with the native peoples, such as an account of the Vasil'ev-Shishmarev expedition to the Arctic of 1819-22 and a translation of V. N. Berkh's account of the expedition. Other articles deal with, for example, the introduction of firearms to Alaska, land tenure and polity of the Bering Strait Eskimos and Eskimo place-names.

774 **The Eskimos of Bering Strait, 1650-1898.**
Dorothy Jean Ray. Seattle; London: University of Washington Press, 1975. 305p. maps. bibliog.

A description and analysis of the changes that took place in the culture of the Eskimos of the Seward Peninsula region of northern Alaska from 1650-1898, from the first reports received in Siberia about Alaskan Eskimos to the time of the Gold Rush. This study concentrates on archaeological and contemporary problems and relies on the primary materials, Russian and American archival documents, teachers' and missionaries' writings, and the author's own field work.

775 **Alaskan Eskimos.**
Wendell H. Oswalt. San Francisco: Chandler, 1967. 297p. maps. bibliog.

This monograph, by a leading anthropologist and ethnographer, describes the Alaskan Eskimos' way of life when they were first encountered by Europeans, excluding the Eskimos of St. Lawrence Island. The opening chapters provide background information on the people, their numbers and the country they occupy. Next, their linguistic affinities, cultural origins and prehistory are discussed. A third chapter discusses the Eskimos as biological beings, as viewed by anthropologists, pathologists and physiologists.

776 **Napaskiak; an Alaskan Eskimo community.**
Wendell H. Oswalt. Tucson, Arizona: University of Arizona Press, 1963. 178p. maps. bibliog.

An attempt to characterize Eskimo village life as it was in 1956 at this community of southwest Alaska. The opening chapter describes the physical environment and a history of contacts outside the settlement. This is followed by a description of a hypothetical family's household and activities during a winter's and a summer's day. The remainder of the text is an account of community society and culture. The final chapter focuses the textual information on the anthropological problems of classifying cultures and societies.

777 **The last of the few.**
Kaare Rodahl. New York: Harper & Row, 1963. 208p. map.
Dr Rodahl and his wife went to Alaska after World War II to develop a physiological laboratory, studying various problems relating to man in the Arctic, and to learn from the Eskimos how best to adapt to a cold environment. Here they describe their life among the still-primitive Eskimos whose culture they studied. Later they returned and observed the changes to the tribal lifestyle brought about by contact with the white man.

778 **Eskimos of the Nushagak River; an ethnographic history.**
James W. Van Stone. Seattle; London: University of Washington Press, 1967. 192p. maps. bibliog.
An attempt to understand Eskimo culture by making a study of the social and economic forces that have acted upon it. Part one of this monograph is an investigation into and an evaluation of how the Eskimos of the Nushagak River region of southwest Alaska have been affected by the arrival of Russian, European and American explorers, fur traders, missionaries and government agents. Part two reconstructs population groupings, settlement trends and the subsistence cycle of these Eskimos as it existed in the late 19th century. A concluding chapter deals with present-day life among these people.

Languages

779 **Yup'ik Eskimo dictionary.**
Compiled by Steven A. Jacobson. Fairbanks, Alaska: University of Alaska, Alaska Native Language Center, 1984. 757p. maps. bibliog.
A dictionary of the Central Yup'ik Eskimo language spoken in southwestern Alaska in the Yukon-Kuskokwin Delta and Bristol Bay areas, which includes dialects.

780 **Alaska native languages: a bibliographical catalogue. Part one: Indian languages.**
Michael E. Krauss, Mary Jane McGary. Fairbanks, Alaska: University of Alaska, Alaska Native Language Center, 1980. 455p.
A bibliography with abstracts of written materials at the library and archive of the Alaska Native Language Center, University of Alaska, a collection which is considered to be exhaustive. The bibliography includes, in addition, sections on Athabascan languages outside Alaska, and on Canadian and Greenlandic Eskimos.

781 **Alaska native languages: past, present and future.**
Michael E. Krauss. Fairbanks, Alaska: University of Alaska, Alaska Native Language Center, 1980. 110p. bibliog.
Alaska is the homeland of two great North American language families, the Eskimo-Aleut and Na-Dene, the former having spread to Canada and Greenland, the latter to Canada and the southwestern United States. The author's paper constitutes a brief

introduction to the subject, the prehistory, history, present status and future of all Alaska native languages. A second paper appended likewise deals with the future of the Alaskan native languages. A third paper deals specifically with the past, present and future of the Alaskan Eskimo languages.

782 **Abridged Iñupiaq and English dictionary.**
Edna Ahgeak MacLean. Fairbanks, Alaska: University of Alaska, Alaska Native Language Center; Barrow, Alaska: Iñupiat Language Commission, North Slope Borough, 1980. 168p. maps.
This dictionary of the North Slope, Alaska Eskimo language (Iñupiaq), focuses primarily on the dialect spoken in Barter Island, Nuiqsut, Barrow, Atqasuk, Wainwright and Point Lay.

783 **Yup'ik Eskimo grammar.**
Irene Reed. Osahito Miyaoka, Steven Jacobson, Paschal Afcan, Michael E. Krauss. Fairbanks, Alaska: University of Alaska, Alaska Native Language Center, Yup'ik Language Workshop, 1977. 330p. map. bibliog.
A grammar of the Yup'ik Eskimo language spoken in the area of western Alaska. Although there are several dialects within this area, Yup'ik is a single language. Alternative vocabulary words are given throughout and the phonology, morphology and syntax are fairly uniform in all the dialects. The grammar is intended as the basis of a two-year college course serving the needs of speakers and non-speakers alike.

784 **English-Eskimo and Eskimo-English vocabularies.**
Roger Wells, John W. Kelly. New York: AMS, 1975. 72p.
A reprint of the 1890 edition published by the US Government Printing Office, Washington, DC and issued as 'circular of information, no. 2' of the US Bureau of Education. Containing 11,318 words, it was intended for the use of teachers as well as government officials and the military in the then Territory of Alaska.

785 **Russian language resources in the Elmer E. Rasmuson Library collections, University of Alaska, Fairbanks.**
Eugene C. West, Tamara Lincoln. In: *Northern libraries colloquy. Proceedings of the eleventh Northern Library Colloquy, Sweden, June 9-12.* Edited by Terje Höiseth, Ann-Christine Haupt. Luleå, Sweden: CENTEC, [1986], p. 41-50.
A description of the Russian subject and language resources in monographic titles in the Rasmuson Library, which is the largest single collection of publications dealing with Alaska.

Missions

786 **A history of the Orthodox Church in Alaska (1794-1917).**
Gregory Afonsky (Bishop). Kodiak, Alaska: St. Herman's
Theological Seminary, 1977. 105p. maps. bibliog.
A study of the Russian Orthodox Church in Alaska, presenting a detailed picture of
the implantation and growth of Orthodox Christianity in America, from the discovery
of Alaska in the early 1700s until the Russian revolution of 1917.

787 **St. Innocent apostle to America.**
Paul D. Garrett. Crestwood, New York: St. Vladimir's Seminary,
1979. 345p.
A life of this priest of the Orthodox Church, who came from Siberia to America in
1823 to evangelize the native Aleut people and subsequently became Bishop in
America and Asia, spending his last years as Metropolitan of Moscow. This biography
makes good use of original correspondence and provides a first-hand account of this
remote region of Russian America and its people.

788 **Alaska and missions of the north Pacific coast.**
Sheldon Jackson. New York: Dodd, Mead, 1880. 400p. map.
A contemporary description, by a leading Presbyterian minister and educator of his
time, of Alaska and its people in the years immediately after the Alaska Purchase from
Russia in 1867, with particular emphasis on the author's efforts to promote religious
instruction and education in the Territory.

789 **Alaskan apostle; the life story of Sheldon Jackson.**
J. Arthur Lazell. New York: Harper & Brothers, 1960. 218p. maps.
An account of the Presbyterian Church missionary and educator who went to Alaska in
1877 and encountered enormous opposition to his attempts to introduce law and order,
schools and justice into this lawless frontier region.

790 **The Russian orthodox religious mission in America, 1794-1837 with
materials concerning the life and works of the monk German, and
ethnographic notes by the hieromonk Gedeon.**
Translated by Colin Bearne, edited by Richard A. Pierce. Kingston,
Ontario: Limestone, 1978. 186p. maps.
This volume, prefaced by three chapters relating to the Russian-American territories,
is a study of the Aleuts and Kokiaks from a religious and moral point of view, as well
as a short history of the Kokiak Mission 1794-1837. The latter history is devoted
principally to reproducing, in two appendixes, translated contemporary correspondence relating to the history of the missionary Father German (Herman) and an account
of Kokiak peoples and their way of life.

Social conditions

791 **Village journey; the report of the Alaska Native Review Commission.**
Thomas R. Berger. New York: Hill & Wang, 1985. 202p. map.

In July 1983 Judge Berger was appointed by the Inuit Circumpolar Conference, an international organization of Eskimos from Alaska, Canada and Greenland, to conduct the Alaska Native Review Commission to review the Alaska Native Claims Settlement Act of 1971. This task took the author to native villages all over Alaska to hear evidence from the Eskimos, Indians and Aleuts. In this book Judge Berger endeavours to put their point of view. Specific topics covered include the subsistence way of life, land use, native sovereignty and the author's final recommendations.

792 **The Alaska Native Claims Settlement Act: conflict and controversy.**
Monica E. Thomas. *Polar Record*, vol. 23, no. 142 (Jan. 1986), p. 27-36. bibliog.

All pending land claims by Alaska natives were extinguished by the Alaska Native Claims Settlement Act of 1971 marking the culmination of over 100 years of expressed Federal concern for the protection of aboriginal land rights in this region. This paper discusses the major events leading to the passage of the act, its key provisions and the major controversies and conflicts facing Alaska natives through the next two decades as a result of the legislation.

Politics and government

793 **Alaska blue book 1985.**
Edited by Scott Foster. Juneau, Alaska: Department of Education, Division of State Libraries, 1985. 7th ed. 329p. map.

A biennial publication listing current statistical, biographical, historical and general information on all aspects of Alaska state government, constitution, and so on.

794 **Alaska state government and politics.**
Edited by Gerald A. McBeath, Thomas A. Morehouse. Fairbanks, Alaska: University of Alaska Press, 357p. maps.

A comprehensive textbook dealing with the state government and politics of Alaska, including its history, structure and authority, public opinion, interest groups and the press. Individual chapters are contributed by a legislator and eleven academics under three main headings: Environment of government in Alaska; Process of Alaska politics; and State government institutions.

795 **Alaska's urban and rural governments.**
T. A. Morehouse, G. A. McBeath, L. Leask. Lanham: University
Press of America, 1984. 261p. bibliog.
A book full of useful and relevant information, derived from both published sources
and personal interviews, concerning the unique system of local government peculiar to
arctic and subarctic territory, where the principal revenue is from oil fields.

796 **Alaska Review of Social and Economic Conditions.**
Anchorage, Alaska: Institute of Social and Economic Research, 1964- .
quarterly.
A periodical featuring well-researched articles on Alaska's social, economic and
political processes. Specific topics covered in recent issues include the effects of
Alaska's economic recession on Anchorage households and Alaska housing and the
recession.

Economic resources and development

797 **Alaska planning information.**
Alaska Department of Labor. Juneau, Alaska: Alaska Department of
Labor, 1985. 105p. maps.
A review of statistical data relating to population, labour and economics in Alaska.

798 **Klondike '70; the Alaskan oil boom.**
Daniel Jack Chasan. New York: Praeger, 1971. 184p.
A journalist's account of Atlantic Richfield Oil Company's great strike on the North
Slope of Alaska in March 1968 which also contains his views on its consequences for
the Alaskan economy and the likely effects on the native people. The early controversy
over the pipeline from Prudhoe to Valdez is also discussed.

799 **Alaskan oil; alternative routes and markets.**
Charles J. Cicchetti. Baltimore, Maryland; London: Johns Hopkins
University Press for Resources for the Future, 1972. 142p. maps.
Presents a well-researched cost-benefit analysis of the Trans-Alaska Pipeline, and some
alternative pipeline routes.

800 **The regulatory aspects of offshore petroleum activity in the Alaska
Beaufort Sea and industry viewpoint.**
Roger C. Herrera. In: *POAC 79; the fifth international conference on
port and ocean engineering . . . vol. 1.* Trondheim, Norway: University
of Trondheim, 1979, p. 449-65. map.
A brief history of oil and gas exploration and development on the North Slope of
Alaska is followed by a factual account of the regulatory procedures involved. The

author concludes that the dialogue that these procedures cause among government, the industry and local people is likely to achieve more than the actual regulations themselves.

801   **Issues in Alaska development.**
       David T. Kresge, Thomas A. Morehouse, George W.
       Rogers.   Seattle; London: University of Washington Press, 1977. 223p.
       maps.
On the assumption that Alaska will continue to play a crucial role in meeting the United States' demands for energy, the studies in this volume explore the social and economic problems that this development will pose. The crucial issue is 'how and to what extent should Alaska's growth be moderated and directed?' This is a difficult problem because of the various interest groups involved – federal and state government, native regional corporations, multinational oil companies, labour unions and local environmental organizations. This volume reports the first major results to come out of the 'Man in the Arctic Program' (MAP), a long-range programme of Alaskan economic and population growth policy analysis.

802   **Development of petroleum reserves in arctic Alaska.**
       Robert E. Smith.   *Cold regions Science and Technology*, vol. 7 (special
       issue), 1983, p. 195-99.
A review of the development of petroleum reserves in arctic Alaska covering the period from 1969, immediately following the discovery of the Prudhoe Bay oil field, through to present activities. Fiscal and technical aspects are described.

803   **Alaska Economic Trends.**
       Alaska Department of Labor, Employment Security Division, [1980]- .
       monthly.
A bulletin of surveys and statistics relating to employment and earnings in the state of Alaska. Short articles deal with such topics as fisheries, the timber industry, the economy, the cost of living, household income and the labour force.

Fisheries and agriculture

804   **The Gulf of Alaska, physical environment and biological resources.**
       Edited by Donald W. Hood, Steven T. Zimmerman.   Washington,
       DC: Superintendent of Documents for Alaska Office, Ocean
       Assessments Division, National Oceanic and Atmospheric
       Administration, 1986. 655p. bibliog.
This volume, consisting of chapters by specialists, constitutes the most current and comprehensive account of the physical and biological environment of the Gulf of Alaska. The chapters are arranged under the following headings: (1) Introduction (physical setting and scientific history); (2) Physical environment; (3) Biological resources; and (4) Issues and perspectives (environmental issues).

805 **Alaska fisheries policy; economics, resources and management.**
Edited by Arlon R. Tussing, Thomas A. Morehouse, James D.
Babb, Jr. Fairbanks, Alaska: Institute of Social, Economic and
Government Research, University of Alaska, 1972. 470p. maps. (ISEG
Report, no. 33).

Fisheries policy making and management are a fundamental responsibility of the
Alaska State government. It is the most labour-intensive of the basic commodity-
producing industries in Alaska and its management most immediately and directly
affects the lives of rural Alaskans. This report on Alaska fisheries covers a broad range
of economic, biological, legal, political and administrative issues under the following
headings: (1) Fisheries economics; (2) Fish stocks; (3) Commercial fisheries; (4)
Fisheries law; (5) Fisheries management; and (6) Marine education (in Alaska).

806 **Agricultural development in Alaska.**
Carol E. Lewis, Roger W. Pearson, Wayne C. Thomas. *Polar Record*,
vol. 23, no. 147 (Sept. 1987), p. 673-82, map. bibliog.

The article identifies four stages of agricultural activity in Alaska during the past 200
years. During the period from first Russian, and later American colonization in the
late 1880s, production was largely for personal consumption. From 1898 to World War
II Federal intervention stimulated local commercial agriculture, and from the late
1940s to the late 1960s commercial production expanded. Since then a state-supported
strategy to develop an export-based agriculture has been tried, but implementation has
not been completed. Alaska has yet to find a workable manner in which to implement
a strategy for agriculture.

Transport

807 **The Alaska Highway: a personal account of the building of the Alaska
Highway.**
Phyllis Lee Brebner. Erin, Ontario: Boston Mills, 1985. 80p.

Presents an illustrated history of the building of the highway, in 1942, from Dawson
Creek to Fairbanks.

808 **Rough road to the north; travels along the Alaska Highway.**
Jim Christy. Toronto: Doubleday Canada; Garden City, New York:
Doubleday, 1980. 197p. map.

An account of this 1,532-mile-long road from Dawson Creek, British Columbia to
Fairbanks, Alaska, covering its construction, the country along its route and characters
encountered.

809 **The Alaska Highway: papers of the 40th anniversary symposium.**
Edited by Kenneth Coates.   Vancouver: University of British
Columbia Press, 1985. 208p. maps.

The papers read to this symposium include descriptions of the construction of the
highway and its significance in the sphere of Canadian-American relations, military
history and the evolution of northern society.

810 **The Alaska railroad.**
Edwin M. Fitch.   New York: Frederick A. Praeger, 1967. 326p. maps.
bibliog.

A history of what was then the federally owned railway running from Seward and
Whittier on the south coast of the Kenai Peninsula, through Anchorage and on to
Fairbanks, a distance of 175 miles. The railway is famous for its scenic route, including
Mount McKinley. This study explores the railroad's history, physical operation and
significance as a government agency, and its effect on the opening up of the interior
'railbelt'.

Environment

811 **Alaska; a challenge in conservation.**
Richard A. Cooley.   Madison, Wisconsin: University of Wisconsin
Press, 1967. 170p. maps. bibliog.

The author, a resource economist, here presents, in layman's language, the problems
and issues facing the people of Alaska in moulding their economic future. He
considers, in terms of modern theories of land management, the mistakes of the past.
He anticipates the conflict that will arise between the need for immediate revenue and
the need for long-term conservation of natural resources. Paramount is the need for
informed planning and development of the total environment for the sustained
prosperity of both the land and the people.

Education

812 **Cross cultural issues in Alaskan education.**
Edited by Ray Barnhardt.   Fairbanks, Alaska: University of Alaska,
Center for Cross-cultural Studies, 1977, 1982. 2 vols.

Chapters in educational theory and practice are contributed by experts. The issues
discussed arise out of the coming together of two different cultural systems, one
reflected in the western institutional structure of the school, and the other in the fabric
of life in Alaskan native communities. The articles in this collection provide many new
insights into the processes underlying cross-cultural education.

813 **Tannik School; the impact of education on the Eskimos of Anaktuvuk Pass.**
Michael S. Cline. Anchorage, Alaska: Alaska Methodist University Press, 1975. 210p. map. bibliog.
A case study by a professional teacher, with experience in Alaska bush schools, which examines the impact of formal education upon the native community of this school at Anaktuvuk Pass, northern Alaska. The first section of the book describes how Nunamiut Eskimos came to settle in the locality. The second section tells how the school came to the Nunamiut, how the teacher is affected by the community and how the community views the school's efforts. Finally, the author analyses the impact of the school on the Nunamiut and suggests how it might better meet their needs.

Science

814 **Alaska Science Conference Proceedings.**
Fairbanks, Alaska. American Association for the Advancement of Science, 1950- . irregular.
The proceedings of this conference (approximately annual), usually in abstract form, cover a broad range of topics in the physical and natural sciences in the context of Alaska, as well as such topics as ecology, land utilization, hydrocarbon exploration and energy conservation.

The arts

815 **Eskimo art; tradition and innovation in north Alaska.**
Dorothy Jean Ray. Seattle; London: University of Washington Press for the Henry Art Gallery, 1977. 298p. bibliog.
The first comprehensive description, analysis and interpretation of all the Eskimo arts and crafts of northern Alaska from the Saint Michael area to the Alaska-Canada border. The arts discussed date from the beginning of the historic record in the late-18th century, with certain themes and forms traced to earlier cultures. The book is illustrated with over 300 photographs of objects discussed in the text. The author's research is based on anthropological field sessions in Alaska between 1950 and 1974.

816 **Eskimo masks. Art and ceremony.**
Dorothy Jean Ray. Seattle; London: University of Washington Press, 1967. 246p. bibliog.
The text is divided into two parts: first there is an analysis and synthesis of all aspects of Alaskan Eskimo life relative to masks, particularly on the interpretation of the mask in ceremonial and religious life; and second, there is a descriptive catalogue of each mask illustrated.

817 **Aleut and Eskimo art; tradition and innovation in south Alaska.**
Dorothy Jean Ray. London: C. Hurst, 1981. 251p. bibliog.
This volume complements the author's earlier work on Eskimo art in north Alaska
(q.v.) and deals with the decorative and sculptural arts of the Eskimo living south of
Saint Michael, Alaska, including the Aleut, Yupik and Pacific Eskimos, from the time
of the first European contact to 1979. The volume is divided into two parts: (1) a
discussion and interpretation of traditional market art; and (2) illustrations of artefacts
with descriptive captions.

Maps

818 **Alaskan maps; a cartobibliography of Alaska to 1900.**
Marvin W. Falk. New York; London: Garland, 1983. 245p. maps.
bibliog. (Garland Reference Library of the Humanities, vol. 409).
A bibliography of published maps of Alaska, including manuscript maps published in
facsimile, up to the year 1900. Citations include (1) an identifying number; (2) the map
title and map maker; (3) the place and date of publication; (4) the size of the map; (5)
where the map appeared, if part of a book or atlas; (6) a reference to one of the major
authorities cited; (7) a citation to where the map has been produced; and (8) comments
on the map. The bibliography is prefaced by a brief history of Alaskan cartography.

Bibliographies

819 **Bibliography of books on Alaska published before 1868.**
Valerian Lada-Mocarski. New Haven; London: Yale University
Press, 1969. 567p.
This listing is devoted primarily to first editions of books on Alaska published before
the end of the Russian period in 1867, and is the first attempt at a chronological,
annotated and critical listing of publications in all major languages. The sequence is
chronological with an index of authors. Detailed paginations and collations with
facsimilies of the title-pages of over 160 books are offered, together with English
translations of Russian titles.

820 **Alaska, a bibliography 1570-1970.**
Compiled by Elsie A. Tourville. Boston, Massachusetts: G. K. Hall,
1974. 738p.
Presents an alphabetical author listing of titles of books and pamphlets, including
native language material, with a classified index.

821 **Documenting Alaskan history; guide to federal archives relating to Alaska.**
George S. Ulibarri.   Fairbanks, Alaska: University of Alaska Press, 1982. 296p.

A comprehensive bibliography of the major record groups, series and subseries of records in the United States National Archives, Washington, DC, pertaining to Alaska. The material is listed under the following headings: aquisition of Alaska; industries and trade; natural resources; land and public buildings; the governing of Alaska and activities of government agencies; fiscal matters; conservation; transportation and communications; people; and military, naval and maritime activities. Appendixes include motion pictures, maps and a selected list of Government Printing Office publications relating to Alaska.

822 **A bibliography of Alaskan literature 1724-1924.**
James Wickersham.   Fairbanks, Alaska: Alaska Agricultural College and School of Mines, 1927. 635p. (Miscellaneous Publications, vol. 1).

Represents a pioneer compilation in the field, containing a title list of some 7,000 books of history, travels, voyages, newspapers, periodicals and public documents in English, Russian, German, French and Spanish.

Soviet Arctic – Siberia

General

823 **Russian settlement in the North.**
Terence Armstrong. Cambridge, England: Cambridge University Press, 1965. 224p. maps. bibliog.

An examination, by a leading Soviet expert, of the causes and effects of Russian settlement of the arctic and subarctic regions, from their first appearance there until 1959. The author examines the causes and effects of their settlement and compares the solutions to some of the problems with those made in arctic North America. After introductory chapters on the area and the early Russian settlers, the book divides into two parts, on the periods before and after 1917. In each, the author discusses the numbers of settlers, the character of the settlement, government policy and foreign influences, and relations with the native peoples.

824 **The Russians in the Arctic; aspects of Soviet exploration and exploitation of the Far North, 1937-57.**
Terence Armstrong. London: Methuen, 1958. 182p. maps. bibliog.

Makes an attempt to estimate the Soviet Union's achievements in the development of her northern regions. Some chapters are concerned with geographical exploration (such as the drift of the *Sedov*) others with exploitation (for example a chapter on the Northern Sea Route) or with the impact on the primitive tribes of northern Siberia of Soviet advance into the Arctic. Finally, there is a chapter on the archaeological finds on the Taymyr Peninsula and the study of a mammoth corpse. The author is a leading British specialist on the Soviet Arctic.

825 **One chilly Siberian morning.**
Douglas Botting. London: Travel Book Club, 1965. 192p. map.

A popular account of a film-making visit to the USSR which included a journey to Yakutia and Kolyma on the shores of the Arctic Ocean.

826 **Architecture of the Russian north 12th-19th centuries.**
B. Fiodorov.   Leningrad: Aurora Art, 1976. 216p. map. bibliog.
This pictorial survey is preceded by a brief architectural history of the cathedrals,
churches, domestic buildings (wooden and stone), and castles in the region to the south
of the White Sea, bounded by Lake Ladoga on the west and Sukhona, Vychegda and
Mezen rivers on the east.

827 **Sibir; my discovery of Siberia.**
Farley Mowat.   Toronto; Montreal: McClelland & Stewart, 1970.
313p. maps.
The author's impressions of the Soviet north are based on extensive travels in 1966 and
1969. Mowat, an experienced traveller in the Canadian Arctic, was able to make many
interesting comparisons. The principle arctic regions visited were Yakutiya and
Chukotka.

828 **Through Siberia the land of the future.**
Fridtjof Nansen.   Translated by Arthur G. Chater. London: William
Heinemann, 1914. 478p. map.
Presents the narrative of the author's visit to Siberia in 1913, made with the intention
of opening up a regular trade connection with the interior of Siberia via the Kara Sea
and the mouth of the Yenisei river, the Siberian Company having been formed for this
purpose by Jonas Lied. At this period of its history the vast resources of Siberia were
largely untapped. All depended on the opening of a regular navigation route through
the icebound waters of what is known today as the Northern Sea Route. The book tells
of Nansen's journey eastwards from Tromsø, Norway, through an open Kara Sea,
eventually reaching the Yenisei river, contacts being made with the native Samoyeds.
A journey was then made up-river, again meeting with the native Yenisei-Ostiak
people, until eventually Krasnoyarsk was reached. The journey finally ended at
Vladivostok, by way of Irkutsk and Lake Baikal.

829 **The land beyond the mountains; Siberia and its peoples today.**
Leonid Shinkarev.   London: Hart-Davis, 1973. 246p. map. bibliog.
The author, a graduate of Gorky State University, has worked and travelled for fifteen
years in Siberia. In this book he reviews Siberia's history from pre-revolutionary times
to the present day, and then discusses contemporary Siberia in terms of its economic
potential and indigenous peoples.

830 **The Soviet Far East; questions and answers.**
Moscow: Novosti Press Agency, 1985. 62p. map.
An illustrated pocket guide to the Soviet Far East, a region of enormous natural
resources whose northeastern regions border the Arctic Ocean. The book is of the
'question and answer' kind which aims to answer 'the most frequently asked questions'
about the region.

831 **The Soviet North.**
Translated from the Russian by David Sinclair-Loutit. Moscow:
Progress Publishers, 1977. 259p.
A collection of literary and scientific articles reflecting the contemporary Soviet Arctic,
ranging from geological prospecting in the Yamal-Nenets National Area of Siberia to
place-names problems in the Arctic.

832 **Sibériana.**
Paris: Centre d'Éudes Arctiques, 1983- . occasional.
A French language journal devoted to translations from Russian language journal
articles relating to Siberia, and covering such fields as the earth sciences,
anthropogeography and natural resources.

Geography

833 **Climates of the U.S.S.R.**
A. A. Borisov. Edited by Cyril A. Halstead. Edinburgh; London:
Oliver & Boyd, 1965. 255p. maps. bibliog.
A translation of the second Russian edition of *Klimatiy SSSR* (Moscow, 1959), a
widely-used textbook and work of reference in the Soviet Union. In the context of this
bibliography the third section of the book, devoted to the climatic regions of the
USSR, probably has the most relevance. This deals with the climates of the northern
seas and eastern seas, the climate of the tundra and that of the mountainous areas.

834 **Diverting Soviet rivers: some possible repercussions for the Arctic
Ocean.**
Howard Cattle. *Polar Record*, vol. 22, no. 140 (May 1985), p. 485-98,
maps. bibliog.
Plans exist in the USSR to divert the southward part of the flow of some Russian and
Siberian rivers, notably the northern Dvina, Pechora, Ob' and Yenisei to alleviate
water shortages in central Asia, Kazakhstan and the Ukraine and to counter falling
water levels in the Aral and Caspian seas. The possible effects of diverting small and
large amounts of river water away from the Arctic are discussed in the light of recent
observations and modelling studies of Arctic Basin hydrology and sea ice distribution.
Current evidence suggests that the small diversions planned to operate before the end
of this century will have little effect on ocean circulation or sea ice distribution.

835 **Geography of the U.S.S.R.**
Paul E. Lydolph. New York: John Wiley, 1977. 3rd ed. maps. bibliog.
A regional geography based on the official Soviet economic regions used for the
purposes of planning and statistical reporting. Each region is discussed in terms of such
things as landform, climate, historical perspectives and ethnology. The whole text is
complemented by the author's *Geography of the U.S.S.R.; topical analysis.* (q.v.).

836 **Geography of the U.S.S.R.; topical analysis.**
Paul E. Lydolph. Elkhart Lake, Wisconsin: Misty Valley, 1979. 522p.
map. bibliog.

An analysis of the Soviet Union, topic by topic, designed as a companion volume to
the author's *Geography of the U.S.S.R.* (q.v.). Topics discussed include territorial
organization, geology, climate, natural vegetation and soils, populations, general
economy, energy, metallurgy and chemicals, manufacturing, fishing, forestry and furs,
water resources and transformation of nature, transportation and domestic trade,
prospects for regional development and international relations.

837 **Geology of the U.S.S.R.**
D. V. Nalivkin. Translated by N. Rast, edited by N. Rast, T. S.
Westoll. Edinburgh: Oliver & Boyd, 1973. 855p. bibliog. maps.

Originally published in 1962 (Moscow; Leningrad: Academy of Sciences) this standard
reference book is described by the publisher as 'the first comprehensive general
account of the geology of the U.S.S.R. ever published'. The editor's preface
summarizes the main advances in the Russian geological sciences to date. The text
includes a section on the western Arctic (p. 380-99). Information on the eastern Arctic
will be found in a section on the Pacific Ocean geosyncline (p. 708-850).

838 **An introduction to town planning and related matters in the Soviet**
North: based upon information collected during the exchange visit by a
Canadian delegation to the Soviet Union – September 25th to October
7th 1977.
Walter Slipchenko, Larry Elkin. Yellowknife, Northwest Territories:
Government of the Northwest Territories, Department of Local
Government, 1980. 426p. maps.

This very comprehensive report is based on the Canadian delegation's discussions with
officials and experts in Moscow and Leningrad and in the Siberian cities of Tyumen
and Nizhnevartovsk. The object of the visit was to identify areas for mutually
beneficial exchanges of information on, for example, architecture, construction and
building materials, the oil and gas and other industries, and transportation. Themes
covered by working groups included methods of planning and development of
populated areas in the Far North, development of municipal services, design and
construction of man-made structures, and construction in low-temperature conditions,
earthmoving operations in permafrost conditions and design and construction of sea
and river ports.

839 **Physical geography of Asiatic Russia.**
S. P. Suslov. Translated by N. D. Gershevsky, edited by Joseph E.
Williams. San Francisco; London: W. H. Freeman, 1961. 549p. bibliog.
maps.

A comprehensive and informative textbook, intended for senior geography students,
which suffers from various defects in translation. The first three parts deal with Siberia,
the last with central Asia. There is a separate chapter in part two covering the arctic
region of eastern Siberia including the adjacent seas and islands, but relevant
information, on permafrost, and the freezing of rivers, for example, will be found in
other chapters.

Soviet Arctic – Siberia. Flora and fauna

840 **The Soviet Union, a systematic geography.**
Leslie Symon, J. C. Dewdney, D. J. M. Hooson, R. E. H. Mellor,
W. W. Newey. London: Hodder & Stoughton, 1983. 266p. maps.
bibliog.
A concise, clearly-written, well-illustrated and up-to-date introduction to the Soviet Union offering contributions by a number of specialists. Following a chapter dealing with the evolution of the Russian state, there are sections on physiography, climate, biogeography, population, agriculture, minerals, fuel and power resources, industry, urban and rural settlement, transport, and a concluding chapter covering the various regions.

Flora and fauna

841 **Vegetation of the Soviet polar deserts.**
V. D. Aleksandrova. Translated by D. Löve. Cambridge, England:
Cambridge University Press, 1988. 228p. maps. bibliog. (Studies in
Polar Research).
A detailed description, by an eminent Soviet botanist, of the arctic polar deserts, focusing primarily on the Barents and Siberian provinces, and concentrating on the work of Soviet scientists. This constitutes the first comprehensive account in English translation of the plants and vegetation of the Soviet arctic polar deserts north of the Eurasian landmass. Also included is an account of the flowering plants of Zemlya Frantsa Iosifa (Franz Josef Land).

Prehistory and archaeology

842 **Prehistory of western Siberia.**
V. N. Chernetsov, W. Moszyńska. Edited by Henry N. Michael.
Montreal; London: McGill-Queen's University Press for the Arctic
Institute of North America, 1974. 377p. maps. bibliog. (Arctic Institute
of North America Anthropology of the North: Translations from
Russian Sources, no. 9).
A selection of major articles in the fields of the archaeology, anthropology and ethnology of Siberian northern native peoples, which were originally published between 1953 and 1961. The peoples most often mentioned are the Khanty and Mansi.

210

843 **The archaeology and geomorphology of northern Asia: selected works.**
Edited by Henry N. Michael. Toronto: University of Toronto Press
for the Arctic Institute of North America, 1964. 512p. maps. bibliog.
(Arctic Institute of North America Anthropology of the North:
Translations from Russian Sources, no. 5).

Offers translations of various articles from the Soviet literature dealing with the
archaeology and Pleistocene geomorphology of northern Asia. Archaeological sites
discussed are situated in the Lena River basin, the upper Amur River, Kamchatka and
the Chukchi Peninsula.

844 **Yakutiya before its incorporation into the Russian state.**
A. P. Okladnikov. Edited by Henry N. Michael. Montreal; London:
McGill-Queen's University Press for the Arctic Institute of North
America, 1970. 499p. maps. bibliog. (Arctic Institute of North America
Anthropology of the North: Translations from Russian Sources, no. 8).

Presents a translation from the Russian of the author's definitive work on the
prehistory and early history of the present Yakut USSR. It discusses the origins and
patterns of life of the Yakuts until their incorporation into the Russian state in the 17th
century. Part one is devoted to the distant past of the aboriginal tribes of Yakutia and
their life in the Stone Age. Part two presents the Yakuts in the 'Age of Metal'. Part
three shows how these nomadic tribes became a nation and describes this nation's
cultural and linguistic traditions.

845 **The ancient culture of the Bering Sea and the Eskimo problem.**
S. I. Rudenko. Translated by Paul Tolstoy. Toronto: University of
Toronto Press for the Arctic Institute of North America, 1961. 186p.
maps. bibliog. (Arctic Institute of North America Anthropology of the
North: Translations from Russian Sources, no. 1).

A translation of the Russian original published in 1947, also including thirty-eight
plates. This fundamental contribution to Eskimo archaeology contains the results of
the author's work in the Chukchi Peninsula, Bering Strait region of the USSR and
makes a significant contribution to the clarification of how man came to settle in the
Arctic and of the various ethnic relationships there.

History

General

846 **To Siberia and Russian America; three centuries of Russian eastward expansion. Vol. 1. Russia's conquest of Siberia 1558-1700: a documentary record.**
Edited and translated by Basil Dmytryshyn, E. A. P. Crownhart-Vaughan, Thomas Vaughan. Portland, Oregon: Western Imprints, Oregon Historical Society Press, 1985. 540p. bibliog.
The early history of the conquest of Siberia told at first-hand through 133 edited and translated contemporary documents taken from many sources held in Russian archives.

847 **To Siberia and Russian America: three centuries of Russian eastward expansion. Vol. 2. Russian penetration of the North Pacific Ocean 1700-1797.**
Edited and translated by Basil Dmytryshyn, E. A. P. Crownhart-Vaughan, Thomas Vaughan. Portland, Oregon: Western Imprints, Oregon Historical Society Press, 1988. 557p. maps. bibliog.
A translation of eighty-six contemporary Russian documents, including reports of trader-explorers and imperial captains in the North Pacific during the 18th century.

848 **Siberia, its conquest and development.**
Yuri Semyonov. Translated from the German by J. R. Foster. London: Hollis & Carter, 1963. 400p. maps. bibliog.
A general introductory history of Siberia, translated from the German edition *Sibirien* (1954). Chapter four deals with the voyages of Bering and chapter seven with the sale of Alaska to the USA.

849 **Russia, Siberia and Great Tartary.**
Philip John von Strahlenberg. New York: Arno and New York Times, 1970. 463p.
A reprint of *An historico-geographical description of the north and eastern parts of Europe and Asia, but more particularly of Russia, Siberia and Great Tartary . . .* (London, 1738), which itself was a translation from the original German edition of 1730. The author was a Swede who, with the Prussian naturalist Messerschmidt, explored the lower basin of the Ob and Yenesei river systems. His map of northern Asia served for a long time as the chief guide to this region.

Voyages and expeditions

850 **The voyage of Semen Dezhnev in 1648: Bering's precursor with selected documents.**
Raymond H. Fisher.   London: Hakluyt Society, 1981. 326p. maps. bibliog. (Hakluyt Society, Second Series, no. 159).

Dezhnev, an illiterate Siberian cosack, was the leader of a party of entrepreneurs who, in the summer of 1648, sailed round the eastern tip of Asia from the Kolyma River, which empties into the Arctic Ocean, reaching a point south of the Anadyr River, which empties into the Pacific Ocean; he thus anticipated Bering's voyage eighty years later. This volume consists of thirty-four selected documents relating to the voyage, together with a discussion of some of the questions raised by it, plus an expanded commentary. Advantage has been taken of the most recent Soviet research in this field.

851 **Bering's expeditions.**
Terence Armstrong.   In: *Studies in Russian historical geography vol. 1.* Edited by James H. Bater, R. A. French.   London: Academic Press, 1983, p. 175-95, maps. bibliog.

This essay views the scope and effectiveness of Bering's two expeditions between 1725 and 1743 in the light of the large amount of research done in Soviet archives in recent years. Here the major emphasis is placed on the Siberian exploration, but outlining the Pacific voyages for the sake of balance and to indicate new material.

852 **Bering's voyages: the reports from Russia.**
Gerhard Friedrich Müller.   Edited and translated by C. Urness.
Fairbanks, Alaska: University of Alaska Press, 1986. 221p. bibliog.
(Rasmuson Library Historical Translation Series, 111).

This translation of Bering's voyages (1725-43), published originally in 1758, is the third to appear in English, the other two being published in 1761 and 1764; these, however, were incomplete. The object of this edition is to fill the gaps and to bring out the way in which Müller used his contemporary sources.

853 **Bering's voyages; whither and why.**
Raymond H. Fisher.   London: C. Hurst, 1977. 217p. maps. bibliog.

Basing his research on a re-examination and a re-translation of some of the source material, including the results of recent Russian research, Fisher sets out in this scholarly book to reinterpret the purpose of Vitus Bering's two voyages of 1728-30 and 1749-41. His thesis maintains that the objective of Peter the Great was not to determine whether Asia and America were joined. The purpose of the first expedition, he suggests, was to find a trade route to America; that of the second expedition was definitely to establish sovereignty in North America, or off-lying islands, and to exploit resources. Thus, by extension, talk of Bering's expeditions as the first great scientific exploration of the 18th century is possibly misplaced.

854 **Bering's voyages; an account of the efforts of the Russians to determine the relation of Asia and America. Vol. 1. The log books and official reports of the first and second expeditions 1725-1730 and 1733-1742. With a chart of the second voyage by Ellsworth P. Bertholf.**
F. A. Golder. New York: American Geographical Society, 1922.
371p. maps. bibliog. (American Geographical Society Research Series, no. 1).

A scholarly account, based on the log books and reports of the Russian navigators, of Vitus Bering's expeditions of 1728-30 and 1733-43, which led to the discovery of Bering Strait, the charting of the Arctic coast of Asia from the White Sea to the Kolyma River, and the North Pacific coast of America from Cape Addington to Bering Island. The index to this work is in volume two (q.v.).

855 **Exploration of Kamchatka; North Pacific scimitar. Report of a journey made to explore eastern Siberia in 1735-41, by order of the Russian Imperial Government.**
Stepan Petrovich Krasheninnikov. Translated with an introduction and notes by E. A. P. Crownhart-Vaughan. Portland, Oregon: Oregon Historical Society Press, 1972. 375p. maps. bibliog.

Offers the first complete and unabridged translation of *Opisaniye zemli Kamchatki* (Description of the land of Kamchatka) (St. Petersburg, 1755). The author, a young scientist on Vitus Bering's second expedition, travelled for three years throughout remote Kamchatka observing the natives and describing their religions, myths, beliefs, customs and language. He also collected specimens of animal and plant life and experimented with agriculture.

856 **Bering's voyages; an account of the efforts of the Russians to determine the relation of Asia and America. Vol. 2. Steller's journal of the sea voyage from Kamchatka to America and return on the second expedition 1741-1742. Translated and in part annotated by Leonhard Stejneger.**
F. A. Golder. New York: American Geographical Society, 1925.
291p. maps. bibliog. (American Geographical Society Research Series, no. 2).

This volume constitutes an account of Bering's second voyage and his visit to Kamchatka in 1741-42. Georg Wilhelm Steller, a German, was the first trained naturalist in the North Pacific. He was an indefatigable explorer and perceptive observer of the native peoples and wildlife. His discoveries in America and Bering Island were to earn him eternal fame. This is the first complete translation into English of his journal. It is prefaced by a biographical note on Steller.

857 **New lands within the Arctic Circle; narrative of the discoveries of the Austrian ship 'Tegetthof' in the years 1872-1874.**
Julius Payer. London: Macmillan, 1876. 2 vols. map.

A translation, with some changes, of the German language edition (Vienna: A. Hölder, 1876). This is the narrative of an Austro-Hungarian expedition in 1872-74, led by Julius Payer and Karl Weyprecht, to explore the Russian Arctic north of Novaya Zemlya, with an account of the *Tegetthof*'s drift in the Barents Sea, the discovery and exploration of Franz Josef Land (Zemlya Frantsa-Iosifa) and the expedition's return by small boat across the Barents Sea to Novaya Zemlya. Included is a great deal of scientific information relating to meteorology, sea ice, aurora as well as the techniques of polar travel and survival.

858 **The voyage of the Vega round Asia and Europe with a historical review of previous journeys along the north coast of the Old World.**
A. E. Nordenskiöld. Translated by Alexander Leslie. London: Macmillan, 1881. 2 vols. maps.

A translation of the Swedish edition (Stockholm: F. & G. Beijer, [1880-81]), offering the narrative of the *Vega* expedition, 1878-1880, led by Nordenskiöld to prove the navigability of the Northeast Passage by steamship. The *Vega* left Sweden in June 1878, passed Cape Chelyuskin on 19 August and was forced by ice conditions to winter at Pitlekay on the north coast of the Chukotsk Peninsula, where scientific work was carried out. In June 1879 the voyage was continued through Bering Strait to Yokohama, Japan, and thence home via China and the Suez Canal. It was the first expedition to complete the through navigation of the present-day Northern Sea Route. Much anthropological work was carried out among the native Samoyeds, Chukchi and Eskimos of northeast Siberia.

859 **A thousand days in the Arctic.**
Frederick G. Jackson. London; New York: Harper & Brothers, 1899. 2 vols. maps.

This is the leader's official narrative of the Jackson-Harmsworth expedition, 1894-97, to Franz Josef Land, an archipelago in the Arctic Ocean. The expedition's headquarters were established at Cape Flora, from which sledge journeys were made to carry out scientific investigations (summarized in the appendixes). The author's journal records the daily course of events and describes in detail such things as weather, ice conditions, food and health. Also described is the famous meeting with Fridtjof Nansen and his companion F. H. Johansen who passed through the camp from the *Fram* expedition described by Nansen in '*Farthest north*' . . . (q.v.)

860 **Charting the Russian Northern Sea Route; the Arctic Ocean hydrographic expedition 1910-1915.**
L. M. Starokadomskiy. Translated and edited by William Barr. Montreal; London: McGill-Queen's University Press for the Arctic Institute of North America, 1976. 332p. maps. bibliog.

This expedition was the first modern attempt to survey arctic waters north of Siberia, five voyages being made by the Imperial Russian Navy icebreakers *Taymyr* and *Vaygach* in as many years; all were wholly successful. An east-west traverse was completed from the Bering Sea to the White Sea and the way was prepared for the subsequent development of the Northern Sea Route as a vital communications artery. This account is based on the author's diaries (he served as medical officer on the *Taymyr*), ships' logs and other writings.

861 **The adventure of Wrangel Island.**
Vilhjalmur Stefansson. New York: Macmillan, 1925. 424p. map.
This well-documented history of a remote Arctic island tells how the Canadian polar explorer Vilhjalmur Stefansson attempted to claim it for the British Empire by organizing a small occupation expedition, consisting of four young white men and one Eskimo woman, to visit it in 1921. The idea was that they should remain there long enough for Stefansson to persuade the British government to assert a claim. Despite long negotiations, no such claim was made. In 1923 a relief expedition was despatched from Alaska which made the dramatic discovery that only the Eskimo woman was alive, the men having perished, some in an attempt to reach the Siberian mainland. The book, with its numerous extracts from diaries and various appendixes, constitutes an apologia. The expedition had the effect of stimulating the interest of the Soviet government which hastened to assert and put into effect its own claim in 1924, a claim which has not since been disputed.

862 **Life on an icefloe.**
Ivan Papanin (et al). Translated from the Russian by Fanny Smitham. London: Hutchinson, [1947]. 240p. map.
A personal account of the purpose, work and personnel of the scientific drifting station 'North Pole' by the leaders of the group (I. D. Papanin, P. P. Shirshov, E. K. Fedorov and E. T. Krenkel) between 1937-38. The expedition was landed by air on an ice floe in the region of the North Pole on 21 May 1937. Papanin kept a full diary of events on which this book is based. A total of 274 days was spent drifting to the south of the Greenland Sea. Papanin's expedition contributed much new scientific data about the central Arctic Ocean, the nature of its currents, and the relief of the seabed. In February 1938 Papanin's party was taken off the ice floe by icebreakers sent by the Soviet government.

863 **Across the top of Russia.**
Richard Petrow. London: Hodder & Stoughton, 1968. 374p. maps.
Gives an account of the voyage of the United States Coast Guard icebreaker *Northwind* in the summer of 1965. Its mission was to test the right of free passage through the fabled Northeast Passage, the Soviet Union's Northern Sea Route, which, since the revolution, has been 'off limits' to all non-Soviet shipping. Eventually the mission was terminated on the orders of the State Department after harassment by the Russians.

Peoples

864 **Who are the 'northern peoples' of the USSR?**
Terence Armstrong. In: *Consequences of economic change in circumpolar regions*. Edited by L. Müller-Wille, H. J. Pelto, Linna Müller-Wille, Regna Darnell. Edmonton, Alberta: University of Alberta, Boreal Institute for Northern Studies, 1978, p. 21-27.
Makes an examination of the practical problem of interpreting what Soviet and other writers mean when they use the phrase 'the northern peoples of the USSR'.

865 **Present-day ethnic processes in the USSR.**
Translated by Campbell Creighton.   Moscow: Progress Publishers,
1982. 277p.
A monograph authored by a group of ethnographers which is primarily concerned with
changes in the cultural features specific to ethnic communities, including languages,
and in identity. The first part of the book examines research methodology, and
describes the ethnic situation processes in pre-revolutionary Russia; the second part
examines aspects of these processes focusing on changes in the material culture,
language, and intellectual life of the peoples of the USSR. The final section describes
the dynamics of ethnic changes, and summarizes the results of the research conducted.

866 **Aboriginal Siberia; a study in social anthropology.**
M. A. Czaplicka.   Oxford: Clarendon, 1969. 374p. map. bibliog.
A comprehensive and concise handbook on the social anthropology of the peoples of
Siberia. Part one is devoted to the geography and ethnology of the region; part two
discusses the social organization customs associated with birth, marriage, death and
future life; part three considers religion; and part four is concerned with pathology,
including the various nervous maladies associated with 'Arctic hysteria'.

867 **Popular beliefs and folklore tradition in Siberia.**
Edited by V. Diószegi.   Bloomington, Illinois: Indiana University; The
Hague: Mouton, 1968. 498p. map. bibliog. (Indiana University
Publications, Uralic and Altaic Series, vol. 57).
A collection of thirty-three specialized papers focusing on the problems of popular
beliefs among the Finno-Ugrian peoples of Siberia, and dealing with such questions as
shamanism, burial rites and totemism from the points of view of ethnography,
ethnology, folklore, linguistics, history and archaeology.

868 **Introduction to Soviet ethnography.**
Edited by Stephen P. Dunn, Ethel Dunn.   Berkeley, California:
Highgate Road Social Science Research Station, 1974. 2 vols. map.
bibliog.
A collection of essays translated from the Russian dealing with aspects of Soviet
ethnography and archaeology, with an introductory essay on 'The intellectual tradition
of Soviet ethnography'.

869 **The Samoyed peoples and languages.**
Péter Hajdú.   Bloomington, Illinois: Indiana University; The Hague:
Mouton, 1963. 114p. bibliog. (American Council of Learned Societies,
Research and Studies in Uralic and Altaic Languages, project no. 99).
A translation from the original Hungarian edition (Budapest, 1949), which is here
revised and updated. A study of the Samoyed people of the Arctic Ocean coast of
Siberia, it includes chapters on their distribution and habitat, physical anthropology,
customs, religion, folklore, history, foreign contacts, language and characteristics.

870 **Karl Marx collective: economy, society and religion in a Siberian collective farm.**
Caroline Humphrey. Cambridge, England: Cambridge University Press; Paris: Editions de la Maison des sciences et de l'homme, 1983. 322p. bibliog.

This book, though based on a study of the Buryat Mongols, a people living outside arctic Siberia, is important for all students of the native peoples of the Soviet Union. It is a very complete and important pioneer analysis of the economic and social bases of farm collectives in the region.

871 **The Yakut.**
Waldemar Jochelson. New York: American Museum of Natural History, 1933. 225p. map. (Anthropological Papers of the American Museum of Natural History, vol. 33, pt. 2).

This account of Yakutiya, in eastern Siberia, and its native peoples is based on expeditions made to the region by the author in 1884-94 and in 1900-02, as a member of the Jessup North Pacific expedition. The subject matter covers habitat, anthropology, language, calender, religion, family and kinship, material culture, art, festivals, leprosy and a history of contact with the Russians.

872 **The peoples of Siberia.**
Edited by M. G. Levin, L. P. Potapov. Chicago; London: University of Chicago Press, 1956. 948p. maps. bibliog.

Offers a translation of *Narodny Sibiri* (Moscow: Academy of Science, 1956). The book consists of a collection of specialist chapters, the first of which discusses the history of Siberia, its culture and anthropological types, together with an historical-ethnographic survey of the Russian population of Siberia in the pre-revolutionary period. The remainder of the volume is devoted to an account of the non-Russian native peoples of southern and northern Siberia and the Far East.

873 **Ethnic origins of the peoples of northeastern Asia.**
M. G. Levin. Edited by Henry N. Michael. Toronto: University of Toronto Press for the Arctic Institute of North America, 1963. 355p. maps. bibliog. (Arctic Institute of North America Anthropology of the North, Translations from Russian Sources, no. 3).

A translation of the original work which was published by the Academy of Sciences of the USSR in 1958, the author being a well-known and prolific writer in the field of anthropology. He has carried out a number of investigations among the Tungus people of northern Cis-Baykal, the Lamuts of the Okhotsk coast, the Yakuts of eastern Siberia and the Chukchi peninsula. These and other peoples are described here, and there is a separate chapter dealing with origins of the Eskimos.

874 **Among the tundra people.**
Harald U. Sverdrup. Translated by Molly Sverdrup. La Jolla,
California: Scripps Institution of Oceanography, 1978. 228p. map.
bibliog.
A translation of the author's *Hos tundra-folket* (Oslo: Gyldenal Norsk Forlag, 1938),
this being an account of the author's life among the primitive Reindeer Chukchi tribe
while a member of Roald Amundsen's *Maud* expeditions of 1918 and 1920-21. During
this time Sverdrup travelled with dog teams along the Chukchi peninsula, Bering
Strait, covering some 2,000 kms. and visiting every native settlement.

Languages

875 **The languages of the Soviet Union.**
Bernard Comrie. Cambridge, England: Cambridge University Press,
1981. 317p. map. bibliog.
This book has two main aims: firstly, to introduce the reader to some of the salient
linguistic features of the various languages and language-families of the USSR;
secondly, to give some indication of how the various languages of the USSR interact in
a multilingual society, especially of how they interact with Russian. The book is
principally concerned with structural features. The main groups discussed are the
Altaic, Uralic, Indo-European, Caucasian, Paleosiberian, and some other languages,
for example Chukotko-Kamchatkan, Eskimo-Aleut and Yukagir.

876 **National languages in the USSR: problems and solutions.**
M. I. Isayev. Moscow: Progress Publishers, 1977. 431p. map. bibliog.
The basic purpose of this book is to show how the Soviet Union has accumulated
exceptionally rich experience in solving the problems of its 130 national languages.
Each language follows its own laws of development, and accordingly the author has
found it appropriate to give a brief account of the evolution of each one.

877 **Multilingualism in the Soviet Union.**
E. Glyn Lewis. The Hague: Mouton, 1972. 332p. map. bibliog.
Few regions of the world have witnessed as much language planning as has the Soviet
Union in connection with a large and diversified set of speech communities and
languages. This book represents an attempt to present the major policies, socio-
linguistic practices and consequences that pertain to the Soviet Union. The author has
examined much linguistic, historical-demographic, chronological and educational data
in the course of this analysis.

878 **An appraisal of the importance of the national languages among the
north Siberian peoples.**
Poul Thoe Nielsen. *Folk*, vols. 14-15, (1972-73), p. 205-53, bibliog.
A review of some twenty-six small north Siberian peoples' groups numbering from 300
to 25,000 persons. Each people speaks its own language and several dialects of the

same language are often found. The development of the present written form is traced and the attitude of central government, particularly as regards school policies, is discussed. The paper contains a useful listing of the geographical and ethnical position of each group and there is discussion of, for example, national-language newspapers, broadcasts and textbooks.

879 **The status of national minority languages in Soviet education: an assessment of recent changes.**
Brian D. Silver. *Soviet Studies*, vol. 26, no. 1 (1974), p. 28-40.
The author concludes that Soviet policy envisages a diminishing use of the languages of many small minority peoples.

Economic resources and development

880 **Siberia, 65° east of Greenwich: oil and people.**
Compiled by Gennady Budnikov. Translated from the Russian by Valery Kryshkin. Moscow: Progress Publishers, 1985. 240p.
This is an account of the Tyumen region of western Siberia, a vast territory stretching from the Urals in the west to the Yenisei River in the east, and from the Arctic Ocean in the north to the Kazakh steppe in the south. It is a land fabulously rich in oil and gas reserves. Gas pipelines link Tyumen Oblast with western Europe. The book consists of contributions by several authors describing the region, its industries and the people who work there.

881 **USSR energy atlas.**
Central Intelligence Agency. Washington, DC: Superintendent of Documents, 1985. 79p. maps.
The exploration, in recent years, of the vast energy resources of Siberia and the Far East is transforming the economy of the Soviet North and has become a major international strategic issue. This atlas uses a wide variety of information, portrayed in maps, graphics, photographs and text, to illustrate many aspects of Soviet energy and to promote a general understanding of the major Soviet energy resources – oil, gas, coal and primary electricity as well as minor fuels and energy resources. The atlas is accompanied by a general map, a gazetteer and an index.

882 **Beyond the Urals; economic developments in Soviet Asia.**
Violet Conolly. London: Oxford University Press, 1967. 420p. bibliog.
An assessment, by a leading Russian specialist, of the economic resources of Asiatic Russia, their role in the Soviet economy and the nature and results of Soviet development plans for Siberia, the Far East and the central Asian republics, based very much on information from the Soviet metropolitan and regional press. The emphasis is on agricultural and industrial development rather than social services and

education. A concluding chapter assesses such topics as the role of Asiatic Russia in the Soviet economy, problems confronting the Soviet government and reactions to Soviet economic policies.

883 **The Soviet energy system: resource, use and policies.**
Leslie Dienes, Theodore Shabad. Washington, DC: V. H. Winston; New York: John Wiley, 1979. 298p. maps. bibliog.
Written by two leading specialists and based on Soviet sources this book is especially relevant to the economic development of present-day Siberia. The authors analyse the alternatives that Soviet planners face in meeting domestic needs and in exporting high-priced energy products as a source of revenue for the purchase of advanced technology from the West. The authors review Soviet supplies of fossil fuel, hydroelectric and nuclear power, and uranium mining centres. Of special relevance are the sections dealing with natural gas development in the Komi ASSR and Tyumen Oblast.

884 **Tapping Siberian wealth: the Urengoi experience.**
Genrick Gurkov, Valeriy Yevseyev. Moscow: Progress Publishers, 1984. 194p.
A popular account of the Urengoi gas field in the Tyumen region of the northern USSR, the source of 4,500 km long pipeling linking Siberia with western Europe. This is probably the costliest and most ambitious project of its kind, planned to develop the vast economic riches to Siberia.

885 **Siberia and the Soviet far east: strategic dimensions in multinational perspective.**
Edited by Rodger Swearingen. Stanford, California: Hoover Institution Press, 1987. 298p. bibliog.
A general review consisting of contributions by specialists whose overall theme is the 'guns for growth' trend of Siberian growth and its implications for regional security and potential trade relationships. The final chapter concerns resources for research on Siberia, listing bibliographies, journals, newspapers, institutes, libraries and publishing houses.

886 **Economics of the Soviet fishing industry. (Ekonomika rybnoi promyshlennosti SSSR).**
N. P. Sysoev. Translated by D. Daneman. Jerusalem: Israel Program for Scientific Translations, 1974. 386p. map. bibliog.
A comprehensive introduction to the economic aspects of the industry, including home and international waters, together with an account of the organizational structure of the administration of the Soviet fishing industry.

887 **The demand for energy in the Soviet Union.**
David Wilson. London; Canberra: Croom, Helm, Rowman & Allanheld, 1983. 310p. maps. bibliog.
The goals of this book are twofold; it undertakes to describe the demand side of the energy situation in the USSR, and then to offer a tentative scenario of the possible development of energy supply and demand to the end of the century. Separate

chapters cover each of the main sectors of energy demand – households and the municipal economy, electricity power industry, ferrous metals, construction materials, chemicals, oil refining, transport, agriculture and exports. It is a useful book for the generalist.

888 **Siberia: problems and prospects for regional development.**
    Edited by A. Wood. London: Croom Helm, 1987. 233p.

A selection of essays including a summary of economic resources and accounts of the oil and gas industry and the transport communications network. Special attention is paid to the newly-constructed Baykal-Amur railway. Subsequent contributions cover military and strategic factors, Siberia's relations with its Asian neighbours and the past and potential involvement of Siberia in the world economy.

889 **Soviet Economy.**
    Silver Spring, Maryland: V. H. Winston, in association with the Joint
    Committee on Soviet Studies of the American Council of Learned
    Societies and the Social Science Research Council, 1985- . quarterly.

The only English language journal devoted exclusively to research on the Soviet economy, economic geography and regional economic issues.

Labour camps

890 **Vorkuta.**
    Edward Buca. Translated from the Polish by Michael Lisinski,
    Kennedy Wells. London: Constable, 1976. 352p.

Edward Buca (pronounced 'Bootsa'), born in eastern Poland, spent a year in a Nazi concentration camp in World War II and after release joined an anti-Soviet movement. He was arrested by the Soviet secret police and sentenced to twenty years hard labour in the Subarctic at a labour camp complex called Vorkuta. In 1953 he organized a revolt against the appalling conditions there and, despite the bloodshed, succeeded in winning a better deal for thousands of Soviet prisoners. This is the story of the strike and of Buca's subsequent adventures leading to his escape to the West in 1971.

891 **Kolyma; the arctic death camps.**
    Robert Conquest. London: Macmillan, 1978. 256p. maps. bibliog.

A documentary account of the Kolyma labour camp in the Subarctic region of north east Siberia, from its earliest beginnings in 1932-33 to the rehabilitations which started to take place in 1954. In its earliest phase the main aim of the administration was to produce gold; in its later period the central aim was to cause the deaths of the prisoners by cold and hunger. This account is based on first-hand reports together with major analyses published in the West or in the Soviet press. The book concludes with an analysis of the deathroll.

892 **Kolyma tales.**
Varlam Shalamov.   Translated from the Russian by John Glad. New
York; London: W. W. Norton, 1980. 222p.

In 1937 Varlam Shalamov was arrested by the Soviet secret police and sent to the
Kolyma gold camps in northeastern Siberia where he spent seventeen years in exile.
He documented these years in a series of powerful stories of which these are a
selection grouped under such headings as 'Survival', 'Hope', 'Defiance', 'The criminal
world', 'The jailer's world', 'The American connection', and 'The release'.

Transport

893 **The Northern Sea Route today.**
Terence Armstrong.   *Cold Regions Science and Technology*, vol. 7
(1983), p. 251-57, map.

A reconstruction, based on limited Soviet published sources and the British
Broadcasting Corporation's *Summary of world broadcasts Part 1, USSR*, of the 1981
Northern Sea Route shipping season. The article includes a review of recent
operations, current uses for the route and future prospects. A list of icebreakers
operating on the route is included. Updates of this information are published regularly
in the journal *Polar Record* (q.v.).

894 **The northern sea route and the economy of the Soviet North.**
Constantine Krypton.   London: Methuen, 1956. 219p. bibliog.

An examination of the actual and potential economic role of the Northern Sea Route,
the seaway along the Arctic coast between Novaya Zemlya and the Bering Strait. In
addition to analysing its economic significance, the study attempts to assess the
strategic value of the route and of Soviet polar aviation in order to throw light on the
non-economic motives for Soviet work in the Arctic. There is much information here
on the industries associated with the region that are served by the sea route, and an
assessment of the navigation, equipment and facilities of the route.

895 **Aeroflot; Soviet air transport since 1923.**
Hugh MacDonald.   London: Putnam, 1975. 323p. maps.

A detailed account of the world's largest carrier of air passengers and cargo, relating
the Soviet air transport effort to the country's vast terrain, its climate and its economy,
and forming a useful (though by now dated) guide to air transport services in the far
north.

896 **The great Baikal-Amur railway.**
Compiled by V. I. Malashenko.   Moscow: Progress Publishers, 1977.
171p.

Gives accounts, in both poetry and prose and by various authors, of the planning and
early construction work on this ambitious attempt to open up the resources of north
eastern Siberia and the Pacific with a railway running to the north of the present
Transiberian Railway.

897 **Soviet merchant ships.**
Kenneth Mason. Homewell, Havant, England: The Author, 1980.
3rd ed. 224p.
A useful illustrated listing based on Loyd's *Register of Shipping* and other sources.
Categories include passenger ships, cargo ships, tankers, whale-oil and fish factory
ships, and icebreakers. Basic information includes shipyard, tonnage, dimensions,
engines and years delivered.

898 **An annotated bibliography on Soviet northern transport 1975-1986.**
R. C. North. Vancouver: University of British Columbia, Department
of Geography, 1987. 163p. (Departmental Paper, 38).
A bibliography of over 1,400 items, mainly in Russian or English, on transport in the
northern regions of the Soviet Union, covering transport, traffic, construction,
operation and organization. Subject and geographical indexes are included.

899 **Gateway to Siberian resources (the BAM).**
Theodore Shabad, Victor L. Mote. New York: John Wiley, Halsted
Press, 1977. 189p. maps. bibliog. (Scripta Series in Geography).
One of the great rail projects of the century is the Baykal-Amur Mainline (BAM)
which is designed to open up new resource areas of Pacific Siberia for trade with the
USA and elsewhere. This book places the significance of BAM as a gateway to
Siberian resources in a development perspective. In addition to basic facts about BAM
it provides concise and readily available references to all Siberian industrial
developments.

900 **Russian transport; an historical and geographical survey.**
Edited by Leslie Symons, Colin White. London: G. Bell, 1975. 192p.
maps. bibliog.
A collection of conference papers which examine the salient features of the transport
systems of the Russian empire and the Soviet Union. Each transport medium and its
development is dealt with by an acknowledged specialist in the field. Chapter five is
devoted to an account of the Northern Sea Route, linking the Atlantic and Pacific by
way of the Arctic coast of Siberia.

Environment

901 **The living tundra.**
Yu I. Chernov. Translated by D. Löve. Cambridge, England:
Cambridge University Press, 1985. 213p. maps. bibliog. (Studies in
Polar Research).
First published in 1980 by Izdatel'stvo 'Mysel', the purpose of this book, written by a
leading Soviet ecologist, is to draw the attention of planners and developers working in
the arctic environment to some of the principles and methods for the utilization and
protection of natural resources. The opening chapter, 'What is the tundra?', defines in

general terms the nature of the treeless landscape situated along the arctic coast and its islands. Subsequent chapters analyse such aspects of the tundra as temperature and humidity, relief and permafrost, snow and its role in the life of the tundra, adaptation of living organisms to conditions in the tundra zone, distribution of animals and plants, interrelationships between organisms and, finally, man and the tundra.

902   **The destruction of nature in the Soviet Union.**
Boris Komarov.   Translated by Michael Vale, Joe Hollander. White Plains, New York: M. E. Sharpe, 149p. bibliog.

This is a translation from the Russian text (Frankfurt/Main, Possev-Verlag, 1978). 'Boris Komarov' is a pseudonym for the Soviet official whose book appeared through unofficial 'samizdat' channels. Though the general public has been kept largely unaware of the threat posed by various economic developments to the natural environment, the Russian scientific community has managed to keep abreast of these developments. Examples discussed include the pollution of Lake Baikal, Siberia, brought about by the construction of cellulose plants. Various hazards associated with the production of atomic energy (pre-Chernobyl) are discussed, and a whole chapter is devoted to ecological hazards posed for arctic Siberia by various developments.

903   **Conservation in the Soviet Union.**
Philip R. Pryde.   Cambridge, England: Cambridge University Press, 1972. 301p. maps. bibliog.

Makes a systematic and comprehensive survey of resource management in the Soviet Union, including the current legal framework. Successive chapters deal with land and soil resources, nature reserves, wildlife and fish management, mineral and forestry resources and environmental pollution. A final chapter evaluates conservation attitudes and the political and philosophical implications of Soviet conservation.

Maps

904   **USSR in maps.**
J. C. Dewdney.   London: Hodder & Stoughton, 1982. 117p. maps. bibliog.

A volume containing forty-nine maps and diagrams, with supporting text, designed to illustrate the present-day geography – physical, human and economic – of the USSR. The arrangement is by topic, such as physical environment, human geography, economic geography, and by regions.

Scandinavian Arctic – Lapland

General

905 **The Lapps.**
Roberto Bosi. London: Thames & Hudson, 1960. 220p. bibliog.
This general review of the Lapps is by a professional archaeologist who travelled in Lapland in the early 1950s. Part one deals with the history of these nomads; part two considers their domestic economy; part three concerns their spiritual beliefs; and part four their origins.

906 **The Lapps today in Finland, Norway and Sweden. II.**
Nordic Lapp Council. [Stockholm]: Universitetsforlaget, [1963], 357p. bibliog.
The second of a series of reports on the Lapps today in northern Scandinavia, recording lectures and discussions from the Nordic Lapp Conferences, 1959-62, and presenting a clear picture of the conditions under which the Lapps were living at this period. The very full bibliography provides a survey of relevant publications issued between 1950-59, covering all topics from history to music and art.

907 **Northern high lights; a journey through the Scandinavian Arctic.**
Joan Sundfeldt, Bengt af Geijerstam, Ake Mokvist. [Stockholm]: Prisma, 1983. 224p. maps. bibliog.
This journey was through arctic Scandinavia north of the Arctic Circle. Prospective visitors to northern Norway, Sweden and Finland (Lapland) would find this travelogue informative background reading, giving hints on where to stay, what to eat and drink, where to go skiing or fishing, and how to hire a dog team.

Geography

908 **Sarek – Stora Sjöfallet – Padjelanta – three national parks in Swedish Lapland.**
Kai Curry-Lindahl.   Stockholm: Raben & Sjörgren, 1968. 141p. map. bibliog. (National parks of Sweden series).
A summary account of the main attractions of these three contiguous Swedish national parks – geology, topography, climate, vegetation, rivers and wildlife. The emphasis of the text is placed on vegetation and vertebrate animals.

909 **Lapland.**
Walter Marsden.   Amsterdam: Time-Life International (Nederland), 1976. 184p. map. bibliog. (The World's Wild Places).
Presents a profusely-illustrated naturalist's account of Lapland, lying within the boundaries of Norway, Sweden and Finland above the Arctic Circle. The emphasis is on the description of the fauna, flora and landscape. A separate chapter by Toby Molenaar describes Sarek Park in Swedish Lapland, regarded as the most inaccessible wilderness in western Europe, populated only by the mountain Lapps.

910 **A geography of Norden; Denmark, Finland, Iceland, Norway, Sweden.**
Axel Sømme.   Oslo: J. W. Cappelens Forlag, 1968. 378p. maps. bibliog.
Though in need of revision this textbook still serves as a valuable introduction to the Scandinavian countries, with contributory expert chapters on the economic background to each. A sequence of eleven colour maps presents information on geographical topics, such as geomorphology, population, forestry, precipitation and surface waters.

Flora and fauna

911 **A tour in Lapland.**
Carl Linnaeus.   New York: Arno and *The New York Times*, 1971. 306p. 2 vols. in 1.
Presents a reprint of *Lachesis lapponica or a tour in Lapland* . . . (London: White & Cochrane, 1811. Vols. 1 & 2). Carl Linnaeus 'the father of botany', explored Lapland for the Swedish Academy of Sciences in 1732, covering some 3,800 miles in five months. In addition to cataloguing the flowers, plants, trees and animals Linnaeus also describes here the physical beauty of the region and the customs and characteristics of its people.

912 **Sarek; Lapland's wild-life sanctuary.**
Edvin Nilsson. Stockholm: Bonniers, 1970. 119p. map.
An account of Sarek National Park in Swedish Lapland, covering an almost unique and
not easily accessible mountain region. The area contains an interesting flora and fauna,
including bears, elks, wolverine, wolves, eagles and falcons. The author is an official
park inspector and the book is illustrated with some outstanding colour photographs.

913 **Arctic summer; birds in north Norway.**
Richard Vaughan. Shrewsbury, England: Anthony Nelson, 1979.
151p. map. bibliog.
An account of a journey made by the author in the summer of 1972 to the Varanger
Peninsula in the county of Finnmark, north Norway, in order to study the varied bird
life of this largely unspoilt region. A systematic list of the birds is appended and the
book is well-illustrated with colour and black-and-white photographs.

Peoples

914 **The trail of the Arctic nomads.**
Hugh Brandon-Cox. London: William Kimber, 1969. 192p. maps.
An account of the author's stay with a Lapp family in northern Norway and a trek
made with them on their long reindeer migration from their winter home to the
summer coastal feeding grounds.

915 **Aspects of the Lappish minority situation.**
Harald Eidheim. Oslo; Bergen; Tromsö: Universitetsforlaget, 1974.
86p. bibliog.
Five essays, concentrating on crucial aspects of the Lappish minority situation in
Norway in the 1950s and 1960s. The first deals with political entrepreneurial activity,
and the second with relationships between nomadic (reindeer-herding) Lapps and
coastal (fishing) Lapps at a time of cultural change. The remaining essays consider
aspects of Lappish identity and social assimilation.

916 **The reindeer people.**
Marie Herbert. London: Hodder & Stoughton, 1976. 187p. map.
bibliog.
A personal account of the reindeer Lapps of northern Norway on the occasion of an
annual spring migration from the high mountain plateaux to the coastal pastures,
involving a cross-country trek by sledge and snow-scooter.

917 **The Skolt Lapps today.**
Tim Ingold. Cambridge, England: Cambridge University Press, 1976.
276p. maps. bibliog.
A study of what the author describes as this 'unique cultural and genetic isolate', based
on his field work carried out in the 1970s in the Skolt Lapp community of Sevettijärvi

in northeast Finland. The study is divided into three parts. The first deals broadly with the 'economy', including reindeer husbandry and fishing. The second part deals with 'society', that is, the patterning of social relations. The final part examines the relationship of the community with the state.

918 **Lapps and Norsemen in olden times.**
Instituttet for Sammenlignende Kulturforskning. Oslo: Universitetsforlaget, 1967. 168p. maps. bibliog.
This publication draws attention to the problems of relations between Lapps and Norsemen in prehistoric and early historic times. It consists of six papers read at a conference in Oslo in 1964. The papers cover linguistic, archaeological, place-name and cultural aspects.

919 **People·of eight seasons.**
Ernest Manker. Gothenburg, Sweden: Tre Tryckare Cagner, 1963. 230p. bibliog.
A history and description of the Lapps by an acknowledged expert, which details, throughout the seasons of the year, the life-cycle of these nomadic peoples. The book is profusely illustrated with pen-and-ink sketches, showing details of, for example, clothing, sledges and equipment.

920 **The Lapps.**
Arthur Spencer. New York: Crane, Russak; Newton Abbot, England: David & Charles, 1978. 160p. bibliog. (This Changing World).
A comprehensive study, for the non-specialist, of the Lapps and their traditional lifestyle. The author also considers the present social and political situation of the Lapps and assesses the future prospects for these people in the light of economic change.

921 **Ethnicity and mobilization in Sami politics.**
Tom G. Svensson. Stockholm: University of Stockholm, Department of Social Anthropology, 1976. 279p. map. bibliog.
This book describes a study of six communities of reindeer-herding mountain Samis (Lapps) in northern Sweden, carried out with the aim of studying their relationship with the dominant ethnic majority (the Swedes) at a time when the position of the Samis has undergone a radical change.

Transport

922 **The Arctic Highway; a road and its setting.**
John Douglas. Newton Abbot, England: David & Charles, 1972. 251p. maps.
An account of the Arctic Highway which begins in Malmö, Sweden, follows the coast to Oslo, then winds its way via Trondheim through Nord-Trondelag and Sør-Trondelag

to reach Mo i Rana and the Polar Circle. This book deals with the final 900 miles from Mo to Kirknes, covering the counties of Nordland, Troms and Finnmark in arctic Norway. Chapters deal with the background and history of the road and offer a detailed description of the road and its branches. A short chapter describes the impact of the highway's construction on the Lapps.

Environment

923 **Absorbing heavy industry in marginal areas. The prospects of petroleum development in northern Norway.**
Tor Halfdan Aase. *Geografisk Tidsskrift*, vol. 40, no. 4 (1986), p. 179-85.
A model study of the socio-economic impact of a hypothetical gas terminal in a real northern Norwegian setting, focusing on the qualitative aspects of the relationship between an industrial complex and the local community.

The Arctic Ocean

924 The Arctic world.
Oceanus, vol. 29, no. 1 (spring 1986), 96p.

Represents a special issue of this journal, published by the Woods Hole Oceanographic Institution, Massachusetts, USA, devoted to the Arctic Ocean. Directed to the non-specialist, the articles cover military aspects, offshore petroleum technology, marine ecosystems, sea ice and climate.

925 Polar oceans.
Edited by M. J. Dunbar. Calgary, Alberta: Arctic Institute of North America, 1977. 682p. maps. bibliog.

The proceedings of the Polar Oceans Conference held at McGill University, Montreal in May 1974 and sponsored by the Scientific Committee on Antarctic Research. These papers, which are all of a specialized nature, are intended as an up-to-date statement of knowledge in a number of different fields. They are presented under four headings: (1) Water masses and circulation; (2) Ice and ice biota; (3) Marine productivity: poles and tropics; and (4) Climatic change and the polar regions.

926 General bathymetric chart of the oceans (GEBCO). Scale 1:10,000,000 at 75°N. lat.
Intergovernmental Oceanographic Commission. Ottawa: Canadian Hydrographic Service for the Intergovernmental Oceanographic Commission, 1979. 5th ed. Sheet 5.17. bibliog.

A chart of the Arctic Ocean showing under-ice terrain features including the Lomonosov Ridge, the Alpha Ridge and Mendeleyev Ridge, the Amundsen Basin and the Canadian Basin among others.

927 **The eastern Bering Sea shelf: oceanography and resources.**
Edited by D. W. Hood, John A. Calder.   Seattle: National Oceanic
and Atmospheric Administration, distributed by the University of
Washington Press, 1981. 2 vols. maps. bibliog.

A compilation of basic information on the Bering Sea shelf, for use by the United
States Bureau of Land Management in connection with the sale of oil and gas leases,
and with the aim of protecting the Bering Sea environment. Its primary purpose is to
present what is now known about the natural science of the region. About seventy
contributions cover such topics as oceanography, ice, geology and geophysics, fisheries,
birds, mammals, microbiology and plankton.

928 **Oceanography of the Bering Sea with emphasis on renewable resources.**
Edited by D. W. Hood, E. J. Kelley.   Fairbanks, Alaska: Institute of
Marine Science, University of Alaska, 1974. 623p. maps. bibliog.
(Occasional Publication, no. 2).

These papers were presented to the International Symposium for Bering Sea Study,
Hakodate, Japan, 31 January–4 February, 1972. Topics covered include physical
processes related to biological productivity, chemistry, renewable resources, ice and its
effects, meteorology, geology and the application of satellite technology to investi-
gative studies.

929 **The nordic seas.**
Edited by Burton G. Hurdle.   New York: Springer-Verlag, 1986.
777p. maps. bibliog.

A comprehensive multidisciplinary scientific description of the nordic seas, intended
for engineers designing and operating systems to be used in this environment, but also
of interest to the general reader. The areas focused upon are the Norwegian and
Greenland seas, the westernmost portion of the Barents Sea and the areas round
Iceland.

930 **USSR/USA Bering Sea experiment.**
Edited by K. Ya Kondrat'ev.   Translated from Russian. New Delhi,
India: Amerind Publishing for National Marine Fisheries Service,
National Oceanic and Atmospheric Administration, 1982. 307p.
bibliog. (TT 76-52017).

Originally published by Gidrometeoizdat, Leningrad (1975) this book consists of a
number of specialized papers reporting on a joint American-Soviet investigation of the
ice dynamics and ice cover of the Bering Sea.

931 **The ocean basins and margins. Vol. 5. The Arctic Ocean.**
Edited by Alan E. M. Nairn, Michael Churkin, Jr., Francis G.
Stehli.   New York, London: Plenum, 1981. 672p. bibliog.

Gives a comprehensive account of research on the tectonics of the Arctic Basin, with
contributions by leading authorities. The geology of the Arctic Ocean and the major
marginal tectonostratigraphic terrain are examined in detail, and there are discussions
of the Arctic continental margin of Alaska, the geology and geophysics of the

American Basin, and the tectonic structure of the Soviet Basin, utilizing a new geosynclinal theory developed by the Geological Institute of the USSR, Academy of Sciences.

932 **Arctic sea ice, 1973-1976: satellite passive-microwave observations.**
Claire L. Parkinson, Josefino C. Comiso, H. Jay Zwalley, Donald J.
Cavalieri, Per Gloersen, William J. Campbell.   Washington, DC:
National Aeronautics and Space Administration (NASA), 1987. 296p.
maps. bibliog. (NASA SP-489).

This atlas constitutes a summary of the observations made of the Arctic by an Electrically Scanning Microwave Radiometer (ESMR) on board the Nimbus 5 polar orbiting meteorological satellite. In addition to a large number of coloured maps depicting various aspects of the state of the the Arctic Ocean in a four-year period in the 1970s, there will be found the information needed to study the details of the changes in the Arctic Ocean that may well ensue if the global warming, now believed to be taking place, accelerates in the years ahead.

933 **The Arctic Ocean; the hydrographic environment and the fate of pollutants.**
Edited by Louis Rey, Bernard Stonehouse.   London, Basingstoke:
Macmillan, 1982. 433p. maps. bibliog.

Papers presented to a conference organized by Comité Arctique International, Monaco, concerned with the exploration and exploitation of the Arctic Ocean. Section one deals with the history and physical characteristics of the Arctic Basin. Section two discusses hydrography, water, ice and atmospheric interactions. Section three is devoted to climatic and atmospheric transport. Section four considers arctic biology and pollution. Section five discusses oils and chemicals in the arctic environment.

934 **The Arctic Ocean and its coast in the Cenozoic era.**
Edited by A. I. Tolmachev.   New Delhi: Amerind Publishing for the
Smithsonian Institution Libraries and the National Science Foundation,
Washington, DC, 1982. 564p. maps. bibliog. (TT 72-52016).

A translation from the Russian *Severniy ledovityi okean i ego poperezh'e v Kainozoe* (1970) consisting of contributions by Soviet scientists on problems of origin, evolution and paleogeography of the Arctic and its coasts during the Tertiary and Quaternary periods. Much emphasis is placed on the evolution of modern Arctic flora and fauna, terrestrial and aquatic.

935 **Biology of the seas of the USSR.**
L. Zenkevitch.   Translated by S. Botcharskaya. London: George
Allen & Unwin, 1963. 955p. bibliog. map.

A definitive work translated from the Russian and covering the northern (Arctic) seas as well as those of the Far East, such as the Sea of Okhotsk and the Bering Sea. Subheadings include the history of exploration; physical geography; hydrology; hydrochemistry and geology; flora and fauna.

Indexes

There follow three separate indexes: authors (personal and corporate); titles of books; and subjects. Title entries are italicized and refer either to the main titles, or to other works cited in the annotations. The numbers refer to bibliographic entry rather than page numbers. Individual index entries are arranged in alphabetical sequence.

Index of Authors

A

Aase, T. H. 923
Adam, K. M. 391
Adams, G. R. 759
Adams, V. M. 350
Adams, W. P. 437, 441, 492, 495, 500-01, 503, 714
Adams-Ray, E. 153
Afcan, P. 783
Afonsky, G. 786
Alaska Department of Labor 797
Albion, R. G. 189
Aleksandrova, V. D. 71, 841
Alexander, B. 557
Allen, K. R. 356
Allen, L. C. van 340
Amedeo, L. 152
Amundsen, R. 154, 159-60
Andersen, S. 292
Andersland, O. B. 407
Anderson, D. M. 407
Anderson, R. M. 648
Anderson, W. R. 163-64
Andrée, S. A. 153
Andrews, M. 491
Archer, C. 317
Archer, W. 558
Armstrong, R. H. 728
Armstrong, T. 18, 39, 263, 823-24, 851, 864, 893
Arobio, E. L. 377
Ashton, G. D. 408
Atkin, R. 596

B

Babb, Jr., J. D. 805
Bach, H. C. 318
Bacharach, A. L. 481
Back, G. 622, 631
Baird, P. D. 19
Baker, F. W. G. 148
Bale, Jr,. S. G. 445
Balkwill, H. R. 37
Bandi, H.-G. 101
Banks, M. 523
Barnhardt, R. 812
Barr, S. 522
Barr, W. 149, 191, 582, 860
Barratt, G. R. 110, 753
Barre, K. de la 707
Barrington, D. 140
Barrow, J. 111
Barry, R. G. 23, 57
Barsness, J. 762
Basse, B. 283
Bater, J. H. 851
Beaglehole, J. C. 142, 217
Beals, C. S. 570
Bearne, C. 790
Beattie, O. 632
Beaufoy, Col. 140
Beaufoy, M. 140
Beechey, F. W. 143
Beeke, C. T. 139
Benedickson, J. 700
Bennet, D. J. 524
Bennett, F. L. 409
Berg, G. 240, 388
Berger, T. R. 791

Bergeron, R. 443
Bergesen, H. O. 319
Berkh, V. N. 773
Berry, F. 451
Berton, P. 760
Bertram, C. 384
Beste, G. 615-16
Beynen, K. 139
Bielawski, E. 591
Bilby, J. W. 654
Binford, L. R. 735
Bird, J. B. 580
Birket-Smith, K. 264
Bixby, W. 395
Bjelke, R. 175
Björn-Rasmussen, S. 447
Blair, C. 164
Bliss, L. C. 63, 588
Blyth, J. D. M. 200-01, 206
Böcher, T. W. 534
Bockstoce, J. R. 344-45, 736
Bogorodsky, V. V. 410
Bone, R. M. 265
Bonner, W. N. 86
Boon, T. C. B. 679
Borisov, A. A. 833
Bosi, R. 905
Botcharskaya, S. 935
Botting, D. 825
Bourassa, R. 695
Bowles, R. P. 700
Bowling, S. A. 59
Bradley, J. 202
Brandon-Cox, H. 914
Bravo, M. T. 597

235

Edholm, O. G. 294,
481-82
Egede Saabye, H. 544
Egeland, A. 60
Eidheim, H. 915
Eidlitz, K. 295
Elbo, J. G. 200, 205-06
Elkin, L. 838
Elkington, T. T. 534
Ellis, R. 90
Ellis, R. D. 114
Ellsworth, L. 159-60
Embry, A. F. 37
Engelhardt, F. R. 432
Erngaard, E. 541
Ervin, A. M. 663
Escher, A. 532
Etienne, J.-L. 176
Evans, P. G. H. 78
Evans, W. E. 94
Eyre, K. C. 321

F

Fahlgren, J. E. J. 712
Fairbanks, R. A. 726
Falk, M. 122, 818
Farrar, V. J. 757
Faulke, A. 539
Fedorov, E. K. 862
Feilberg, J. 535
Feilden, H. W. 145
Ferguson, W. O. 440
Fiennes, R. 170, 173
Finley, J. C. 708
Fiodorov, B. 826
Fisher, R. H. 850, 853
Fitch, E. M. 810
Fitzhugh, W. 104
Flanders, N. E. 296
Flayderman, E. N. 466
Fleetwood, P. 162
Fleming, A. L. 680
Fletcher, R. J. 586
Foighel, I. 564
Folk, Jr., G. E. 233
Folk, M. A. 233
Food and Agriculture
    Organization 367, 372
Ford, C. 751
Fortuine, R. 297
Foster, M. 444
Foster, S. 793
Fowler, H. S. 392

Fraenkel, K. 153
Francis, D. 357, 600
Francis, E. T. 511
Franklin, J. 622-24, 628
Fraser, C. 41
Frederiksen, T. 555
Fredskild, B. 535
Freeman, E. J. 313
French, R. A. 851
Freuchen, D. 269
Freuchen, P. 221
Friends of the Earth 358
Fries, G. 544
Friis, H. R. 151, 445
Fristrup, B. 533
Fukuda, M. 417
Fuller, W. A. 64
Funston, B. W. 691

G

Gad, F. 543
Galpin, G. M. 470
Galpin, V. 502
Garnett, E. 219
Garrett, P. D. 787
Garwood, E. J. 512
Gathorne-Hardy, G. M.
    131
Gavrilo, V. P. 410
Geddes, F. 338
Geiger, J. 632
Geijerstam, B. af 907
George, O. 765
Gershevsky, N. D. 839
Gerwick, Jr., B. C. 413
Giaever, J. 453
Giddings, J. L. 741
Glad, J. 892
Glen, A. R. 213, 514
Glines, C. V. 182
Gloersen, P. 932
Goetzmann, W. H. 756
Golder, F. A. 751, 854,
    856
Goldschmidt, V. 565
Gonzalez, R. R. 298
Goodwin, C. R. 708
Goodwin, R. 503
Gordon, M. R. 441
Gordon-Cooper, H. 454
Gough, B. M. 629
Govornkha, L. S. 22
Graburn, N. H. H. 248

Graf-Baumann, T. 301
Gray, D. M. 42, 391
Greely, A. W. 645
Green, L. 646
Greenaway, K. 571
Gregory, J. W. 512
Greve, T. 508
Grierson, J. 183-84
Grounds, G. W. 382
Gruening, E. 743-44, 746
Guimont, P. 443
Gulland, J. A. 368
Gunderson, E. K. E. 294
Gurkov, G. 884
Gutteridge, W. 322
Guttridge, L. F. 147

H

Haber, E. 67
Hajdú, P. 285, 869
Haley, D. 91
Hall, C. F. 615, 642
Hall, D. K. 43
Hall, S. 249
Halliday, E. M. 207
Halstead, C. A. 833
Hamelin, L.-E. 582
Hamilton, J. 467
Hammerich, L. L. 286
Hansen, T. 617
Hantzsch, B. 649
Haraldson, S. R. S. 299
Harbron, J. D. 398
Hardy, A. 123
Hardy, R. N. 65
Hare, K. F. 57
Harper, K. 276
Harrington, R. 661
Harris, S. A. 44
Harrison, R. J. 92, 97
Hastings, R. 338
Hauan, M. A. 521
Haupt, A.-C. 491, 785
Hauser, M. 566
Hayes, I. I. 639
Heal, O. W. 63
Hearne, S. 618
Helle, R. K. 373
Heller, H. L. 761
Helm, J. 250
Helmer, J. W. 281
Hendry, C. E. 681
Henson, L. 486

237

Index of Titles

Index of Subjects

Map of The Arctic

REGIONAL SECTIONS as numbered on the map featured overleaf.

1. Arctic Basin
2. Arctic seas
3. Arctic Shelf seas
4. Chukchi Sea
5. Bering Strait
6. Bering Sea
7. Aleutian Islands
8. Aleutian waters
9. Alaska, northern
10. Alaska
11. Alaska, Gulf of
12. Alaska, southeast
13. Yukon Territory
14. Beaufort Sea
15. Mackenzie District
16. Northwest Territories
17. Keewatin District
18. Canadian Arctic Islands (Banks and Prince Patrick Islands and islands eastward as far as, but excluding, Ellesmere and Baffin Islands)
19. Canadian Arctic Islands waters (waters within the archipelago)
20. Ellesmere Island
21. Smith Sound—Robeson Channel
22. Jones Sound
23. Lancaster Sound
24. Baffin Island (including offshore islands)
25. Southampton Island
26. Hudson Strait
27. Hudson Bay
28. Manitoba, northern
29. Ontario, northern (including offshore islands
30. James Bay
31. Quebec, northern (including Ungava Peninsula)
32. Ungava Bay
33. Labrador (including offshore islands)
34. Labrador Sea
35. Baffin Bay—Davis Strait
36. Greenland, west
37. Greenland, north
38. Greenland—Inland Ice
39. Greenland, East (south from Danmarks Fjord to Lindenows Fjord)
40. Denmark Strait
41. Jan Mayen
42. Greenland Sea
43. Svalbard (archipelago, including Bjørnøya)
44. Svalbard waters (straits, fjords and waters within the archipelago)
45. Vestspitsbergen (including offshore islands to the west)
46. Nordaustlandet
47. Kong Karls Land
48. Bjørnøya
49. Barents Sea
50. Scandinavia and Finland
51. Kola Peninsula
52. White Sea
53. Archangel Oblast
54. Novaya Zemlya
55. Zemlya Frantsa Iosifa (Franz Josef Land)
56. Zemlya Frantsa Iosifa (waters)
57. Kara Sea
58. Omsk Oblast (now Tyumenskaya)
59. Krasnoyarsk Kray
60. Severnaya Zemlya
61. Laptev Sea
62. New Siberian Islands
63. Yakutskaya A.S.S.R.
64. East Siberian Sea
65. Wrangel Island
66. Kamchatka Oblast
67. Okhotsk, Sea of
68. Kamchatka Peninsula
69. Commander Islands

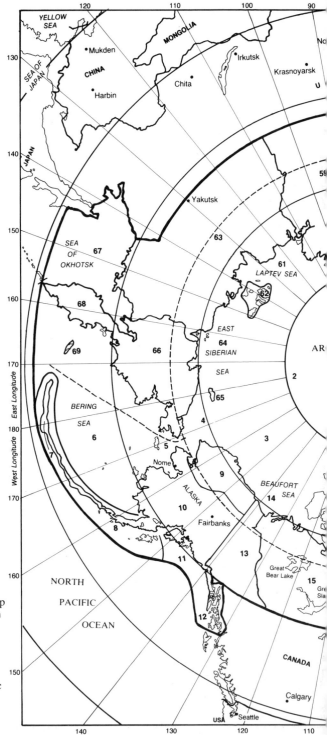

Adapted from the map originally published in *Arctic bibliography*, prepared for, and in cooperation with, the US Department of Defense under the direction of the Arctic Institute of North America, Washington DC, 1953.

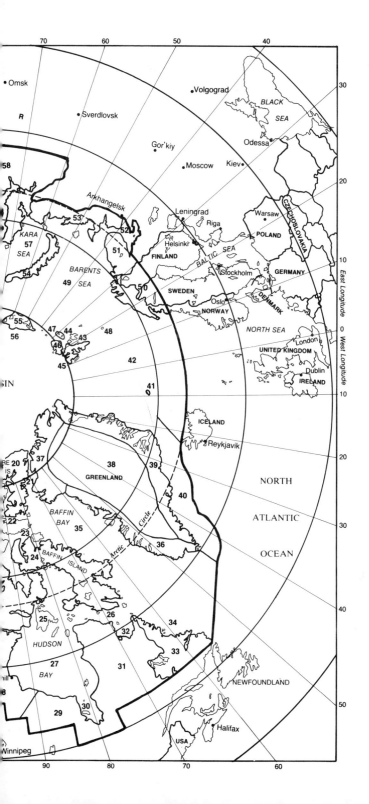